Detroit, MI 48201

Minnie's Sacrifice
Sowing and Reaping
Trial and Triumph

《《》》

Black Women Writers Series

《《》》

Minnie's Sacrifice
Sowing and Reaping
Trial and Triumph

《《》》

Three Rediscovered Novels by
Frances E. W. Harper

EDITED BY
Frances Smith Foster

Beacon Press
25 Beacon Street
Boston, Massachusetts 02108-2892

Beacon Press books
are published under the auspices of
the Unitarian Universalist Association of Congregations.

99 98 97 96 95 94   8 7 6 5 4 3 2 1

Text design by Kathleen Szawiola

Library of Congress Cataloging-in-Publication Data

Harper, Frances Ellen Watkins, 1825–1911.
    Minnie's sacrifice; Sowing and reaping; Trial and triumph:
    three rediscovered novels / by Frances E. W. Harper; edited
    by Frances Smith Foster.
        p.   cm.
    ISBN 0-8070-8332-1
    I. Afro-Americans—Fiction. I. Foster, Frances Smith.
II. Title: Minnie's sacrifice.   III. Title: Sowing and reaping.
IV. Title: Trial and triumph.
PS 1799.H7A6   1994
813'.3—dc20   93-38597

This book is for Quinton
and all other men
who love, respect, and work alongside
today's Minnies, Belles, and Annettes.

Contents

《《 》》

Acknowledgments

These three novels are restored to us through the cooperation and consideration of many individuals. The project has taken several years and more people than I can name have contributed their time and effort. They have looked up, for, around, and through all kinds of documents in every place we could imagine might yield more of the texts or more information about their author. However, I am especially thankful to Leslie Callahan, Chanta Haywood, Karen Kornweibel, Sara McIntyre, Maggie Sale, Maia Sorrells, and Lauren Wilson, students who made my search their own personal quests and who continually reaffirmed for me the importance of my project. I also want to thank Deborah McDowell, the founding editor of Beacon Press's Black Women Writers series, who persuaded me that these books should be published as a part of this series. The volume you are now reading is the result of efforts by these and many other generous and considerate individuals. I sincerely hope that readers of this volume will judge it *utile dulci*. Most of all, I hope it will lead to the discovery of the remaining missing chapters of Harper's novels and to the lost novels of other African American authors.

Introduction

The three novels collected in this volume represent a major discovery in American literary history. Most obviously, they increase the number of known publications by U.S. writers between 1868 and 1888, a period of profound social, economic, and political development instigated in part by extensive European immigration and international expansion by the United States, but determined most particularly by the abolition of slavery and its aftermath. In their depictions from the perspective of African Americans of life in bondage and freedom these novels are essential to our understanding of a crucial era in U.S. history. The mid-nineteenth century was also a time of monumental change in U.S. literary history. It was a moment when the emergence of new authors, new subjects, and new literary techniques combined with the explosive growth of the publishing industry and the rapid increase in the number and influence of readers to produce a new kind of "American" literature. The texts published here, written for an audience with a sizeable contingent of newly literate readers and appearing in approximately ten-year intervals in the *Christian Recorder*, the journal of the African Methodist Episcopal Church, provide a special opportunity to chart the evolution of American popular fiction. They were written by a woman and do demonstrate many of the elements that characterized the fiction of nineteenth-century American women. They are also texts with a decidedly political focus and a clear enunciation of aesthetic principles that differ significantly from those traditions attributed to most "women's fiction." Consequently, these three works provide a basis for revising our understanding of nineteenth-century women's literature.

As African American literature, the importance of these texts is even more striking, for there are only four or five novels known to have been published before *Minnie's Sacrifice* (1869) and most bibliographies list fewer than two dozen novels written by African Americans before the twentieth century. Of those, fewer than a half-dozen are readily available and form the core of the current critical discussion concerning the development of African American fiction.

These three novels will enhance the already substantial reputation of their author, Frances Ellen Watkins Harper. Long recognized as the most popular African American poet prior to Paul Laurence Dunbar, Harper can now claim her place as a prolific and innovative prose pioneer as well. Coming as they do between Harper's short story, "The Two Offers" (1859), and her novel, *Iola Leroy* (1892), these three texts offer an unprecedented opportunity to witness the development of a nineteenth-century African American writer's concerns and style over a forty-year period. The place of publication and the circumstances of their recovery offer a criticism of prevailing forms of African American scholarship and an argument for continued collegial corroboration. And, finally, but probably most important, these three novels are interesting, provocative works that should enlarge and diversify the current readership of African American literature.

By any standard Frances Ellen Watkins Harper, the woman

who wrote these novels, was an extraordinary individual. By the standards of the nineteenth century, and particularly those for African American women of that era, she was almost without peer. Born free in the slave state of Maryland in 1825, Harper received a liberal education at the Watkins Academy for Colored Youth and became the first female instructor at Union Seminary (the precursor of Wilberforce University in Ohio). In 1854, at a time when few women were allowed to speak in public on any subject, Frances Ellen Watkins Harper was employed by the Maine Anti Slavery Society to carry the abolitionist message across New England to audiences that included women and men of all races and backgrounds. Her proficiency and popularity soon led to invitations for her to travel from the Atlantic seaboard to the western frontiers of Ohio and Michigan and to share the same platforms as Frederick Douglass, Sojourner Truth, William Lloyd Garrison, Lydia Maria Child, and other prominent spokespersons. Since she numbered Underground Railroad conductors such as William Still and the Reverend J. W. Loguen among her personal friends and since her letters often inquired about the welfare of individual fugitive slaves, contained cash donations, and volunteered for additional assignments, it is highly probable that Frances Ellen Watkins Harper was herself an active agent and may well have escorted passengers along that line. She was a friend and confidant of radical reformers, such as Henry Highland Garnet, William C. Nell, and John Brown, and like Rosa Parks a century later, Harper once refused to give up her seat on the segregated streetcars of Philadelphia. Like Rosa Parks, also, Frances Harper was frequently described as "slender and graceful" with a "soft musical voice" and commended for her "chaste" language and her discreet demeanor. Orator, writer, activist, and "lady," Harper's roles were many but they were unified by her life goal: the building up of "true men and true women," individuals whom she describes as those who would "make every gift, whether gold or talent, fortune or genius, subserve the cause of crushed humanity and carry out the greatest idea of the present age, the glorious idea of human brotherhood."[1]

After slavery was abolished, Harper turned her energies to the work of Reconstruction. She was especially concerned with helping women understand that they could and should use their time and talents to achieve "high and lofty goals," that their hands were made to rock the cradles of their own children and the cradle of civilization. Harper argued that "women as a class are quite equal to the men in energy and executive ability" and that "mothers are the levers which move in education" (271). Harper advocated academic and vocational education for everyone according to her or his inclinations and abilities. She organized Sunday Schools, YMCAs, and women's clubs. She served on the national boards of the Women's Christian Temperance Union, the American Equal Rights Association, and the National Council of Negro Women and was a featured speaker at conferences such as the World Congress of Representative Women, the National Council of Women of the United States, and the Mothers' Peace Day. Frances Harper became a leader in the American Association for Education of Colored Youth, the Universal Peace Union, the American Women's Suffrage Association, and the John Brown Memorial Association of Women. Her reputation was so great and she was so admired that women from Pittsburgh, Pennsylvania, to St. Louis, Missouri, and St. Paul, Minnesota, formed F. E. W. Harper Leagues. Although a Unitarian herself, she was listed in *The Heroines of African Methodism* and cited by the *African Methodist Episcopal Church Review* as a "Woman of Our Race Worthy of Imitation." Named in Phebe A. Hanaford's *Daughters of America* as "one of the colored women of whom white women may be proud," Harper was also the only African American woman to be awarded a day on the Red Letter Calendar of the Women's Christian Temperance Union.

For more than sixty years, Frances Ellen Watkins Harper was a leader among the African American litterateurs. She published at least eight books of poetry, innumerable prose pieces, and so many journal articles that she became known as the "journalistic mother" of the African American press. Harper was, for example, a frequent contributor to the *Provincial Freeman*, *Frederick Douglass's Paper*, the *New York Independent*, the *Weekly Anglo African*, the *Women's Era*, and *The African Methodist Episcopal Church Review*. She was on the editorial board of the *Anglo-African Magazine*, a periodical founded in New York in 1859 and generally assumed to be the first literary journal for, by, and about African Americans. Frances Harper was one of very few African Americans who published regularly in both the religious press and the secular press, in venues read largely by blacks and in venues read primarily by whites. She is credited as the first African American to publish a short story, and her novel *Iola Leroy* is probably the best known and most reprinted African American novel published before Zora Neale Hurston's *Their Eyes Were Watching God* (1937). In her lifetime, as now, Frances Harper was represented in virtually every major anthology of African American literature. Today she is included in encyclopedias of African Americans and in every comprehensive dictionary of American women writers. There is even a Frances Ellen Watkins Harper doll available.

Thus, it is a curiosity of scholarship that there is no full-length study of her literature and that anthologies limit themselves primarily to her abolitionist poetry. Such indifference or neglect makes sense only when viewed in the context of the history of African American literary scholarship and criticism. While traditional histories of American literature have generally ignored the productions by African Americans, the fact remains that African Americans were writing and publishing literature almost as soon as Anglo-Americans were. While they did not always value or understand these literary productions, Europeans and Americans began reading and discussing this literature before there was a United States of America or, if we are to be technical, before there were many African Americans. The earliest extant poem by a black inhabitant of the North American colonies appeared around 1746 and is credited to Lucy Terry Prince. According to Sidney Kaplan in *The Black Presence in the Era of the American Revolution 1770–1880*,[2] both Lucy Terry Prince and her daughter, Durexa, earned reputations as poets and storytellers and their home was a popular gathering place for black literary activity. Generally, writings by an individual black person were claimed as evidence, positive or negative, not only of that person's genius but of that of most, if not all, of their race. The publication of Phillis Wheatley's *Poems on Various Subjects, Religious and Moral* in 1773 prompted the observations of *The Monthly Review* in London that while "most of those people [blacks] have a turn for imitation, though they have little or none for invention," Wheatley "has written many good lines, and now and then one of superior character has dropped from her pen."[3] In 1784, Thomas Jefferson entered his thoughts on black literature in his *Notes on the State of Virginia* when he hazarded that "among the blacks is misery enough, God knows, but no poetry. Religion, indeed has produced a Phyllis Whately [*sic*]; but it could not produce a poet."[4] Henri Grégoire's *An Enquiry Concerning the Intellectual and Moral Faculties, and Literature of the Negroes, Followed with an Account and the Life and Works of Fifteen Negroes & Mulattoes, Distinguished in Science, Literature and the Arts* (1808) was both a rebuttal to Jefferson's thesis and further evidence that African American literature excited international interest.

By the mid-nineteenth century, the idea of African American writers was not alien to most readers. Letters, essays, poems, and narratives by individuals such as Frederick Douglass, Frances Ellen Watkins Harper, and William Wells Brown were occasionally printed in periodicals or publishing series normally reserved for white writers. More frequently these and many other black writers were published under the auspices of a growing black publishing industry or by their own entrepreneurial efforts. Slave narratives were sometimes disparaged as "literary negritudes" and "little tadpoles of the press,"[5] but even their detractors had to acknowledge that they were, in fact, best-sellers. The poetic legacy established by Lucy Terry Prince, George Moses Horton, Phillis Wheatley, and others was not abandoned during the antebellum period, but generally critics and scholars of nineteenth-century African American literature have focused upon the nonfiction. This may be part of the reason why it has been readily assumed that while the mid-nineteenth century is marked by the emergence of a large and influential number of American women novelists, African American women, a group well represented among the earliest colonial women to be published in the United States, did not participate in that renaissance.

As a genre, the novel requires of its author more time and sometimes greater financial stability than most nineteenth-century Americans could muster. Certainly free blacks' struggle to survive and enslaved blacks' circumscribed lives made the leisure necessary for writing longer literary forms a rare commodity. Perhaps this accounts for the tendency of many scholars and anthologists to ignore the production of fiction by African Americans before the Harlem Renaissance or to settle for quick references to Frederick Douglass's "The Heroic Slave" (1852) as the "first" novella, William Wells Brown's *Clotel* (1853) as the "first" novel, Frances Ellen Watkins Harper's "The Two Offers" (1859) as the "first" short story without much questioning of how or why the longer forms came first.

It has long been known that African Americans did publish fiction in the nineteenth century. During the "second black renaissance" of the 1970s, when literary archaeologists had both the funding and the inclination to poke around in the graveyards of

African American literature, the bibliographies of nineteenth-century fiction began to grow. Yet it is still a common assumption that the novel did not become a viable genre for African Americans until the 1890s. Anthologies and surveys of African American literary history often include mention of or excerpts from history books or personal narratives, but generally ignore nineteenth-century novels. Some acknowledge that being a fugitive slave was not such a handicap that William Wells Brown could not publish at least three distinct versions of his novel, several autobiographical narratives, a few plays, some textbooks, and anthologies. Some even record the existence of the full-length biography of her father that Josephine Brown published in 1856 and reveal Frances Rollin as the person who used the pseudonym "Frank Rollin" for her biography of Martin R. Delany in 1868. The pioneering studies of African American novels, such as Benjamin Brawley's *The Negro Genius: A New Appraisal of the Achievement of the American Negro in Literature and the Fine Arts* (1937), Hugh Gloster's *Negro Voices in American Fiction* (1948), and Robert Bone's *The Negro Novel in America* (1957), all report that there were at least three antebellum novelists. Still, it was not until 1983 when Henry Louis Gates, Jr., announced his discovery that *Our Nig; Or, Sketches from the Life of a Free Black* had been published in 1859 by Harriet E. Wilson that scholars began to consider seriously the possibility that our information about the African American novelistic tradition may have been based upon inadequate data.

Our knowledge of earlier African American literature has increased dramatically since then. Studies on the various versions of William Wells Brown's *Clotel* have appeared. More people are examining Frederick Douglass's "The Heroic Slave." *Our Nig* has become almost *de rigueur* for any discussion of antebellum prose literature, and even Frank J. Webb's *The Garies and Their Friends* (1857) is getting some overdue attention. The Schomburg Library of Nineteenth Century Black Women Writers will certainly give birth to more critical discussions on African American women's literature, and one hopes that the work of scholars such as Dickson Bruce, Jr., and Richard Yarborough will stimulate more consideration of nineteenth-century novels. Overall, however, most scholars continue to repeat the assessment of Robert Bone in *The Negro Novel in America*: "In the beginning was slavery, and it prevented the Word from becoming flesh. Leisure and education are the necessary conditions of literary activity, and the antebellum South did not recklessly indulge its slaves in either. . . . By its very nature slavery limited the creative expression of the Negro bondsman to folk forms."[6]

Frances Harper's novels in this volume correct the assertions of more than one recent (and generally very good) historical study of African American literature that from William Wells Brown's fourth version of *Clotel* in 1867 until James Howard's *Bond and Free* in 1886, there were no new African American novels published. They remind us also that long before the antebellum period, not every African American was in bondage and not every slave was a stranger to the written word. They make it very difficult to continue to believe that slaves and free blacks alike confined their literary expression to folktales and spirituals.

These novels and the circumstances of their publication contradict much of our received knowledge about African American literature and culture. By and large our African American ancestors have been stereotyped as illiterate slaves, as beings so oppressed and so restricted that whatever creativity survived the Middle Passage, the whips and chains, the hunger and deprivation of slavery, that creativity, we are told, was manifest in music, dance, and storytelling (both folktales or tall tales and lying, prevaricating, shucking, and jiving). Some would add our mother's gardens and their quilts and jams and jellies to the list of African American cultural contributions, but basically our received knowledge about African American culture prior to the Harlem Renaissance boils down to the idea that it was visual, tactile, oral, and aural. This has contributed in no small way to the neglect of early African American publications and to the persistence of inadequate discussion and outmoded theories about the development of the African American novel.

While it is customary now for survey courses to include one or two early works, they are generally given as evidence of a few extraordinary individuals' ability to read and write or as examples of abolitionist protest literature. The common interpretation is that in either case, they wrote primarily for white folks and that, as in the idea of the dog who walks on two legs, the wonder is not what or how well they wrote but that they wrote at all. Early African American literature, we continue to believe, is more valuable as artifact than artistry. We rightfully recall that during the eighteenth and nineteenth centuries, when the majority of black people in the United States were slaves and when the majority of white people in the United States were unsure just where in the great chain of being those of African ancestry fit, early African Americans did write to prove themselves prepared for citizenship or at least to be included within the general category of human being. Thus, for example, the trope of the talking book manifests some black writers' attempts to unlock the doors of literature and to claim their places within the Western literary heritage as well as their attempts to demonstrate their "own membership in the human community."[7]

It is a fact that at certain periods in our history, literacy, including literacy at its most fundamental level, the basic ability to sign one's name or to read the words on a bag of cotton seed, for African Americans was forbidden by law or proscribed by custom or unattainable simply because most African Americans had no one to teach them nor anywhere they could safely go to for lessons if and when they had the energy after having worked from can see to can't. But, it is equally a fact that despite the social systems that were consciously crafted to repress and to dehumanize, if not to destroy black people, literacy was neither unknown nor unmanifest in African American culture. Moreover, African American literacy was not restricted to the ability to read and write in English. The slave trade was an equal opportunity employer. It did not discriminate in regards to religion, ethnicity, or educational level. Consequently, some of those kidnapped slaves included priests and holy women, business people, students, griots, and poets. There are extant texts of autobiographies written in Arabic and of large portions of the Koran inscribed from memory by Africans enslaved in this country. Among those Africans whose abductors took them first to Holland or Haiti or Mexico or elsewhere were individuals who arrived here writing and reading in Dutch, French, Spanish, and other languages. Literacy in the slave South is not well documented for blacks or for whites, but it is quite possible that the rates for slaves and poor whites were similar—probably few of either group could "read their titles clear." In the northern colonies and states, black Americans compared favorably with white Americans in their abilities to make their marks. In 1850, the census reported that 86 percent of black Bostonians were literate. By 1860 the number had risen to 92 percent.[8] New England and the Atlantic seaboard have never been typical of the entire United States. Both the reliability of census figures, especially concerning people of color, and the definition of literacy are problematic, but the basic point should be clear. Long before Emancipation, long before the American Missionary Association sent its army of teachers behind the Union troops to wage war on ignorance, some African Americans were more than able to sign their names and read the labels that distinguished the parcel of sugar from the parcel of salt.

In cities such as Philadelphia, New York, and Baltimore, African Americans fought for public schools or founded private ones to educate their youth. The adults created literary societies and libraries for themselves. In Boston, for example, women organized the Afric American Female Intelligence Society in 1832, and in 1838 the Adelphia Union Library Association was established as a forum for intellectual debate, dramatic performances, and literary exercises. Moreover, the actual number of readers defines neither the impact of nor appreciation for a written literature. Reading aloud and recitations were popular practices in private and in public places all across the United States. From the mid-eighteenth century on, African Americans also read, appreciated, and appropriated the works of Shakespeare, Milton, Whittier, Longfellow, and Lowell. There are extant letters, poems, and essays by African Americans—slave and free, women and men—addressed to or commenting upon the work of Thomas Jefferson, George Washington, Samuel Sewall, George Whitfield, Charles Sumner, Charles Dickens, Lord and Lady Byron, Mary and Percy Shelley, and others. But, and this is most important, black Americans also read and supported their own writers. Phillis Wheatley, Benjamin Banneker, Frederick Douglass, Harriet Jacobs, and others assumed that their black brothers and sisters would read and would critique their works, and they wrote to earn and to keep their respect.

It is not the fault of the writers nor that of their contemporaries that so few present-day readers and critics know or have thought carefully about the implications of black literacy for their writing and our understanding of their texts. Nonetheless systematic consideration of the implications of the fact that before Emancipation there was a significant population of African Americans with sufficient education to calculate the harvest of the crops, to read the Bible and compose sermons, and to write letters to relatives, friends, acquaintances, and public figures has not been a part of the work of most scholars of early African American literature. We have discounted the impact of a combined oral and written tradition wherein those who could, read to those who could not. We have celebrated the rare instances of those who wrested the bachelor degree from Harvard, Amherst, Dartmouth, Bowdoin, Oberlin, and such and those who claimed Ph.D.s from these and from universities in Germany, France, and England, but we have not calculated the influence of those lesser-known individuals who taught in or attended the private or "colored" schools in the North and the many unnamed courageous and ingenious ones—slave and free, women and men—who conducted and attended the secret "Sunday Schools" in the slave South, schools that like phoenixes appeared, were discovered, and destroyed only to reappear again and again.

I have lingered over what might be called a litany of literary legacy because I want to make it perfectly clear why we can no longer subscribe to the common conclusion that when African American writers such as Phillis Wheatley, William Wells Brown, Frank Webb, or Frances Harper wrote, their implied or actual audiences were white or that their works should be read as attempts—weak and inadequate, but given their situation, rather heroic—to imitate the literary productions of Euro-Americans. And I want it to be clear why we must not uncritically accept a major myth derived from such "general knowledge," the myth that the oral folk tradition—particularly as manifest in the secular arena: the work songs and the blues, the trickster tales and the barroom toasts—is the only authentically black art prior to the twentieth century. The latter statement does not intend to subtract from the artistry or the integrity of the secular or of the oral tradition, but to add to our understanding of African American literary production. When we reaffirm the complexity of culture and communication, their continuities as well as their dissonances, we are in a better position to read and understand both the written and the oral traditions. While rhetorical strategies for oral and written communication are not always the same, neither are they totally distinct. Comments such as "this letter sounds just like her" or "I can just hear him saying this" reveal one way this occurs in everyday life. For those who aspire to publication or rhetorical eminence, literature also invites the author to replicate oral features in writing and vice versa. Once we acknowledge that in the nineteenth century, as now, African Americans were as capable of appropriating as they were of assimilating, that they could not only signify in conversation but also in correspondence, then some of our interpretations of early African American literary productions must change. Greater respect for the genius, strength, and resiliency of African American culture would allow different readings of the evangelists who published their religious experiences and the sailors and soldiers who narrated their "uncommon sufferings and surprizing deliverances," the escaped slaves who described how they ran "a thousand miles to freedom," and the scholars and theologians who published textbooks, disciplines, and spiritual meditations. For example, if we were to take seriously the idea that Christianity was not manufactured in Europe and did in fact contain beliefs and practices common to many African religions and the idea that in many African cultures, poetry was used to instruct, correct, and commemorate, then Phillis Wheatley might be read as an audacious, even a subversive, poet. She was a slave woman but she was also a born-again Christian scholar of Greek and Latin mythology, and it was as both that she dared to reprimand the students at the University of Cambridge in New England for their reputed preference of concentrations in cards and spirits rather than books and spirituality. Wheatley was versed in the rhetorical traditions of the British neoclassicists, but she revised and resisted several of them, substituting or adding elements of the praise song and signifying.

Such readings are further supported when we factor in the numerous schools, literary societies, newspapers, and magazines created by African Americans despite economic and political conditions designed to exorcise the intellectual and aesthetic spirit. When we seriously think about those journalists and poets, scientists and novelists, preachers, teachers, and politicians who wrote for publication and who, when the established media refused their submissions or disrespected their cultural contributions, founded their own newspapers, magazines, and publishing companies, often risking and sometimes losing both their savings and their lives, the commitment of a significant portion of African Americans to a viable written literature becomes clear. The commitment to African American literacy and literature was one not simply of individuals but of institutions. One of the first acts of the newly established African Methodist Episcopal Church was to establish a school for children and adults. In 1817, it created the AME Book Concern to make sure that appropriate reading materials were available, and since then virtually every African American denomination has created its own publishing company. While a major concern was to promulgate the songs, liturgies, and biblical interpretations of each group, these publishers also disseminated nationally works on politics, art, science, and history. The *Christian Recorder*, the source of the three Harper novels for this volume, was one of the results of this commitment. Consideration of such factors requires us to revise our notions that early African American publications were directed to white readers or that the black readership was too small and too dependent to count for much. A perspective that gives greater weight to the existence of a viable black readership encourages us to understand that just because law and custom made it difficult, law and custom did not make it impossible—law and custom did in fact create a necessity for a distinctly African American literature.

In the nineteenth century, especially, religion and politics, secular and sacred, were not carefully distinguished. For example, what is frequently asserted to have been the earliest extant black newspaper in the United States, *Freedom's Journal* founded in 1827, was edited by John B. Russwurm and the Reverend Samuel Cornish and was "a tenacious abolitionist newspaper with a decidedly religious orientation." At the same time, the prospectus of a church publication begun in 1859, the *Repository of Religion and Literature, and of Science and Art*, announced that "OUR GREAT OBJECT will be to diffuse useful knowledge; to cultivate and develop latent talent; to elevate the intellectual, moral and religious status of the people whom we serve." The Afro-Protestant press rarely if ever confined itself to what we might understand as "religious" subjects. To the publishers and contributors, as to their intended readers, the sacred and the secular were not discrete elements of their lives and their experiences. Advertisements for lectures and poetry readings, for books and pamphlets appeared in the Afro-Protestant press along with book reviews, bibliographical essays, and discussions about literary theory. The publishers solicited and printed original contributions by both well-known professional and amateur writers. Surveys of the literature by African Americans published in the Afro-Protestant press suggest that the aesthetic assumptions and requirements for written literature were based upon assumptions strikingly compatible with those that directed the oral literature, the music, and the material culture.

Consider, for instance, the implications of Frances Harper's essay "Christianity" having been published in the *Christian Recorder* before it was included in her book *Poems on Miscellaneous Subjects*—a book published in both Boston and Philadelphia in 1854, reprinted in 1855, 1856, revised and enlarged in 1857, and reprinted at least twenty more times. That essay articulates a theory of aesthetics that seems to have influenced many early African American writers. Harper argues that because Christianity was a "system claiming God for its author, and the welfare of man for its object," all literature must be subordinated to this purpose or be rejected as mere "idle tales." "Learning," she writes, "may bring her ample pages and her ponderous records. . . . Philosophy and science may bring their abstruse researches and wondrous revelations—Literature her elegance, with the toils of the pen, and the labors of the pencil—but they are idle tales compared to the truths of Christianity." It should not be a surprise then to learn that Frances Harper's writings were functional and theological. But the Christianity that Harper espoused was what Clarence Walker in *A Rock in a Weary Land* terms a "civic religion," hers was a church militant whose congregation included several radicals named Moses. "I like the character of Moses," Harper wrote in her 1859 essay "Our Greatest Want." "He is the first disunionist we read of in the Jewish Scriptures. . . . He would have no union with the slave power of Egypt" (103–4). In a speech to the National Woman's Rights Convention in 1866, she evoked the name of another Moses saying, "We have a woman in our country who has received the name of 'Moses,' not by lying about it, but by acting it out—a woman who has gone down into the Egypt of slavery and brought out hundreds of our people into liberty" (47). Among the other Moses figures that she identifies in her writing are John Brown of Harper's Ferry fame and Abraham Lincoln.

Reprinting these three novels will contribute, I hope, to the current reconsideration of the best theories and methods for scholastic inquiry and critical discussion. But to give priority to the texts themselves, I will suspend further discussion of reasons why the existence of these novels revises our knowledge of African American literary history and offers evidence for reinterpretation of previously known texts and turn now to *Minnie's Sacrifice* (1869), *Sowing and Reaping* (1876–77), and *Trial and Triumph* (1888–89).

First of all, these novels are fun to read. They are interesting and compelling stories about ideas, dilemmas, and choices; loves lost and won; identities uncovered and recovered; purposes defined, risks taken, rewards reaped. The novels are also convenient to read. Written for serial publication, each chapter has enough complication of plot and mystery of outcome to invite the reader to obtain the next installment, but at the same time they are not cliff-hangers. Each chapter offers an episode complete enough in itself to be read and enjoyed in short periods of time. While continuity is important, episodes build upon one another, and the developments are not predictable. The serial format contains enough exposition in each unit to enable a reader to imagine what came before. One need not block out large periods of time in order to get into the story. And finally, these works were written for sharing because their format lends itself to reading aloud.

There is something else about these novels that makes them special to me. Not everyone shares my historical interests, my inclinations toward controversial subject matter, and my tolerance for technical experimentation. My parents, for example, do not like to read books that include violence, sex, or profanity. Try as I might, I cannot convince them that *Native Son*, *The Color Purple*, or *Middle Passage* are worth reading. My sister-in-law is not interested in stories about slavery and racial discrimination. She experiences enough of that in everyday life, she says, and prefers the semifactual escape that historical romances provide. Each of Harper's novels is potentially interesting to them, for Harper's writings may be read unblushingly and pleasurably by people like those in my own family whose preferences and values have caused them to ignore much of the contemporary African American canon. Harper's novels are a welcome relief from the black-as-victim-of-racism-and-discrimination depictions that permeate some other nineteenth-century stories. Yet they are not "raceless" melodramas of life in middle-class resorts or heroic tales of impoverished isolates making their ways through moral and material minefields to worldwide acclaim and material or psychic riches. And finally, these novels are clearly not protest stories or guided tours of black folk culture designed primarily to convert and convict readers outside of the African American culture. These books speak about and to African Americans themselves. If at least one of our goals as scholars and critics is to provide a larger appreciation of African

American literature to a larger and more diverse readership, the potential value of these three texts, and others like them, is impressive.

Minnie's Sacrifice was published in twenty chapters over a period of six months. Despite its title, there are really two major characters, Minnie and Louis. Unrelated and unknown to each other, each child is the progeny of a white master and his black slave. Both children are sent to live in the North where they obtain a good education and grow up to be paragons of virtue, intelligence, sensitivity, and all the other fine things that make up the ideal nineteenth-century hero and heroine. Neither knew the identities of their biological parents and both had been reared as if they were—indeed they assumed themselves to be—Anglo-Americans. But, of course they were not, and the story revolves around their reactions to learning their racial heritage. Both must decide if they will continue to pass as white, thereby living lives of social privilege, or publicly identify themselves as black and dedicate themselves to helping their kinspeople rise up from slavery and assume the rights and privileges due them as citizens of the United States and as joint heirs in Christ.

Harper's readers today may recognize that the author gives Minnie and Louis attitudes that combine those now commonly associated with Martin Luther King, Jr., and Malcolm X. The young couple argue that racial progress must be achieved using the Bible, the ballot box, and, if necessary, bullets. Those who have read *Iola Leroy* may recognize certain basic similarities in the two plots, and knowing that Harper was experimenting with certain themes, characters, and structures some twenty-five years before she published *Iola Leroy* invites further comparison of the two texts in terms of technique, characterization, and social and political contexts. These and many other insights will reward the reader of this unusual story. But for this discussion, focus upon the fact that

Minnie's Sacrifice was published in a black paper, by a black woman, for black readers—during Reconstruction. It shares certain elements of the tragic mulatto themes found in earlier African American novels, but *Minnie's Sacrifice* is not simply a variation on a theme or evidence of intertextuality among *Clotel*, *The Garies and Their Friends*, and even *Our Nig*. It is also a deliberate retelling of the Old Testament Moses story. This is evident from certain patterns and tropes in the text and because Harper makes it explicit in the very first chapter. Camille, Louis's half-sister, decides to save the little blond slave child, not because she knows they share the same father, but because she recognizes an opportunity to reenact the "beautiful story in the Bible" where the king's daughter rescues another beautiful child from bondage by adopting it into the royal family. In the manner of Moses' sister and mother, Louis's grandmother, Miriam, encourages, even manipulates, the young girl in this decision. *Minnie's Sacrifice* is a very clear appropriation of the Judeo-Christian mythology into African American literature. Written about the same time as Harper's other literary experiment, *Moses: A Story of the Nile*, this novel invites the interpretation of that epic poem as a Reconstruction fable and a subversive use of a Bible story to critique a contemporary political situation. Such intertextual comparisons reveal this serialized novel, which resembles a contemporary soap opera, to be also a clever articulation of liberation theology and makes all the more interesting the fact that *Minnie's Sacrifice* was published in the religious press but *Moses: A Story of the Nile*, while advertised in the *Christian Recorder*, was not published in that paper.

Each of the novels reveals ways in which Frances Harper experimented with genre, literary technique, and theme; but *Sowing and Reaping* is especially helpful because it is clearly connected with some of Harper's other works. *Sowing and Reaping* is subtitled "A Temperance Story," but while temperance is the subject most consistently discussed and most critical to the sequence of actions, the central theme, the importance of doing the right thing, is essentially the same as that of *Minnie's Sacrifice. Sowing and Reaping*, a more complicated literary exercise than *Minnie's Sacrifice*, has many more characters and several interwoven subplots. At first, Harper (or the publisher) struggles to control these various strands and makes mistakes such as giving both Jeanette and her lover, Charles, the same last name in the beginning of the story. But overall the story makes a fascinating and integrated display. In *Sowing and Reaping*, Harper complicates the technique of using paired protagonists so common to fiction of that era and found in both "The Two Offers" and *Minnie's Sacrifice* by presenting two sets of paired protagonists. Perhaps to underscore this parallel, the first two installments were both designated as "Chapter One."

The August 10, 1876, episode begins with a dialogue between Paul Clifford and John Anderson, two businessmen who have been friends since their schooldays but whose ideas and actions are virtually opposite. John has decided that his highest ambition is to become rich and for this he is willing not just to "sacrifice time, talent, energy and every faculty" but to "spend honor, conscience and manhood, in an eager search for gold." Paul is also ambitious to succeed financially, but he puts a higher priority on justice, charity, and integrity. Paul Clifford is a staunch temperance man. He advocates equal rights for women and marriages that are shared partnerships. Paul practices "lending a helping hand" upon every opportunity, refusing, for example, to press his claim with a creditor's widow even though his own business is in jeopardy. On August 24, the second Chapter One, subtitled "The Decision" (and included here as the second part of chapter I), begins with a conversation between Jeanette Roland and Belle Gordon. Like Janette Alston and Laura Lagrange in "The Two Offers," Jeanette and Belle are cousins who when faced with a similar dilemma make opposing choices. Using dialogue as exposition, Harper identifies the dilemmas and describes the choices that each of the four makes. Having shown the "sowing," the narrator, who is so intrusive a voice as to be another character, then reveals the results of their various choices. This summary may make the novel seem formulaic and predictable but this is not the case. The dialogue, the logic, and the moral dilemmas presented form the basis for sufficient suspense and interest. The plot is further complicated by the inclusions of several other characters and their stories. There's Josiah Gough, the alcoholic who, through the intervention of Paul and Belle, signs the pledge and reforms, and his wife, Mary, a seamstress whose abusive marriage is in part the fruit of her impulsive decision to elope. There's the story of John and Annette's daughter, Sophronia, who runs away with a phony English count. There's even a tale of what the narrator calls "Intemperance and Sensuality" which comes from the mixture of guns, liquor, and lust.

Comparison of *Sowing and Reaping* to "The Two Offers" is merited not simply because they have similar themes but also because in many ways situations in the novel seem to be elaborations upon those in the short story. For example, Belle's sacrifice of her love for Charles Romaine may be a more detailed exposition of Janette Alston's unrequited love to which the earlier story alluded. John and Annette Anderson's marriage, the descriptions of their material wealth and their impoverished characters, even the fate of their son, Frank, appear to be an elaboration upon the brief sketch of the parents of Laura Lagrange's husband. And, finally, the characters in both "The Two Offers" and *Sowing and Reaping* are racially ambiguous. Their raven hair and flashing eyes might be those of fair-skinned African Americans such as Minnie and Louis or of Americans of other ancestry. Harper does not imply that their circumstances and their conflicts, their choices and their consequences are more appropriate to one race or ethnic group than to another.

Harper's experimentation with literary genre is evident in several ways. Many situations in *Sowing and Reaping* replicate or revise themes in poems such as "Advice to Girls," "The Contrast," "Something and Nothing," "Save the Boys," and "The Fatal Pledge" that Harper published during that same period. Another version of Mary Gough's exploitation as a seamstress is found in Harper's newspaper column "Fancy Sketches." Echoes of language from previous works and certain phrases that will appear in later works are abundant. For example, Belle Gordon describes Charles Romaine as "drifting where he ought to steer" and "floating down the stream" rather than "holding the helm and rudder of his young life." In *Iola Leroy*, the narrator says that Iola's father, Eugene, "had learned to drift where he should have steered, to float with the current instead of nobly breasting the tide."[9] In both cases, these well-meaning but undisciplined men fail to make the right choices and cause great tragedy to befall their loved ones.

At the conclusion of *Trial and Triumph*, as in the conclusion of *Iola Leroy*, the narrator says that under the guise of fiction she has woven a story that will not only delight but also motivate and instruct its readers. Such is the case with each of Harper's novels, but *1888* *Trial and Triumph* differs from the earlier ones because it focuses specifically on the current weaknesses and the potential power of the African American community. As in the other texts, the characters are described more in terms of their values and actions than physical characteristics, and there are still a large number of raven-haired and flashing-eyed individuals; but racial signifiers are everywhere and there is no doubt that the major characters are African American and that the primary conflicts and the best solutions come from that group.

In what may be her most autobiographical writing, Harper presents Annette Harcourt, a strong-willed, outspoken, and sometimes mischievous young woman. Born to an unmarried mother and orphaned in her childhood, Annette is reared by her grandmother and encouraged by several respectable members of her community, but she is ostracized by other members of her family and community. She confronts racial discrimination in the classroom, but graduates with honors only to encounter sexism and racism during her quest to become a teacher and a poet. The now familiar melodramatic elements of Harper's fiction reappear in *Trial and Triumph*. Lovers meet and are separated. Strangers suddenly appear to disrupt lives and change futures. There are fatal illnesses and pathetic deathbed scenes. But *Trial and Triumph* is also explicitly concerned with race and intraracial progress. Its narrator criticizes class distinctions, religious hypocrisy, economic potential, and other issues of direct and immediate concern to late-nineteenth-century African Americans faced with the death of Reconstruction, the birth of Jim Crow laws, and the rise of racial violence. The novel emphasizes the dangers of class divisions based upon appearance, material possessions, and affectations of manner; the differences between the rituals of Christianity and the practices of a true Christian; the ways some African Americans participate in the exploitation and oppression of other African Americans and others work for the greater social good. It introduces a broad spectrum of African American characters. They include Reverend Lomax, a politically conscious and intellectual minister who desires to do more than sway the emotions of his congregation; Mrs. Lasette, a genteel and generous matron who opens her home to gifted and talented individuals of good moral conduct regardless of their family name or the cut of their clothes; and Mr. Thomas, a teacher who loses his position when the schools are integrated. These individuals emphasize racial pride and aspirations by teaching young people to emulate the beauty of the African Cleopatra, advising them of the emotional and psychological consequences of racial passing, and encouraging them to become writers and readers of African American literature.

The presentation of these three novels promises good reading for a variety of individuals. Scholars can more easily assess the life and works of Frances Ellen Watkins Harper and other writers. We now recognize that the richness of our American literary tradition is more vast and the task of recovery more complicated than we may have imagined. As readers, scholars, and critics we are not immune to unwarranted or unexamined assumptions; we would benefit from examination and reexamination of our own interests and those of others; we can accomplish more together than alone. These are, I realize, very general, vague, and even sentimental assertions. They are ones not likely to be challenged but neither are they likely to be taken seriously. To argue for their serious consideration and to show more directly how the rediscovery of *Minnie's Sacrifice, Sowing and Reaping,* and *Trial and Triumph* specifies and reinforces these ideas is my true intention.

Until 1991, no published bibliography of Frances Harper and no discussion of the African American novel that I have seen has mentioned the existence of these three novels. But that is probably because few literary scholars or social historians thought to look in the Afro-Protestant press or to read the research of theologians and church historians and vice versa. And that is probably because as readers we are too prone to assume that the way things are is better than, or at least the same as, the way things were. Since the gulf between the church and state, between belle lettres and bestsellers is large and enlarging, we have been content to assume it has always been so. Such ahistorical and overdisciplined ways of thinking compel many of us in cultural studies, for example, to walk past six storefront churches and two cathedrals while looking for a bar or rap group where we can get in touch with the "real" folk.

Instead, we must make increased efforts to see our ancestors, our neighbors, and ourselves in the complexity and the multiplicity of real life. As a case in point I am suggesting that not only does the examination of the Afro-Protestant press demonstrate that some of our received knowledge about African American literary heritage is misinformed and incomplete, but it also offers the potential to reinterpret, to understand in new ways the literature that we have. Whatever our fields of expertise, it does us well to look beyond our immediate tasks and converse with our fellow plowers once in a while. The presentation of *Minnie's Sacrifice*, *Sowing and Reaping*, and *Trial and Triumph* is intended to provide pleasure and instruction. The process by which they were rediscovered is recorded in the Editor's Note as a testimony for a mode of cooperation that has been viable for years but is not as well known and as extensively practiced today as it should be. These three novels are presented with the hope that reading them will encourage greater curiosity about, more discussion concerning, and higher appreciation for African American literature, then and now.

Notes

1. Frances Ellen Watkins, "Our Greatest Want," in *A Brighter Coming Day: A Frances Ellen Watkins Harper Reader*, ed. Frances Smith Foster (New York: Feminist Press, 1990), 104. Unless otherwise stated, subsequent references to Harper's works are from this source and page numbers are given in the text.

2. Sidney Kaplan, *The Black Presence in the Era of the American Revolution, 1770–1800* (Greenwich, Conn.: New York Graphic Press, 1973), 211.

3. Quoted in Julian D. Mason, Jr., *The Poems of Phillis Wheatley* (Chapel Hill: University of North Carolina Press, 1989), 25.

4. Quoted in ibid., p. 30.

5. "Black Letters; or Uncle Tom-Foolery in Literature," *Graham's Magazine* (May 1853): 214.

6. Robert Bone, *The Negro Novel in America* (New Haven: Yale University Press, 1965), 11.

7. Henry Louis Gates, Jr., *The Signifying Monkey: A Theory of Afro-American Literary Criticism* (New York: Oxford University Press, 1988), 128.

8. James Oliver Horton and Lois E. Horton, *Black Bostonians: Family Life and Community Struggle in the Antebellum North* (New York: Holmes & Meier Publishers, 1979), 12.

9. Frances E. W. Harper, *Iola Leroy* (New York: Oxford University Press, 1988), 86.

Editor's Note

The discovery of these three texts is important because it demonstrates the efficacy of current academic collegiality and argues, I hope, for an even more widespread practice of scholastic sharing. The recovery of these works began with fairly casual conversations about research interests and plans. Later, Nellie McKay, a colleague at the University of Wisconsin well known for her dedication and generosity, recalled my interests when Florence Howe mentioned that the Feminist Press was interested in including Frances Ellen Watkins Harper in its series of "lost" or undervalued women writers. I was invited to submit a prospectus. I did. And that was the beginning which led to the recovery of these works.

Most of Harper's known books had been privately published and it was quite difficult to obtain some of them. Most extant volumes did not circulate and were not microfilmed. Many were often too fragile to photocopy or they were owned by libraries too underfunded and understaffed to provide that service for out-of-town scholars. But in every case, the librarians and archivists were supportive and helpful when I came in person. Examination of the various editions of Harper's books showed that some shared the same title but their contents varied significantly, and some with different titles or copyright dates were essentially the same as others. I quickly learned that whenever I encountered a new title or a different date, I needed to get my hands on the volume itself. Eventually I had seen enough major revisions or entirely new poems, essays, and descriptive prose to understand that Harper's literary production was far more extensive than current scholarship had documented. After nearly five years of traveling about the country and poring over copies often too fragile to photocopy, I thought I had a fairly good idea of the shape and scope of her canon. I had submitted the typescript for the Harper anthology when Jean Fagan Yellin told me that in the course of researching Harriet Jacobs she had collected many citations about other nineteenth-century African American women and offered to share what she had on Frances Harper. When I compared Yellin's bibliography on Harper with my own, four of her entries were particularly intriguing. Each was from the *Christian Recorder*, a newspaper published by the African Methodist Episcopal Church, and each had a single title but multiple dates. Knowing that Harper had written fairly regularly to newspapers about her travels or issues of contemporary importance and knowing that between 1865 and 1870 Harper had undertaken at least three lengthy tours of the Reconstruction South, I thought I knew what to expect, but I was curious enough to go to the Library Company of Philadelphia and to the Philadelphia Historical Society to make sure. When I turned to the June 12, 1869, issue of *The Christian Recorder* and began to read "Minnie's Sacrifice," I was stunned.

My excitement was tempered by the fact that several chapters, including the first six, were missing, but I knew then that this was a historical find. Within a week, I had found *Sowing and Reaping* and *Trial and Triumph* and my elation had given way to curiosity, embarrassment, and frustration. With all the scholarship that had been undertaken on African American fiction and on Frances Harper, why had no published bibliography mentioned these texts? Embarrassed at my own complicity and obtuseness, I wondered why I, too, had been so quick to assume that a writer who pioneered the short story and whose *Iola Leroy* is clearly a revision of Brown's *Clotel* and the antecedent of Charles Chesnutt's fiction had abandoned fiction for thirty-three years? My frustration came about because the preservation of *The Christian Recorder*, as the preservation of many black periodicals, had been incomplete and chapters were missing from each of the three novels. This particular frustration continues, though abated, to this moment. After two years of inquiry and searching, I did find a few more chapters, including the first six to *Minnie's Sacrifice*. Again this discovery was the result of collegial generosity. I had checked every listed collection and every archive and library that I imagined might have an unindexed cache of *Christian Recorders*. The story seemed to be the same. The fragmented and decaying copies had been collected, microfilmed into the most comprehensive and permanent record possible, then apparently most archives had disposed of the originals. If there were any additional copies, I was told, they were in private collections. I had decided it was a lost cause and took up another project, but I continued to ask any and every one I thought might know. While at Harvard Divinity School researching the role of the Afro-Protestant press in the development of African American literature, I met Randall Burkett of the DuBois Institute and Mike Roy of the Black Periodical Literature Project. Neither knew of any secret caches of the *Christian Recorder*, but they both encouraged me to keep looking and they allowed me access to their materials. I read through countless microfilms and thumbed through great stacks of photocopied excerpts, and one afternoon I found chapters one through six of *Minnie's Sacrifice*. In June 1992, encouraged by Ken Rowe, the archivist at Drew University, I visited Drew where I found the last missing chapter of *Trial and Triumph*. Try as I might, I've not found any more, but I hope that through this publication, someone will come forward who knows where the few remaining missing pages are, the complete texts will be published, and the final chapter of this search will have a happy ending.

My intention is to present these novels as accurately as possible. Thus, I have been very conservative in editing. I have made only those changes that seem imperative. Nonetheless, this is not intended as a definitive edition of these stories. The *Christian Recorder* is riddled with typographical errors, so much so that it is not uncommon to find letters from readers objecting to the quality of editing and responses by the editor complaining about inadequate funding for staff and late or illegible manuscripts included in its pages. On the other hand, nineteenth-century spellings, grammar, and idioms vary from our own, and thus it is difficult to determine whether a particular wording is intentional or not. And of course, Frances Harper had her own stylistic preferences. Obvious typographical errors (for example, missing quotation marks or periods) have been silently emended. In cases that are grammatically or stylistically different from today's standard practices but which seem to form a consistent pattern or represent an idiomatic expression, I have elected to preserve the original. Thus, the frequent use of run-on sentences and the use of semi-colons instead of commas, idiosyncratic capitalization (or the lack of it), variations in spelling, and the combining of various speakers' statements in the same paragraph have all been preserved.

When it appears that a word or phrase was inadvertently omitted, I have added it within brackets. In some places, the original source is blurred, torn, or otherwise mutilated. When it is fairly clear what the word or phrase is, I have bracketed it with a question mark. Where a character's name in the original is clearly in error, or in a few places where the context strongly suggests a revision, I have revised and provided the original in a note following Harper's novel. In other places, even though the original wording may be confusing or is perhaps the result of an error committed by the *Christian Recorder*, the original has been preserved.

And finally, some installments of *Minnie's Sacrifice, Sowing and Reaping*, and *Trial and Triumph* are in missing issues of the *Christian Recorder*. I have indicated in this volume where installments are missing. With the hope that readers may know where these missing installments might be found, I include the following list of the issues in which they most likely appeared. In some cases, the issue exists but the pages (given in parentheses) are mutilated or missing. All issues dated earlier than 1854 may have been called the *Christian Herald*. Please send any suggestions to Frances Smith Foster in care of Beacon Press, 25 Beacon Street, Boston, Massachusetts 02108.

May 29, 1869
June 5, 1869
June 19, 1869 (pp. 1–2)
August 7, 1869 (pp. 1–2)
September 18, 1869

August 31, 1876 (pp. 1–2)
September 14, 1876 (pp. 1–3 and 6–7)
September 21, 1876 (pp. 5–6)
November 2, 1876 (pp. 5–6)
November 9, 1876 (pp. 1–2)
November 16, 1876 (pp. 1–2)

January 18, 1877
January 25, 1877

Minnie's Sacrifice

Chapter I

Miriam sat in her lowly cabin, painfully rocking her body to and fro; for a great sorrow had fallen upon her life. She had been the mother of three children, two had died in their infancy, and now her last, her loved and only child was gone, but not like the rest, who had passed away almost as soon as their little feet had touched the threshold of existence. She had been entangled in the mazes of sin and sorrow; and her sun had gone down in darkness. It was the old story. Agnes, fair, young and beautiful, had been a slave, with no power to protect herself from the highest insults that brutality could offer to innocence. Bound hand and foot by that system, which has since gone down in wrath, and blood, and tears, she had fallen a victim to the wiles and power of her master; and the result was the introduction of a child of shame into a world of sin and suffering; for herself an early grave; and for her mother a desolate and breaking heart.

While Miriam was sitting down hopelessly beneath the shadow of her mighty grief, gazing ever and anon on the pale dead face, which seemed to bear in its sad but gentle expression, an appeal

from earth to heaven, some of the slaves would hurry in, and looking upon the fair young face, would drop a word of pity for the
weeping mother, and then hurry on to their appointed tasks. All
day long Miriam sat alone with her dead, except when these kindly
interruptions broke upon the monotony of her sorrow.

In the afternoon, Camilla, the only daughter of her master, entered her cabin, and throwing her arms around her neck exclaimed, "Oh! Mammy, I am so sorry I didn't know Agnes was
dead. I've been on a visit to Mr. Le Grange's plantation, and I've
just got back this afternoon, and as soon as I heard that Agnes was
dead I hurried to see you. I would not even wait for my dinner. Oh!
how sweet she looks," said Camilla, bending over the corpse, "just
as natural as life. When did she die?"

"This morning, my poor, dear darling!" And another burst of
anguish relieved the overcharged heart.

"Oh! Mammy, don't cry, I am so sorry; but what is this?" said
she, as the little bundle of flannel began to stir.

"That is poor Agnes' baby."

"Agnes' baby? Why, I didn't know that Agnes had a baby. Do
let me see it?"

Tenderly the grandmother unfolded the wrappings, and presented the little stranger. He was a beautiful babe, whose golden
hair, bright blue eyes and fair complexion showed no trace of the
outcast blood in his veins.

"Oh, how beautiful!" said Camilla; "surely this can't be Agnes'
baby. He is just as white as I am, and his eyes—what a beautiful
blue—and his hair, why it is really lovely."

"He is very pretty, Miss, but after all he is only a slave."

A slave. She had heard that word before; but somehow, when
applied to that fair child, it grated harshly on her ear; and she said,
"Well, I think it is a shame for him to be a slave, when he is just as
white as anybody. Now, Mammy," said she, throwing off her hat,

and looking soberly into the fire, "if I had my way, he should never be a slave."

"And why can't you have your way? I'm sure master humors you in everything."

"I know that; Pa does everything I wish him to do; but I don't know how I could manage about this. If his mother were living, I would beg Pa to set them both free, and send them North; but his mother is gone; and, Mammy, we couldn't spare you. And besides, it is so cold in the North, you would freeze to death, and yet, I can't bear the thought of his being a slave. I wonder," said she, musing to herself, "I wonder if I couldn't save him from being a slave. Now I have it," she said, rising hastily, her face aglow with pleasurable excitement. "I was reading yesterday a beautiful story in the Bible about a wicked king, who wanted to kill all the little boys of a people who were enslaved in his land, and how his mother hid her child by the side of a river, and that the king's daughter found him and saved his life. It was a fine story; and I read it till I cried. Now I mean to do something like that good princess. I am going to ask Pa, to let me take him to the house, and have a nurse for him, and bring him up like a white child, and never let him know that he is colored."

Miriam shook her head doubtfully; and Camilla, looking disappointed, said, "Don't you like my plan?"

"Laws, honey, it would be fustrate, but your Pa wouldn't hear to it."

"Yes, he would, Mammy, because I'll tell him I've set my heart upon it, and won't be satisfied if he don't consent. I know if I set my heart upon it, he won't refuse me, because he always said he hates to see me fret. Why, Mammy, he bought me two thousand dollars worth of jewelry when we were in New York, just because I took a fancy to a diamond set which I saw at Tiffany's. Anyhow, I am going to ask him." Eager and anxious to carry out her plan,

Camilla left the cabin to find her father. He was seated in his library, reading Homer. He looked up, as her light step fell upon the threshold, and said playfully, "What is your wish, my princess? Tell me, if it is the half of my kingdom."

Encouraged by his manner, she drew near, perched upon his knee, and said; "Now, you must keep your word, Pa. I have a request to make, but you must first promise me that you will grant it."

"But I don't know what it is. I can't tell. You might want me to put my head in the fire."

"Oh no, Pa, you know I don't!"

"Well, you might wish me to run for Congress."

"Oh no, Pa, I know that you hate politics."

"Well, darling, what is your request?"

"No; tell me first that you will grant it. Now, don't tease me, Pa; say yes, and I will tell you."

"Well, yes; if it is anything in reason."

"Well, it is in reason, let me tell you, Pa. To-day, after I came home, I asked Annette where was Agnes, and she told me she was dead. Oh I was so sorry; and so before I got my dinner I hastened to Mammy's cabin, and found poor Mammy almost heart-broken, and Agnes lying dead, but looking just as natural as life."

"She was dead, but had left one of the dearest little babies I ever saw. Why, Pa, he is just as white as we are; and I told Mammy so, but she said it didn't matter; 'he is a poor slave, just like the rest of us.' Now, Pa, I don't want Agnes' baby to be a slave. Can't you keep him from growing up a slave?"

"How am I to do that, my little Abolitionist?"

"No, Pa, I am not an Abolitionist. I heard some of them talk when I was in New York, and I think they are horrid creatures; but, Pa, this child is so white, nobody would ever know that he had one drop of Negro blood in his veins. Couldn't we take him out of that cabin, and make all the servants promise that they would never breathe a word about his being colored, and let me bring him up as a white child?"

"Well," said Mr. Le Croix, bursting into a hearty laugh, "that is a capital joke; my little dewdrop talk of bringing up a child! Why, darling, you would tire of him in a week."

"Oh no, Pa, I wouldn't! Just try me; if it is only for a week."

"Why, Sunbeam, it is impossible. Who ever heard of such a thing as a Negro being palmed upon society as a white person?"

"Negro! Pa, he is just as white as you are, and his eyes are as blue as mine."

"Still he belongs to the Negro race; and one drop of that blood in his veins curses all the rest. I would grant you anything in reason, but this is not to be thought of. Were I to do so I would immediately lose caste among all the planters in the neighborhood; I would be set down as an Abolitionist, and singled out for insult and injury. Ask me anything, Camilla, but that."

"Oh, Pa, what do you care about social position? You never hunt, nor entertain company, nor take any part in politics. You shut yourself up in your library, year after year, and pore over your musty books, and hardly any one knows whether you are dead or alive. And I am sure that we could hide the secret of his birth, and pass him off as the orphan child of one of our friends, and that will be the truth; for Agnes was our friend; at least I know she was mine."

"Well, I'll see about it; now, get down, and let me finish reading this chapter."

The next day Camilla went again to the cabin of Miriam; but the overseer had set her to a task in the field, and Agnes' baby was left to the care of an aged woman who was too old to work in the fields, but not being entirely past service, she was appointed as one of the nurses for the babies and young children, while their mothers were working in the fields.

Camilla, feeling an unusual interest in the child, went to the overseer, and demanded that Miriam should be released from her tasks, and permitted to attend the child.

In vain the overseer plead the pressure for hands, and the busy season. Camilla said it did not matter, she wanted Miriam, and she would have her; and he, feeling that it was to his interest to please the little lady, had Miriam sent from the field to Camilla.

"Mammy, I want you to come to the house. I want you to come and be my Mammy. Agnes is dead; your husband is gone, and I want you to come and bring the baby to the house, and I am going to get him some beautiful dresses, and some lovely coral I saw in New Orleans, and I am going to dress him so handsomely, that I believe Pa will feel just as I do, and think it a shame that such a beautiful child should be a slave."

Camilla went home, and told her father what she had done. And he, willing to compromise with her, readily consented; and in a day or two the child and his grandmother were comfortably ensconced in their new quarters.

The winter passed; the weeks ripened into months, and the months into years, and the child under the pleasant dispensations of love and kindness grew to be a fine, healthy, and handsome boy.

One day, when Mr. Le Croix was in one of his most genial moods, Camilla again introduced the subject which she had concealed, but not abandoned.

"Now, father, I do think it is a shame for this child to be a slave, when he is just as white as anybody; I am sure we could move away from here to France, and you could adopt him as your son, and no one would know anything of his birth and parentage. He is so beautiful, I would like him for my brother; and he looks like us anyhow."

Le Croix flushed deep at these words, and he looked keenly into his daughter's face; but her gaze was so open, her expression so frank and artless, he could not think that her words had any covert meaning in reference to the paternity of the child; but to save that child from being a slave, and to hide his origin was with her a pet scheme; and, to use her own words, "she had set her heart upon it."

Chapter II

Mr. Bernard Le Croix was the only son of a Spanish lady, and a French gentleman, who were married in Hayti a few months before the revolution, which gave freedom to the Island, and made Hayti an independent nation.

His father, foreseeing the storm which was overshadowing the land, contrived to escape, bringing with him a large amount of personal property; and preferring a climate similar to his own, he bought a plantation on Red river, and largely stocked it with slaves. Only one child blessed their union; Bernard Le Croix, who grew up sensitive, shy and retiring, with a taste for solitude and literary pursuits.

During the troubles in Hayti, his uncle and only daughter escaped from the Island, leaving every thing behind except the clothing upon their persons, and a few jewels they had hastily collected. Broken in spirits, feeble in health, Louis Le Croix reached Louisiana, only to die in his brother's arms and to leave his orphan daughter to his care. She was about ten years old and Bernard was twelve, and in their childhood was commenced a friendship which ripened into love and marriage. Bernard's father and mother lived long enough to see their first and only grandchild, and then died, leaving their son a large baronial estate, 500 slaves, and a vast amount of money.

Passionately fond of literature, aesthetic in his tastes, he devoted himself to poetry and the ancient classics; filled his home with the finest paintings and the most beautiful statuary, and had his gardens laid out in the most exquisite manner. And into that beautiful home he brought his young and lovely bride; but in that fair house where velvet carpets hushed her tread, and magnificence surrounded her path, she drooped and faded. Day by day her cheek grew paler, her footsteps slower, until she passed away like a thing of love and light, and left her heart-broken husband and a child of six summers to mourn her loss.

Bernard, ever shy and sensitive, grew more so after the death of his wife. He sought no society; seemed to lose all interest in politics; and secluded himself in his library till he had almost passed from the recollection of his nearest neighbors. He superintended the education of his daughter, because he could not bear the thought of being separated from her. And she, seeing very little of society, and reading only from the best authors, both ancient and modern, was growing up with very little knowledge of the world, except what she learned from books.

Without any female relatives to guide her, she had no other associates than the servants of her household, and the family of Mr. Le Grange. Her mother's nurse and favorite servant had taken the charge of her after her death, and Agnes had been her nurse and companion.

Camilla, although [adored?] and petted by every one, and knowing no law but her own will, was still a very lovely child. Her father, wrapped in his literary pursuits, had left the entire control of his plantation to overseers, in whom he trusted almost implicitly. And many a tale of wrong and sorrow came to the ear of Camilla; for these simple-minded people had learned to love her, and to trust in her as an angel of mercy. Often would she interfere in their behalf, and tell the story of their wrongs to her father. And at her instance, more than one overseer had been turned away; which, coming to the ears of others, made them cautious how they offended the little lady, for young as she was they soon learned that she had great influence with her ease-loving father, who would comply with almost any fancy or request rather than see her unhappy or fretting.

And Camilla, knowing her power, insisted that Agnes' child should be raised as a white child, and the secret of his birth effectually concealed. At first, Mr. Le Croix thought it was a passing whim that she would soon forget; that the child would amuse and interest her for awhile; and then she would tire of him as she had of other things; such as her birds, her squirrel, and even her Shetland pony. But when he found that instead of her intention being a passing whim it was a settled purpose, he made up his mind to accede to her wishes.

His plan was to take the child North, to have him educated, and then adopt him as his son. And in fact the plan rather suited him; for then he could care for him as a son, without acknowledging the relationship. And being a member of two nations having a Latin basis, he did not feel the same pride of race and contempt and repulsion for weaker races which characterizes the proud and imperious Anglo-Saxon.

The next Summer Mr. Le Croix took a journey to the North, taking Louis and Camilla with him. He found a very pleasant family school in New England; and having made suitable arrangements, he left Louis in the care of the matron, whose kindness and attentions soon won the child's heart; and before he left the North, Louis seemed perfectly contented with his new home.

Camilla was delighted with her tour; the constant companion of her father, she visited with him every place of amusement or interest they could find. She was much pleased with the factories; and watched with curious eyes the intelligent faces of the operatives, as they plied with ready fingers their daily tasks. Sometimes she would contrast their appearance with the laborers she had seen wending their way into their lowly huts; and then her face would grow sober even to sadness. A puzzled expression would flit over her countenance, as if she were trying to solve a problem which was inexplicable to her.

One day on the hunt for some new excitement, her father passed down Tremont St., and saw advertised, in large letters, on the entrance to Tremont Temple, "Anti Slavery Meeting;" and never having been in such a place before he entered, impelled by a natural curiosity to hear what could be said against a system in which he had been involved from his earliest recollections, without taking the pains to examine it.

The first speaker was a colored man. This rather surprised him. He had been accustomed to colored men all the days of his life; and as such, he had known some of them to be intelligent, shrewd, and wide awake; but this was a new experience. The man had been a slave, and recounted in burning words the wrongs which had been heaped upon him. He told that he had been a husband and a father: that his wife had possessed (for a slave) the "fatal gift of beauty;" that a trader, from whose presence her soul had recoiled with loathing, had marked her as his prey. Then he told how he had knelt at his master's feet, and implored him not to sell her, but it was all in vain. The trader was rich in sin-cursed gold; and he was poor and weak. He next attempted to describe his feelings when he saw his wife and children standing on the auction block; and heard the coarse jests of the spectators, and the fierce competition of the bidders.

The speaker made a deep impression upon the minds of the audience; and even Le Croix, who had been accustomed to slavery all his life, felt a sense of guilt passing over him for his complicity in the system; whilst Camilla grew red and pale by turns, and clutching her little hands nervously together, said, "Father, let us go home."

Le Croix saw the deep emotion on his daughter's face, and the nervous twitchings of her lips, and regretted that he had introduced her to such an exciting scene.

When they were seated in their private parlor, Le Croix said: "Birdie, I am sorry that we attended that meeting this morning. I didn't believe a word that nigger said; and yet these people all drank it down as if every word were gospel truth. They are a set of fanatics, calculated to keep the nation in hot water. I hope that you will never enter such a place again. Did you believe one word that negro said?"

"Why, yes, Pa, I did, because our Isaac used to tell me just such a story as that. If I had shut my eyes, I could have imagined that it was Isaac telling his story."

"Isaac! What business had Isaac telling you any such stories?"

"Oh, Pa, don't get angry with Isaac. It wasn't his fault; it was mine.

"You know when you brought him home to drive the carriage, he used to look so sorrowful, and I said to him one day, Isaac, what makes you so sad? Why don't you laugh and talk, like Jerry and Sam?

"And he said, 'Oh Missus, I can't! Ise got a mighty heap of trouble on my mind.' And he looked so down-hearted when he said this, I wanted to know what was the matter; but he said, 'It won't do, for a little lady like you to know the troubles of we poor creatures,' but one day, when Sam came home from New Orleans he brought him a letter from his wife, and he really seemed to be overjoyed, and he kissed the letter, and put it in his bosom, and I never saw him look half so happy before. So the next day when I asked him to get the pony ready, he asked me if I wouldn't read it for him. He said he had been trying to make it out, but somehow he could not get the hang of the words, and so I sat down and read it to him. Then he told me about his wife, how beautiful she was; and how a trader, a real mean man, wanted to buy her, and that he had begged his master not to sell her; but it was no use. She had to go; but he was glad of one thing; the trader was dead, and his wife had got a place in the city with a very nice lady, and he hoped to see her when he went to New Orleans. Pa, I wonder how slavery came to be. I should hate to belong to anybody, wouldn't you, Pa?"

"Why, yes, darling, but then the negroes are contented, and wouldn't take their freedom, if you would give it to them."

"I don't know about that, Pa; there was Mr. Le Grange's Peter. Mr. Le Grange used to dress him so fine and treat him so well that he thought no one would ever tempt Peter to leave him; and he came North with him every year for three or four summers, and he always made out that he was afraid of the abolitionists—bob-olitionists he used to call them—and Mr. Le Grange just believed that Peter was in earnest, and somehow he got Mrs. Le Grange to bring his wife North to wait on her. And when they both got here, they both left; and Mrs. Le Grange had to wait on herself, until she got another servant. She told me she had got enough of the North, and never wanted to see it again so long as she lived; that she wouldn't have taken three thousand dollars for them."

"Well, darling, they would have never left, if these meddlesome abolitionists hadn't put it in their heads; but, darling, don't bother your brain about such matters. See what I have bought you this morning," said he, handing her a necklace of the purest pearls; "here, darling, is a birth-day present for you." Camilla took the necklace, and gazing absently upon it said, "I can't understand it."

"What is it, my little philosopher, that you can't understand?"

"Pa, I can't understand slavery; that man made me think it was something very bad. Do you think it can be right?"

Le Croix's face flushed suddenly, and he bit his lip, but said nothing, and commenced reading the paper.

"Why don't you answer me, Pa?" Le Croix's brow grew darker, but he tried to conceal his vexation, and quietly said, "Darling, never mind. Don't puzzle your little head about matters you cannot understand, and which our wisest statesmen cannot solve."

Camilla said no more, but a new train of thought had been awakened. She had lived so much among the slaves, and had heard so many tales of sorrow breathed confidentially into her ears, that she had unconsciously imbibed their view of the matter; and without comprehending the injustice of the system, she had learned to view it from their standpoint of observation.

What she had seen of slavery in the South had awakened her sympathy and compassion. What she had heard of it in the North had aroused her sense of justice. She had seen the old system under a new light. The good seed was planted, which was yet to yield its harvest of blessed deeds.

Chapter III

"What is the matter?" said St. Pierre Le Grange, as he entered suddenly the sitting-room of his wife, Georgietta Le Grange, and saw her cutting off the curls from the head of little girl about five years old, the child of a favorite slave.

"Matter enough!" said the angry wife, her cheeks red with excitement and her eyes half blinded with tears of vexation. "This child shan't stay here; and if she does, she shall never again be taken for mine."

"Who took her for yours? What has happened that has brought about all this excitement?"

"Just wait a minute," said Georgietta, trying to frame her excitement into words.

"Yesterday I invited the Le Fevres and the Le Counts, and a Northern lady they had stopping with Mrs. Le Fevre, to dine with us. Today I told Ellen to have the servants all cleaned up, and looking as well as possible; and so I distributed around more than a dozen turbans, for I wanted Mrs. King to see how much better and happier our negroes looked here than they do when they are free in the North, and what should Ellen do but dress up her little minx in her best clothes, and curl her hair and let her run around in the front yard."

"So she overdid the thing," said Le Grange, beginning to comprehend the trouble.

"Yes, she did, but she will never do it again," exclaimed Mrs. Le Grange, her dark eyes flashing defiantly.

Le Grange bit his lip, but said nothing. He saw the storm that was brewing, and about to fall on the head of the hapless child and mother, and thought that he would do nothing to increase it.

"When Mrs. Le Fevre," continued Georgietta, "alighted from the carriage, she noticed the child, and calling the attention of the whole party to her, said, 'Oh, how beautiful she is! The very image of her father.' 'Mrs. Le Grange,' said she, after passing the compliments of the day, 'I congratulate you on having such a beautiful child. She is the very image of her father. And how large she is for her age.' Just then Marie came to the door and said 'She's not my sister, that is Ellen's child.' I saw the gentlemen exchange glances, and the young ladies screw up their mouths to hide their merriment, while Mrs. Le Fevre, with all her obtuseness, seemed to comprehend the blunder, and she said, 'Child, you must excuse me, for my poor old eyes are getting so good for nothing I can hardly tell one person from the other.' I blundered some kind of answer, I hardly know what I said. I was almost ready to die with vexation; but this shall never happen again."

"What are you going to do?"

"You see what I have begun to do. I am going to have all this curling business broken up, and I am going to have her dressed in domestic, like the other little niggers. I'll let Ellen know that I am mistress here; and as soon as a trader comes along I mean to sell her. I want a new set of pearls anyhow."

Le Grange made no reply. He was fond of the child, but knowing what a termagant his wife was, he thought that silence like discretion was the better part of valor, and hastily beat a retreat from her presence.

"Take these curls and throw them away," said Mrs. Le Grange to Sally, her waiting-maid. "Move quick, and take this child into the kitchen, and don't let me see her in the front yard again. Do you hear what I say?" said Georgiette in a sharp, shrill tone. "Don't you let me see that child in the front yard again. Here, before you go, darken this room, and let me see if I can get any rest. I am so nervous, I am almost ready to fly."

Sally did as she was bidden; and taking the child to the kitchen, exclaimed to Milly, the cook, "Hi! Oh! there's been high times upstairs to-day."

"What's the matter?" said Milly, wiping the dough from her hands, and turning her face to Sally.

"Oh! Missus mad 'bout Ellen's child. She's mad as a March hare. See how she's cut all her hair off."

"A debil," said Milly. "What did she do dat for? She is allers up to some debilment. What did that poor innercence child do to her? I wonder what she'll get at next!"

"I don't know, but to-day when Mrs. Le Ferre come'd here she kissed the child, and said it was the very image of its father, and Missus just looked mad enough to run her through."

Milly, in spite of her indignation could not help laughing. "Well, that's a good joke. I guess Missus' high as ninety. What did Massa say?"

"He neber said a word; he looked like he'd been stealin' a sheep; and Missus she jist cut up high, and said she was going to keep her hair cut short, and have her dressed in domestic, and kept in the kitchen, and when she got a good chance she meant to sell her, for she wanted a new set of pearls anyhow. Massa neber said beans. I jist b'lieve he's feared of her. She's sich a mity piece. I spect some night the debil will come and fly way wid her. I hope so anyhow."

To which not very pious wish Milly replied, "I am fraid there is no such good luck. Nothin' don't s'prise me that Miss Georgiette does 'cause she's a chip off the old block. Her mother's poor niggers used to be cut up and slashed all the time; for she was a horse at the mill. De debil was in dat woman big as a sheep. Dere was Nancy, my fellow servant; somehow she got a spite agin Nancy's husban', said he shouldn't come dere any more. Pore Nancy, her and Andy war libing together in dar nice little cabin, and Nancy did keep ebery ting shinin' like a new pin, 'cause she would work so hard when she was done her task for Missus. But one day Missus got de debil in her, and sayed Andy shouldn't come der any more, and she jist had all Nancy's tings took out de cabin and shut it up, and made her come and sleep in de house. Pore Nancy, she cried as if her heart would break right in two; and she says why does you take my husban' from me? and Missus said I did it to please my own self, and den Nancy kneeled at her feet and said, 'Missus I'll get up before day and set up till twelve or one o'clock at night and work for you, but please don't take me from my husban'.' An' what do you think ole Missus did? Why she jist up wid her foot and kicked Nancy in de mouf, and knocked out two of her teef. I seed her do it wid my own blessed eyes. An' I sed to myself de debil will never git his own till he gits you. Well she did worry dat pore cretur almost to death. She used to make her sleep in the room wid her chillen, and locked de door ebery night, and Sundays she'd lebe some one to watch her, she was so fraid she'd git to see her husban'. An' dis Miss Georgiette is de very moral of her Ma, and she's jist as big as a spitfire."

"Hush," said Milly, "here comes Jane. Don't say no more 'bout Missus, cause she's real white people's nigger, and tells all she knows, and what she don't."

Chapter IV

"I am really sorry, Ellen, but I can't help it. Georgiette has taken a dislike to the child, and there is no living in peace with her unless I sell the child or take it away."

"Oh! Mr. St. Pierre, you would not sell that child when it is your own flesh and blood?" Le Grange winced under these words.

"No, Ellen, I'll never consent to sell the child, but it won't do for her to stay here. I've made up my mind to send her North, and have her educated."

"And then I'll never see my darling any more."

"But, Ellen, that is better than having her here to be knocked around by Georgiette, and if I die to be sold as a slave. It is the best thing I can do,—hang old Mrs. Le Fevre's tongue; but I guess it would have come out some time or the other. I just tell you what I'll do, Ellen. I'll take the child down to New Orleans, and make out to Georgiette that I am going to sell her, but instead of that, I'll get a friend of mine who is going to Pennsylvania to take her with him, and have her boarded there, and educated. Nobody need know anything about her being colored. I'd send you both, Ellen, but, to tell you the truth, the plantation is running down, and the crops are so short this year I can't afford it; but when times get better, I'll send you up there and tell you where you can find her."

"Well, Mr. St. Pierre, that is better than having Missus knocking her around or selling her to one of those old mean nigger traders, and never having a chance to see my darling no more. But, Mr. St. Pierre, before you take her away won't you please give me her likeness? Maybe I won't know her when I see her again."

Le Grange consented, and when he went to the city again he told his wife he was going to sell the child.

"I am glad of it," said Georgiette. "I would have her mother sold, but we can't spare her; she is so handy with her needle, and does all the cutting out on the place."

Le Grange's Plan

"The whole fact is this Joe, I am in an awkward fix. I have got myself into a scrape, and I want you to help me out of it. You were good at such things when we were at College, and I want you to try your hand again."

"Well, what's the difficulty now?"

"Well, it is rather a serious one. I have got a child on my hands, and I don't know what to do with it."

"Whose child is it?"

"Now, that's just where the difficulty lies. It is the child of one of my girls, but it looks so much like me, that my wife don't want it on the place. I am too hard up just now to take the child and her mother, North, and take care of them there. And to tell you the truth I am too humane to have the child sold here as a slave. Now in a word do you think that among your Abolitionist friends in the North you could find any one who would raise the child and bring it up like a white child."

"I don't know about that St. Pierre. There are a number of our people in the North, who do two things. They hate slavery and hate negroes. They feel like the woman who in writing to her husband said, they say (or don't say) that absence conquers love; for the longer you stay away the better I love you. But then I know some who, I believe, are really sincere, and who would do anything to help the colored people. I think I know two or three families who would be willing to take the child, and do a good part by her. If you say so, I will write to a friend whom I have now in mind, and if they will consent I will take the child with me when I go North, provided I can do it without having it discovered that she is colored, for it would put me in an awkward fix to have it known that I took a colored child away with me."

"Oh, never fear," said St. Pierre, slapping his friend on the shoulder. "The child is whiter than you are, and you know you can pass for white."

True to his promise, Josiah Collins wrote to a Quaker friend, whom he knew in Pennsylvania, and told him the particulars of the child's history, and the wishes of her father, and the compensation he would give. In a few days he received a favorable response in which the friend told him he was glad to have the privilege of rescuing one of that fated race from a doom more cruel than the grave; that the compensation was no object; that they had lost their only child, and hoped that she would in a measure fill the void in their hearts.

Highly gratified with the kind letter of the friend, Le Grange gave the child into the charge of Josiah Collins, and putting a check for five hundred dollars in his hand, parted with them at the [station].

He went back into the country, and told his wife that he had found a trader, who thought the child so beautiful, and that he had bought her to raise as a fancy girl, and had given him five hundred dollars for her. "And here," said he, handing her a set of beautiful pearls, "is my peace offering."

Georgette's eyes glistened as she entertwined the pearls amid the wealth of her raven hair, and clasped them upon her beautifully rounded arms.

What mattered it to her if every jewel cost a heart throb, and if the whole set were bought with the price of blood? They suited her style of beauty, and she cared not what they cost. Proud, imperious, and selfish, she knew no law but her own will; no gratification but the enjoyment of her own desires.

Passing from the boudoir of his wife, he sought the room where Ellen sat, busily cutting and arranging the clothing for the field hands, and gazing furtively around he said, "here is Minnie's likeness. I have managed all right." "Thank Heaven!" said the sad hearted mother, as she paused to dry her tears, and then resumed her needle. "Anything is better—than Slavery."

Chapter V

Before I proceed any further with my story, let me tell the reader something of the Le Granges, whom I have so unceremoniously introduced.

Le Grange, like Le Croix, was of French and Spanish descent, and his father had also been a Haytian refugee. But there the similitude ends; unlike Le Croix, he had grown up a gay and reckless young man, fond of sports, and living an aimless life.

His father had on his plantation a beautiful quadroon girl, named Ellen, whom he had bought in Richmond because she begged him to buy her when he had bought her mother, who had been recommended to him as a first-rate cook. They had been servants in what was called one of the first families of Virginia, and had been treated by their mistress with more kindness and consideration than generally fell to the lot of persons in their condition. As long as she lived, they had been well fed and well clothed, and except the deprivation of their freedom, had known but few of the hardships so incident to slave life; but a reverse had fallen upon them.

Their mistress had intended to set them free, but, dying suddenly, she had failed to carry out her intention. Her property fell into the hands of distant heirs, who sold it all, and divided it among themselves. Ellen and her mother were put up at auction, when a kindly looking old Frenchman bought the mother. Ellen stood trembling by; but, when she saw her mother's new master, she started forth, and kneeling at his feet, she begged him to buy her. The mother joined in and said, "Do, Massa, and I'll serve you faithful day and night; there is a heap of work in these old bones yet."

Mr. Le Grange told her to be quiet, and he would buy her. And, true to his word, although the bidding ran high, and the competition was fierce, he bought her; and the next day, he started with them for his plantation on Red River.

His son, Louis, had just graduated, and was spending the winter at home, in just that mood of which it is said that Satan finds some mischief for idle hands to do. Milly, who knew the wiles of the world better than Ellen, tried to keep her as much as possible out of his way; but her caution was all in vain. She saw her child engulfed, as thousands of her race had been.

Mrs. Le Grange, when she became apprised of the condition of things, grew very angry; but, instead of venting her indignation upon the head of her offending son, she poured out the vials of her wrath upon the defenseless girl. She made up her mind to sell her off the place, and picked the opportunity, while her son was absent, to send her to a trader's pen in the city. When Louis came home, he found Milly looking very sullen and distressed, and her eyes red with weeping.

"What is the matter?" said Louis.

"Matter enough," said Milly. "Missus done gone and sold Ellen."

"Sold Ellen! Why, how did that happen?"

"Why, she found out all about her, and said she should not stay on the place another day, and so she sent her down to Orleans to the nigger trader's, and my heart's most broke," and Milly sat down, wiping her tears with her apron.

"Never mind, Milly," said Louis, "I'll go down to New Orleans and bring her back. Mother sha'n't do as she pleases with me, as if

I were a boy, and must always be tied to her apron string. I've got some money of my own, and I mean to find Ellen if I have to look all over the country."

"He entered the dining room, and saw his mother seated at the tea table, looking as bland and pleasant as a Spring morning, and asked, "Where is Ellen?"

The smile died from her lips, and she answered, curtly, "She is out of *your* reach [?]. I've sold her."

"But where have you sold her?"

"Out of your reach, and that is all I am going to tell you."

Louis, without saying another word went out to the coachman, and asked what time the cars left the station.

"Ten minutes to nine."

"Can you take me there in time to reach the train? I want to go to the city tonight."

"Dunno, massa; my best horse is lame, and what—"

"Never mind your excuse; here," said he, throwing him a dollar, "hitch up as quick as possible, and take me there without any 'buts' or 'ifs.'"

"All right, massa," said Sam, grinning with delight. "I'll have you over there in short order."

The carriage harnessed, Samuel found no difficulty with his horses, and reached the depot almost a half hour before the time.

Louis arrived in the city after midnight, and the next day he devoted to hunting for Ellen. He searched through different slave pens, inquired of all the traders, until at last, ready to abandon his search in hopelessness, he heard of a private jail in the suburbs of the city. Nothing daunted by his failure, he found the place and Ellen also.

The trader eyed him keenly, and saw from his manner that he was in earnest about having the girl.

"She is not for sale in this city. Whoever buys her must give me a pledge to take her out of this city. That was the bargain I made with her mistress. She made me promise her that I would sell her to no one in the vicinity of the city. In fact, she wanted me to sell her out of the way of her son. His mother said she had dedicated him to the Blessed Virgin, and I reckon she wanted to keep him out of the way of temptation. Now what will you give me for her?"

"Will you take a thousand for her?"

"Now you ain't saying nothing," said the trader, shutting one eye, and spitting on the floor.

"How will twelve hundred do?"

"It won't do at all, not for such a fancy article as that. I'd rather keep her for myself than sell her at such a low figure. Why, just look at her! Why, she's pretty as a picture! Look at that neck, and her shoulders. See how she carries her head! And look at that splendid head of hair. Why some of our nabobs would give three thousand dollars; but I'll tell you what I'll do, I'll let you have her for two thousand dollars; fancy article is cheap at that."

Louis demurred, but the trader was inexorable, and rather than let the opportunity to rescue Ellen from him escape he paid the exorbitant price, and had her brought to his hotel. His next work was to get a house for Ellen, and have her taken there, installed as his mistress. He then went back to the plantation as if nothing had happened, and his mother soon thought he was reconciled about the loss of Ellen. Only Milly knew his secret, and she kept it as a secret thing.

"I've got some pleasant news for you, Louis," said Mrs. Le Grange, one day to her son: "your uncle and cousin are coming down from Virginia, and I want you to be all attention to your cousin, for she is very rich. She has a fortune in her right, which was left her by her grandmother, and besides she will have another one at her father's death, added, to which they say, she is a very beautiful girl."

Great preparations were made for the expected guests. Georgiette was Mrs. Le Grange's brother's child, and having been separated from him for more than fifteen years she was full of joyful anticipations, when he apprised her of his intention of visiting her in company with his daughter. At length the welcome day arrived, and Mrs. Le Grange stood arranging her jewels and ribbons to receive the guests.

"You are welcome to Louisiana," said she, removing Georgiette's shawl, and tenderly kissing her, "and you too, brother," she said, as Mr. Monteith followed his daughter. "How beautiful Georgiette has grown since I saw her. Why darling you look charming! I'm afraid I shan't be able to keep you long for some of the beaux will surely run away with you." "My son," said Mrs. Le Grange, introducing Louis, who just then entered the door.

««»»

Louis bowed very low, and expressed his pleasure in seeing them; and hoped they would have a happy time, and that nothing should be wanting on his part, to make it so. Very pleasantly passed the time away; Georgiette was in high and charming spirits; and many a pleasant ride and delightful saunter she took with her cousin through the woods, or in visiting other plantations. She was very popular among the planters' sons; admired by the young men, but feared and envied by the girls.

And thus the hours passed in a whirl of pleasurable excitement, until Louis actually imagined himself in love with her, and found himself one pleasant afternoon offering her his hand and heart.

She blushed and sighed, and referred him to her papa; and in a few weeks they were engaged.

At length the time of their departure came; and Louis, after accompanying them to New Orleans, returned to make ready for the wedding. His father made him a present of a large plantation, which he stocked from his own purse, with three hundred slaves; and installed Ellen there as housekeeper till the arrival of the new mistress.

Chapter VI

"Thee is welcome to S.," said the cheerful voice of Thomas Carpenter, as Josiah Collins alighted, bringing with him his charge; "and is this the little child thee wrote me about? I am heartily glad thee has rescued her from that dreadful system!"

"Anna," said he, turning to his wife, who had just entered the room, "here is our friend, Josiah Collins, and the little girl I told thee about."

"I am glad thee has come," said Anna. "sit down and make thyself at home. And this is the little girl thee wrote Thomas about. She is a beautiful child," continued Anna, gazing admiringly at the child. "I hope she will be contented. Does she fret about her mother?"

"Not much; she would sometimes ask, 'where is mamma?' But the ladies in the cars were very kind to her, and she was quite at home with them. I told them I was taking her North; that I thought the North would better agree with her; and that it was not convenient for her mother to come on just now. I was really amused with the attention she received from the Southern ladies; knowing how they would have shrunk from such offices if they had known that one drop of the outcast blood ran in her veins."

"Why, Josiah," said Anna, "I have always heard that there was more prejudice against the colored people in the North than in the South. There is a difference in the manifestations of this feeling, but I do not think there is as much prejudice here as there. [Here?] we have a prejudice which is [formed from?] traditional ideas. We see in many parts of the North a very few of the colored people, and our impressions of them have received their coloring more or less from what the slaveholders have said of them."

"We have been taught that they are idle, improvident, and unfitted for freedom, and incapable of progression; and when we see them in the cities we see them overshadowed by wealth, enterprise, and activity, so that our unfavorable impressions are too often confirmed. Still if one of that class rises above this low mental condition, we know that there are many who are willing to give such a one a healthy recognition."

"I know that there are those that have great obstacles to overcome, but I think that while Southerners may have more personal likings for certain favorite servants, they have stronger prejudices than even we have, or if they have no more than we have, they have more self-restraint, and show it more virulently."

"But I [think?] they do not seem to have any horror of personal contact."

"Of course not; constant familiarity with the race has worn away all sense of physical repulsion but there is a prejudice which ought to be an American feeling; it is a prejudice against their rising in the scale of humanity. A prejudice which virtually says you are down, and I mean to keep you down. As a servant I tolerate you; you are useful as you are valuable, but rise one step in the scale of being, and I am ready to put you down. I see this in the treatment that the free colored people receive in parts of the South; they seem to me to be the outcasts of an outcast race. They are denied the right to walk in certain public places accessible to every class unless they go as nurses, and are forbidden to assemble in evening meetings, and forced to be in the house unless they have passes, by an early hour in the night, and in fact they are hampered or hemmed in on every side; subject to insults from any rude, coarse or brutal white, and in case of outrages, denied their testimony. Prejudiced as we are in Pennsylvania, we do not go that far."

"But, Josiah, we have much to blush for in Pennsylvania; colored people are denied the privilege of riding in our street cars. Only last week when I was in Philadelphia I saw a very decent-looking colored woman with a child, who looked too feeble to walk, and the child too heavy for her to carry. She beckoned to a conductor, but he swept by and took no more heed of her than if she had been a dog. There was a young lady sitting in the car, who remarked to her mother, as a very filthy-looking white man entered, 'See, they will let that filthy creature ride and prohibit a decent respectable colored person!' The mother quietly assented.

"From her dress I took her to be a Quakeress, for she had a lovely dress of dove-colored silk. The young lady had scarcely uttered the words when a young man who sat next the mother deliberately arose, and beckoned to the man with the sooty clothes to take his seat; but fortunately for the Quakeress, a lady who was sitting next her daughter arose just at that moment, and left the seat, and the old man without noticing the manoeuvre passed over to the other side, and thus avoided the contact. I was amused, however, about one thing; for the young man who gave up his seat was compelled to ride about a mile standing."

"Served him right," said Thomas Carpenter; "it was a very contemptible action, to attempt to punish the hardihood of the young lady by attempting to soil her mother's dress; and yet little souls who feel a morbid satisfaction in trampling on the weak, always sink themselves in the scale of manhood."

While this conversation was going on, the tea bell rang, and Josiah and his little charge sat down to a well supplied table; for the Friends, though plain and economical, are no enemies to good living.

Anna had brought the high-chair in which their own darling had sat a few months before, when she had made gladness and sunshine around her parent's path.

There was a tender light in the eye of the Quakeress as she dusted the chair, and sat Minnie at the table.

"Do you think," said Thomas, addressing Josiah, "that we will ever outgrow this wicked, miserable prejudice?"

"Oh, yes, but it must be the work of time. Both races have their work to do. The colored man must outgrow his old condition of things, and thus create around him a new class of associations.

This generation has known him as a being landless, poor, and ignorant. One of the most important things for him to do is to acquire land. He will never gain his full measure of strength until (like Anteus) he touches the earth. And I think here is the great fault, or misfortune of the race; they seem to me to readily accept their situation, and not to let their industrial aspirations rise high enough. I wish they had more of the earth hunger that characterizes the German, or the concentration of purpose which we see in the Jews."

"I think," said Thomas, "that the Jews and Negroes have one thing in common, and that is their power of endurance. They, like the negro, have lived upon an idea, and that is the hope of a deliverer yet to come; but I think this characteristic more strongly developed in the Jews than in the Negroes."

"Doubtless it is, but their origin and history have been different. The Jews have a common ancestry and grand traditions, that have left alive their pride of race. 'We have Abraham to our father,' they said, when their necks were bowed beneath the Roman yoke."

"But I do not think the negro can trace with certainty his origin back to any of the older civilizations, and here for more than two hundred years his history has been a record of blood and tears, of ignorance, degradation, and slavery. And when nominally free, prejudice has assigned him the lowest positions and the humblest situations. I have not much hope of their progress while they are enslaved in the South."

"Well, Josiah, I have faith enough in the ultimate triumph of our principles to believe that slavery will bite the dust before long."

"I don't know, friend Carpenter; for the system is very strongly rooted and grounded in the institutions of the land, and has entrenched itself in the strongholds of Church and State, fashion, custom, and social life. And yet when I was in the South, I saw on every hand a growing differentiation towards the Government."

"Do you know, Josiah, that I have more hope from the madness and folly of the South than I have from the wisdom and virtue of the North? I have read too 'whom the gods would destroy they first make mad.'"

Chapter VII

Ten years have elapsed since Minnie came to brighten the home of Thomas Carpenter, and although within the heart of Anna there is a spot forever green and sacred to the memory of her only child, yet Minnie holds an undivided place in their affections.

There is only one subject which is to them a source of concern. It is the connection of Minnie with the colored race. Not that they love her less on account of the blood that is in her veins, but they dread the effect its discovery would have upon the pleasant social circle with which she is surrounded, and also the fear that the revelation would be painful to her.

They know that she is Anti-Slavery in her principles. They have been careful to instil into her young mind a reverence for humanity, and to recognize beneath all externals, whether of condition or color, the human soul all written over with the handmarks of divinity and the common claims of humanity.

She has known for years that their home has been one of the stations of the underground railroad. And the Anti-Slavery lecturer, whether white or colored, has always been among the welcomed guests of her home. Still they shrink from the effect the knowledge would have on her mind. They know she is willing to work for the colored race; but they could not divine what it cost her to work with them.

"It seems to me, Anna, that we ought to reveal to Minnie the fact of her connection with the colored race. I am afraid that she will learn in some way that will rudely shock her; whereas we might break it to her in the tenderest manner. Every time a fugitive comes I dread that our darling will be recognized."

"Nay, Thomas; thy fears have made thee over sensitive. Who would imagine he saw in this bright and radiant girl of fifteen the little five-year-old child we took to our hearts and home? I never feel any difference between her and the whitest child in the village as far as prejudice is concerned. And if every body in the village knew her origin I would love her just as much as I ever did, for she is a dear good child."

"Well, dear, if you think it is best to keep it a secret, I will not interfere. But we must not forget that Minnie will soon be a young lady; that she is very beautiful, and even now she begins to attract admiration. I do not think it would be right for us to let her marry a white man without letting her know the prejudices of society, and giving her a chance to explain to him the conditions of things."

"Yes," said Anna, "that is true; I have heard that traces of that blood will sometimes reappear even in grandchildren, when it has not been detected in the first. And to guard against difficulty which might arise from such a course, I think it is better to apprise her of the facts in the case."

"It is time enough for that. I want her to finish her education before she thinks of marrying, and I am getting her ready to go to Philadelphia, where she will find an excellent school as I have heard it very highly spoken of. She is young and happy, trouble will come time enough, let me not hasten its advent."

But if time has only strewed the path of Minnie with flowers, and ripened the promised beauty of her childhood, it has borne a heavy hand upon the destiny of the La Croix family.

La Croix is dead; but before his death he took the precaution to have Louis emancipated, and then made him a joint heir with his daughter. The will he entrusted to the care of Camilla; but the deed of emancipation he placed in the hands of Miriam, saying,

"Here are your free papers, and here are Louis'. There is nothing in this world sure but death; and it is well to be on the safe side. Some one might be curious enough to search out his history; and if there should be no legal claim to his freedom, he might be robbed of both his liberty and his inheritance; so keep these papers, and if ever the hour comes when you or he should need them, you must show me."

Miriam did as she was bidden; but her heart was lighter when she knew that freedom had come so near her and Louis.

Le Croix, before his death, had sold the greater part of his slaves, and invested the money in Northern bonds and good Northern securities. Camilla had married a gentleman from the North, and is living very happily upon the old plantation. She does not keep an overseer, and tries to do all in her power to ameliorate the condition of her slaves; still she is not satisfied with the system, and is trying to prepare her slaves for freedom, by inducing them to form, as much as possible, habits of self-reliance, and self-restraint, which they will need in the freedom which she has determined they shall enjoy as soon as she can arrange her affairs to that effect. But she also has to proceed with a great deal of caution.

The South is in a state of agitation and [foment?]. The air is laden with rumors of a [rising?] conflict between the North and the South, and any want of allegiance to Southern opinions is punished either as a crime if the offender is a man, or with social ostracism and insult if a woman.

The South in the palmy days of her pride and power would never tolerate any heresy to her creed, whose formula of statement might have been written we believe in the divine right of the Master, to take advantage of the weakness, ignorance, and poverty of the slave; that might makes right, and that success belongs to the strongest arm.[1]

Some of her former friends were beginning to eye her with

coldness and suspicion because she would not join in their fanatical hatred of the North and because she would profess her devotion to the old flag, while they were ready to spit upon and trample it under foot.

Her adopted brother was still in the North, and strange to say he did not share her feelings; his sympathies were with the South, and although he was too young to take any leading part in the events there about to transpire, yet year after year when he spent his vacations at home, he attended the hustings and political meetings, and there he learned to consider the sentiment, "My country right or wrong," as a proper maxim for political action.

This difference in their sentiments did not produce the least estrangement between them; only Camilla regretted to see Louis ready to raise his hand against the freedom of his mother's race, although he was perfectly unconscious of his connection with it, for the conflict which was then brewing between the North and the South was in fact a struggle between despotism and idea; between freedom on one side and slavery on the other.

Chapter VIII

"Commencement over, what are you going to do with yourself?"

"I don't know; loaf around, I suppose."

"Why don't you go to Newport?"

"Don't want to; got tired of it last year."

"Saratoga?"

"A perfect bore!"

"Niagara?"

"Been there twice."

"A pedestrian tour to the White Mountains?"

"Haven't got energy enough."

"What will you do?"

"Stay at home and fight mosquitoes."

"Very pleasant employment. I don't envy you, but I can tell you something better than that."

"What is it?" said his companion, yawning.

"Come, go home with me."

"Go home with you! Where is that, and what is the attraction?"

"Well, let me see, it is situated in one of the most beautiful valleys of Western Pennsylvania, our village is environed by the most lovely hills, and nestling among the trees, with its simple churches and unpretending homes of quiet beauty and good taste, it is one of the most pleasant and picturesque places I ever saw. And, besides, as you love to hunt and fish, we have one of the finest streams of trout, and some of the most excellent game in the woods."

"Is that all?"

"Why, isn't that enough? You must be rather hard to please this morning."

"Think so?"

"Yes, but I have not told you the crowning attraction."

"What is it?"

"Oh, one of the most beautiful girls I ever saw! We call her the lily of the valley."

"Describe her."

"I can't. It would be like attempting to paint a sun beam or doing what no painter has ever done, sketch a rainbow."

"You are very poetical this morning, but I want you to do as our President sometimes tells us, proceed from the abstract to the concrete."

"Well, let me begin: she has the most beautiful little feet. I never see her stepping along without thinking of Cinderella and the glass slipper. As to eyes, they are either dark brown or black, I don't know which; but I do know they are beautiful; and her hair, well, she generally wears that plain in deference to the wishes of her Quaker friends, but sometimes in the most beautiful ripples of golden brown I ever saw."

"That will do, now tell me who she is? You spoke of her Quaker friends. Is she not their daughter?"

"No, there seems to be some mystery about her history. About ten years ago, my father brought her to Josiah Carpenter's but he's always been reticent about her, in fact I never took the pains to inquire. She's a great favorite in the village, and everybody says she is as beautiful as she is good, and vice versa."

"Well, I'd like to see this paragon of yours. I believe I'll go."

"Well, let us get ready."

"When do you start?"

"To-morrow."

"All right. I'll be on hand." And with these words the two friends parted to meet again the next day at the railroad station.

The first of the speakers is the son of Josiah Collins, and his friend is Louis Le Croix, Camilla's adopted brother. He is somewhat changed within the last ten years. Time has touched the golden wealth of his curls with a beautiful deep auburn, and the rich full tones of his voice tell that departed is written upon his childhood.

He is strongly Southern in his feelings, but having been educated in the North, whilst he is an enthusiast in defense of his section, as he calls the South, he is neither coarse and brutal in actions, nor fanatical in his devotion to slavery. He thinks the Negroes are doing well enough in slavery, if the Abolitionists would only let matters rest, and he feels a sense of honor in defending the South. She is his mother, he says, and that man is an ingrate who will not stand by his mother and defend her when she is in peril.

He and Charles Collins are fast friends, but [on the subject of slavery they are entirely opposed ?]. And so on that point they have agreed to disagree. They often have animated and exciting discussions, but they [pass?] and Josiah and Louis are just as friendly as they were before.

There were two arrivals the next evening in the [quiet ?] village of S. One was Charles Collins, the other his Southern friend, who was received with the warmest welcome, and soon found himself at home in the pleasant society of his friend's family. The evening was enlivened with social chat and music, until ten o'clock, when Josiah gathered his children and having read the Bible in a deeply impressive manner, breathed one of the most simple and fervent prayers he had ever heard.

While they were bending at prayer in this pleasant home, a shabby looking man came walking slowly and wearily into the village. He gazed cautiously around and looked anxiously in the street as though he were looking for some one, but did not like to trust his business to every one.

At length he saw an elderly man, dressed in plain clothes, and a broad brim hat, and drawing near he spoke to him in a low and hesitating voice, and asked if he knew a Mr. Thomas Carpenter.

"My name is Carpenter," said the friend, "come with me."

There was something in the voice, and manner of the friend that *assured* the stranger. His whole manner changed. A peaceful expression stole over his dark, sad face, and the drooping limbs seemed to be aroused by a new infusion of energy.

"Come in," said Thomas, as he reached his door, "come in, thee's welcome to stop and rest with us."

"Anna," said Thomas,[2] his face beaming with kindness, "I've brought thee a guest. Here is another passenger by the Underground Railroad."

"I'm sure thee's welcome," said Anna, handing him a chair, "sit down, thee looks very tired. Where did thee come from?"

Moses, that was the fugitive's name, hesitated a moment.

"Oh, never fear, thee's among friends; thee need not be afraid to tell all about thyself."

Moses then told them that he had come from Kentucky.

"And how did thee escape?"

He said, "I walked from Lexington to Covington."

"Why, that was almost one hundred miles, and did thee walk all that way?"

"Yes, sir," said he, "I hid by day, and walked by night."

"Did no one interrupt?"

"Yes, one man said to me, 'Where's your pass?' I suppose I must have grown desperate, for I raised my fists and said dem's my passes; and he let me alone. I don't know whether he was friendly or scared, but he let me alone."

"And how then?"

"When I come to Covington I found that I could not come across the river without a pass, but I watched my chance, and hid myself on a boat, and I got across. I'd heard of you down home."

"How did you?"

"Oh, we's got some few friends dere, but we allers promise not to tell."

Anna and Thomas[3] smiled at his reticence, which had grown into a habit.

"Were you badly treated?"

"Not so bad as some, but I allers wanted my freedom, I did."

"Well, we will not talk about thee any more; if thee walked all that distance thee must be very tired and we'll let thee rest. There's thy bed. I hope thee'll have a good night's rest, and feel better in the morning."

"Thankee marm," said Moses, "you's mighty good."

"Oh no, but I always like to do my duty by my fellow men! Now, be quiet, and get a good night's sleep. Thee looks excited. Thee mustn't be uneasy. Thee's among friends."

A flood of emotions crept over the bosom of Moses when his kind friends left the room. Was this freedom, and was this the long wished for North? and were these the Abolitionists of whom he had heard so much in the South? They who would allure the colored people from their homes in the South and then leave them to freeze and starve in the North? He had heard all his life that the slaveholders were the friends of the South, and the language of his soul had been, "If these are my friends, save me from my foes." He had lived all his life among the white people of the South, and had been owned by several masters, but he did not know that there was so much kindness among the white race, till he had rested in a Northern home, and among Northern people.

Here kindness encouraged his path, and in that peaceful home every voice that fell upon his ear was full of tenderness and sympathy. True, there were rough, coarse, brutal men even in that village, who for a few dollars or to prove their devotion to the South, would have readily remanded him to his master, but he was not aware of that. And so when he sank to his rest a sense of peace and safety stole over him, and his sleep was as calm and peaceful as the slumber of a child.

The next morning he looked refreshed, but still his strength was wasted by his great physical exertion and mental excitement; and Thomas[4] thought he had better rest a few days till he grew stronger and better prepared to travel; for Thomas[5] noticed that he was nervous, starting at the sound of every noise, and often turning his head to the door with an anxious, frightened look.

Thomas would have gladly given him shelter and work, and given him just wages, but he dared not do so. He was an American citizen it is true, but at that time slavery reigned over the North and ruled over the South, and he had not the power under the law of the land to give domicile, and break his bread to that poor, hunted and flying man; for even then they were hunting in the South and sending out their human bloodhounds to search for him in the North.

Throughout the length and breadth of the land, from the summit of the rainbow-crowned Niagara to the swollen waters of the

Mexican Gulf; from the golden gates of sunrise to the gorgeous portals of departing day, there was not a hill so high, a forest so secluded, a glen so sequestered, nor mountain so steep, that he knew he could not be tracked and hailed in the name of the general government.

"What's the news, friend Carpenter? any new arrivals?" said Josiah Collins in a low voice to Thomas.

"Yes, a very interesting case; can't you come over?"

"Yes, after breakfast. By the way, you must be a little more cautious than usual. Charley came home last night, and brought a young friend with him from college. I think from his conversation that he is either a Southerner himself, or in deep sympathy with the South."

Both men spoke in low tones, for although they were Northerners, they were talking about a subject on which they were compelled to speak with bated breaths.

After breakfast Josiah came over, but Moses seemed so heavy and over wearied that they did not care to disturb him. There was a look of dejection and intense sadness on the thin worn face, and a hungry look in the mournful eyes, as if his soul had been starving for kindness and sympathy. Sometimes he would forget his situation, and speak hopefully of the future, but still there was a weariness that he could not shake off, a languor that seemed to pervade every nerve and muscle.

Thomas thought it was the natural reaction of the deep excitement, through which he just passed, that the tension of his nerves had been too great, but that a few days rest and quiet would restore him to his normal condition; but that hope soon died away.

The tension, excitement, and consequent exhaustion had been too much. Reason tottered on its throne, and he became a raving maniac; in his moments of delirium he would imagine that he was escaping from slavery; that the pursuers were upon his back; that they had caught him, and were rebinding him about to take him back to slavery, and then it was heartrending to hear him beg, and plead to be carried to Thomas Carpenter's.

He would reach out his emaciated hands, and say "Carry me to Mr. Carpenter's, that good man's house," for that name which had become more precious to him than a household to his soul, still lingered amid shattered cells. But the delirium spent its force, and through the tempests of his bosom the light of reason came back.

One night he slept more soundly than usual; and on the next morning his faithful friends saw from the expression of his countenance and the light in his eyes that his reason had returned. They sent for their family physician, a man in whose honor they could confide. All that careful nursing and medical skill could do was done, but it was in vain; his strength was wasted; the silver cord was loosed, and the golden bowl was broken; his life was fast ebbing away. Like a tempest tossed mariner dying in sight of land, so he passing away from earth, found the precious, longed for, and dearly bought prize was just before, but his hand was too feeble to grasp, his arms too powerless to hold it.

His friends saw from the expression of his face that he had something to say; and they bent down to catch the last words of the departing spirit.

"I am dying," he said, "but I am thankful that I have come this near to freedom."

He attempted to say no more, the death rattles sounded in his throat; the shadows that never deceive flitted o'er his face, and he was dead. His spirit gone back to God, another witness against the giant crime of the land.

Josiah came again to see him, and entered the room just as the released spirit winged its flight. Silently he uncovered him as if paying that reverence to the broken casket which death exacts for his meanest subjects. With tenderness and respect they prepared the body for the grave, followed him to the silent tomb, and left him to his dreamless sleep.

««»»

[Installment missing.]

Chapter IX

"Friend Carpenter, I have brought a friend to see you. He is a real hot-headed Southerner, and I have been trying to convert him, but have been almost ready to give it up as a hopeless task. I thought as you are so much better posted than I am on the subject, *you* might be able to convert him from the error of his ways. He is a first-rate fellow, my College chum. He has only one fault, he will defend Slavery. Cure him of that, and I think he will be as near perfect as young men generally are."

Friend Carpenter smiled at this good-natured rally, and said, "It takes time for all things. Perhaps your friend is not so incorrigible as you think he is."

"I don't know," said Charley, "but here he is; he can speak for himself."

"Oh the system is well enough of itself, but like other things, it is liable to abuse."

"I think, my young friend," said Thomas, "thee has never examined the system by the rule of impartial justice, which tells us to do to all men as we would have them do to us. If thee had, thee would not talk of the abuses of Slavery, when the system is an abuse itself. I am afraid thee has never gauged the depth of its wickedness. Thy face looks too honest and frank to defend this system from conviction. Has thee ever examined it?"

"Why, no, I have always been used to it."

Louis, who liked the honest bluntness of the Quaker, would have willingly prolonged the conversation, simply for the sake of the argument, but just then Minnie entered, holding in her hand a bunch of flowers, and started to show them to her father, before she perceived that any company was in the room.

"Oh father," said she, "see what I have brought you!" when her eye fell upon the visitors, and a bright flush overspread her cheek, lending it additional beauty.

Charles immediately arose, and giving her his hand, introduced her to his friend.

"I am glad to see you, Minnie; you are looking so well this summer," said Charles, gazing on her with unfeigned admiration.

"I am glad you think so," said she, with charming frankness.

Some business having called friend Carpenter from the room, the young people had a pleasant time to themselves, talking of books, poetry, and the current literature of the day, although being students, their acquaintance with these things was somewhat limited. By the time they were ready to go, Thomas had re-entered the room and bidding them good-bye, cordially invited them to return again.

"What do you think of her?" said Charles to his friend.

"Beautiful as a dream. The half had not been told. Her *acquaintance* pays me for my trip; yes, I would like to become better acquainted with her; there was such a charming simplicity about her, and such unaffected grace that I am really delighted with her. How is it that you have never fallen in love with her?"

"Oh, I have left that for you; but in fact we have almost grown together, played with each other when we were children, until she appears like one of our family, and to marry her would be like marrying my own sister."

"How does thee like Charles' friend?" said Minnie, to her adopted father.

Thomas spoke slowly and deliberately, and said, "He impresses me rather favorably. I think there's the making of a man in him. But I hear that he is pro-slavery."

"Yes, he is, but I think that is simply the result of former associations and surroundings. I do not believe that he has looked deeper than the surface of Slavery; he is quite young yet; his reflective faculties are hardly fully awakened. I believe the time will come, when he will see it in its true light, and if he joins our ranks he will be an important accession to our cause. I have great hopes of him. He seems to be generous, kind-hearted, and full of good impulses, and I believe there are grand possibilities in his nature. How do you like him?"

"Oh, I was much pleased with him. We had a very pleasant time together."

In a few days, Charles and Louis called again. Minnie was crocheting, and her adopted mother was occupied with sewing; while Thomas engaged them in conversation, the subject being the impending conflict; Louis, taking a decided stand in favor of the South, and Thomas being equally strong in his defense of the North.

The conversation was very animated, but temperate; and when they parted, each felt confident of the rightfulness of his position.

"Come, again," said Thomas, as they were leaving; "we can't see eye to eye, but I like to have thee come."

Louis was very much pleased with the invitation, for it gave him opportunity to see Minnie, and sometimes she would smile, or say a word or two when the discussion was beginning to verge on the borders of excitement.

The time to return to College was drawing near, and Louis longed to tell her how dear she was to him, but he never met her alone. She was so young he did not like to ask the privilege of writing to her; and yet he felt when he left the village, that it would afford him great satisfaction to hear from her. He once hinted to Friend Carpenter that he would like to hear from his family, and that if he was too busy perhaps Miss Minnie might find time to drop a line, but Thomas did not take the hint, so the matter ended;

he hoping in the meantime to meet her again, and renew their very pleasant acquaintance.

Chapter X

[Text missing.]

Chapter XI

"Is Minnie not well?" said Thomas Carpenter, entering one morning, the pleasant room, where Anna was labelling some preserves. "She seems to be so drooping, and scarcely eats anything."

"I don't know. I have not heard her complain; perhaps she is a little tired and jaded from her journey; and then I think she studies too much. She spends most of her time in her room, and since I think of it, she does appear more quiet than usual; but I have been so busy about my preserves that I have not noticed her particularly."

"Anna," said Thomas suddenly, after a moment's pause, "does thee think that there is any attachment between Louis and Minnie? He was very attentive to her when we were in Boston."

"Why, Thomas, I have never thought anything about it. Minnie always seems so much like a child that I never get her associated in my mind with courtship and marriage. I suppose I ought to though," said Anna, with the faintest sigh.

"Anna, I think that something is preying on that child's mind, and mother, thee knows that you women understand how to manage these things better than we men do, and I wish thee would find out what is the matter with the child. Try to find out if there is anything between her and Louis, and if there is, by all means we must let her know about herself; it is a duty we owe her and him."

"Well, Thomas, if we must we must; but I shrink from it. Here she comes. Now I'll leave in a few minutes, and then thee can tell her; perhaps thee can do it better than I can."

"What makes thee look so serious?" said Thomas, as Minnie entered the room.

"Do I, father?"

"Yes, thee looks sober as a Judge. What has happened to disturb thee?"

"Nothing in particular; only I was down to Mr. Hickman's this morning, and they have a colored woman stopping with them. She is a very interesting and intelligent woman, and she was telling us part of her history, and it was very interesting, but, mother, I do think it is a dreadful thing to be a colored person in this country; how I should suffer if I knew that I was hated and despised for what I couldn't help. Oh, it must be dreadful to be colored."

"Oh, don't talk so, Minnie, God never makes any mistakes."

"I know that, mother; but, mother, it must be hard to be forced to ride in smoking cars; to be insulted in the different thoroughfares of travel; to be denied access to public resorts in some places,—such as lectures, theatres, concerts, and even have a particular seat assigned in the churches, and sometimes feel you were an object of pity even to your best friends. I know that Mrs. Heston felt so when she was telling her story, for when Mrs. Hickman said, 'Well, Sarah, I really pity you,' I saw her dark eyes flash, and she has really beautiful eyes, as she said, 'it is not pity we want, it is justice.'"

"In the first place, mother, she is a widow, with five children. She had six. One died in the army,—and she had some business in Washington connected with him. She says she was born in Virginia, and had one little girl there, but as she could not bear the idea of her child growing up in ignorance, she left the South and went to Albany. Her husband was a barber, and was doing a good business there. She was living in a very good neighborhood, and sent her child to the nearest district school.

"After her little girl had been there awhile, her teacher told her she must go home and not come there any more, and sent her mother a note; the child did not know what she had done; she had been attentive to her lessons, and had not behaved amiss, and she was puzzled to know why she was turned out of school.

" 'Oh! I hated to tell Mrs. Heston,' said the teacher; 'but the child insisted, and I knew that it must come sooner or later. And so, said she, I told her it was because she was colored.'

" 'Is that all.' Poor child, she didn't know, that, in that fact lay whole volumes of insult, outrage, and violence. I made up my mind, she continued, that I would leave the place, and when my husband came home, I said, 'Heston, let us leave this place; let us go farther west. I hear that we can have our child educated there, just the same as any other child.' At first my husband demurred, for we were doing a good business; but I said, let us go, if we have to live on potatoes and salt.

" 'True, it was some pecuniary loss; but I never regretted it, although I have been pretty near the potatoes and salt. My husband died, but I kept my children together, and stood over the wash-tub day after day to keep them at school. My oldest daughter graduated at the High School, and was quite a favorite with the teachers. One term there was a vacancy in her room, caused by the resignation of one of the assistant teachers, and the first teacher had the privilege of selecting her assistants from the graduates of the High School, their appointment, of course, being subject to the decision of the Commissioner of Public Schools.

" 'Her teacher having heard that she was connected by blood with one of the first families of Virginia, told the Commissioner that she had chosen an Assistant, a young lady of high qualifications, and as she understood, a descendant of Patrick Henry.

"'Ah, indeed,' said the Commissioner, 'I didn't know that we had one of that family among us. By all means employ her;' but as she was about to leave, she said: 'I forgot to tell you one thing, she is colored.'

"A sudden change came over him, and he said: 'Do you think I would have you walk down the street with a colored woman? Of course not. I'll never give my consent to *that*.' And there the matter ended. And then she made us feel so indignant when she told us that on her way to Washington to get her son's pension, she stopped in Philadelphia, and the conductor tried to make her leave the car, and because she would not, he ran the car off the track."

"Oh, father," said she, turning to Thomas, "how wicked and cruel this prejudice. Oh, how I should hate to be colored!"

Anna and Thomas exchanged mournful glances. Their hearts were too full; and as Minnie left the room, Thomas said, "Not now, Anna. Not just yet." And so Minnie[6] was permitted to return again to school with the secret untold.

««»»

"Minnie, darling, what are you doing? moping as usual over your books? Come, it is Saturday morning, and you have worked hard enough for one week; got all good marks; so now just put up that Virgil, and come go out with me."

"Where do you wish to go?" said Minnie, to her light-hearted friend, Carrie Wise.

"I want to go out shopping. Pa has just sent me twenty dollars, and you know a girl and her money are soon parted."

"What do you wish to get?"

"Well, I want a pair of gloves, some worsted to match this fringe, and a lot of things. Come, won't you go?"

"Oh, I don't know, I didn't intend going out this morning."

"Well, never mind if you didn't, just say you will go. Where's your hat and mantle?" said Carrie, going to her wardrobe.

"Well, just wait till I fix my hair; it won't take long."

"Oh, Minnie, do let me fix it for you! If ever I have to work for my living, I shall be a hair-dresser. I believe it is the only thing that I have any talent for."

"What an idea! But do, Minnie, won't you, let me arrange your hair? You always wear it so plain, and I do believe it would curl beautifully. May I, Minnie?"

"Why yes."

So Carrie sat down, and in a short time, she had beautifully arranged Minnie's hair with a profusion of curls.

"Do you know what I was thinking? said Carrie, gazing admiringly upon her friend. "You look so much like a picture I have seen of yours in your father's album. He was showing me a number of pictures which represent you at different ages, and the one I refer to, he said was our Minnie when she was five years old. Now let me put on your hat. And let me kiss you for you look so pretty?"

"Oh, Carrie, what an idea! You are so full of nonsense. Which way will we go first?"

"First down to Carruther's. I saw a beautiful collar there I liked so much; and then let us go down to Mrs. Barguay's. I want to show you a love of a bonnet, one of the sweetest little things in ribbon, lace, and flowers I ever saw."

Equipped for the journey the two friends sauntered down the street; as they were coming out of a store, Carrie stopped for a moment to speak to a very dear friend of her mother's, and Minnie passed on.

As she went slowly on, loitering for her friend, she saw a woman approaching her from the opposite side of the street. There was something in her look and manner which arrested the attention of Minnie. She was a tall, slender woman about thirty five years old, with a pale, care-worn face—a face which told that sorrow had pressed her more than years. A few threads of silver mingled with the wealth of her raven hair, and her face, though wearing a sad and weary expression, still showed traces of great beauty.

As soon as her eyes fell on Minnie, she raised her hands in sudden wonder, and clasping her in her arms, exclaimed: "Heaven is merciful! I have found you, at last, my dear, darling, long-lost child. Minnie, is this you, and have I found you at last?"

Minnie trembled from head to foot; a deadly pallor overspread her cheek, and she stood still as if rooted to the ground in silent amazement, while the woman stood anxiously watching her as if her future were hanging on the decision of her lips.

"Who are you? and where did you come from?" said Minnie, as soon as she gained her breath.

"I came from Louisiana. Oh, I can't be mistaken. I have longed for you, and prayed for you, and now I have found you."

Just then, Carrie, who had finished speaking with her friend, seeing Minnie and the strange woman talking together, exclaimed, "What is the matter?"

Noticing the agitation of her friend, "Who is this woman, and what has she said to you?"

"She says that she is my mother, my long-lost mother."

"Why, Minnie, what nonsense! She can't be your mother. Why don't you see she is colored?"

"Where do you live?" said Minnie, without appearing to notice the words of Carrie.

"I don't live anywhere. I just came here yesterday with some of the Union soldiers."

"Come with me then, and I will show you a place to stop."

"Why, Minnie, you are not going to walk down the street with that Nig—colored woman; if you are, please excuse me. My business calls me another way."

And without any more ceremony Carrie and Minnie parted. Silently she walked by the side of the stranger, a thousand thoughts revolving in her mind. Was this the solution of the mystery which enshrouded her young life? Did she indeed belong to that doomed and hated race, and must she share the cruel treatment which bitter, relentless prejudice had assigned them?

Thomas Carpenter and Anna were stopping in P., at the house of relatives who knew Minnie's history, but who had never made any difference in their treatment of her on that account.

"Is father and mother at home?" said Minnie to the servant, who opened the door. She answered in the affirmative.

"Tell them to come into the parlor, they are wanted immediately."

"Sit down," said Minnie to the stranger, handing her a chair, "and wait till father comes."

Anna and Thomas soon entered the room, and Minnie approaching them said, "Father, this woman met me on the street today, and says she is my mother. You know all about my history. Tell me if there is any truth in this story."

"I don't know, Minnie, I never saw thy mother."

"But question her, father, and see if there is any truth in what she says; but tell me first, father, am I white or colored?"

"Minnie, I believe there is a small portion of colored blood in thy veins."

"It is enough," said Minnie, drawing closer to the strange woman. "What makes you think that I am your child?"

"By this," said she, taking a miniature from her bosom. "By this, which I carried next to my heart for more than twelve years, and never have been without it a single day or night."

Thomas looked upon the miniature; it was an exact likeness of Minnie when she first came to them, and although she had grown and changed since the likeness was taken, there was too close a resemblance between it and one which had been taken soon after she came, for him to doubt that Minnie was the original of that likeness.

Thomas questioned the woman very closely, but her history

and narrative corresponded so well with what he had heard of Minnie's mother, that he could not for a moment doubt that this was she, and as such he was willing to give her the shelter of his home, till he could make other arrangements.

"But why," said Anna, somewhat grieved at the shock, that Minnie had received, "did thee startle her by so suddenly claiming her in the street? Would it not have been better for thee to have waited and found out where she lived, and then discovered thyself to her?"

"I'spect it would, 'Mam," said Ellen, very meekly and sorrowfully, "but when I saw her and heard the young lady say, Minnie, wait a minute, I forgot everything but that this was my long-lost child. I am sorry if I did any harm, but I was so glad I could not help it. My heart was so hungry for my child."

"Yes, yes," said Anna sadly, "I understand thee; it was the voice of nature."

Minnie was too nervous and excited to return to her school that day; the next morning she had a very high fever, and Thomas concluded it would be better to take her home and have her mother accompany her.

And so on Monday morning Anna and Thomas left P., taking Minnie and her mother along.

Once again in her pleasant home, surrounded by the tenderest care (for her mother watched over her with the utmost solicitude) the violence of her fever abated, but it was succeeded by a low nervous affection which while it produced no pain yet it slowly unstrung her vitality.

Ellen hovered around her pillow as if she begrudged every moment that called her from her daughter's side, and never seemed so well contented as when she was performing for her some office of love and tenderness. A skilful nurse, she knew how to prepare the most delicate viands to tempt the failing appetite, and she had the exquisite pleasure of seeing her care and attention rewarded by the returning health and strength of her child.

One morning as she grew stronger, and was able to sit in her chair, she turned her eyes tenderly towards Ellen and said, "Mother, come and sit near me and let me hold your hand."

"Mother," Oh how welcome was that word. Ellen's eyes filled with sudden tears.

"Mother," she said, "It comes back to me like a dream. I have a faint recollection of having seen you before, but it is so long I can scarcely remember it. Tell me all about myself and how I came to leave you. I always thought that there was some mystery about me, but I never knew what it was before, but now I understand it."

"Darling," said the mother, "you had better wait till you get a little stronger, and then I will tell you all."

"Very well," said Minnie, "you have been so good to me and I am beginning to love you so much."

It was touching to see the ripening love between those two long-suffering ones. Ellen would comb Minnie's hair, and do for her every office in her power. Still Minnie continued feeble. The suffering occasioned by her refusal of Louis; the hard study and deep excitement through which she had passed told sadly upon her constitution; but she was young, and having a large share of recuperative power she slowly came back to health and strength, and when the spring opened Thomas decided that she should return again to her school in P.

Chapter XII

Let us now return to Carrie Wise, whom we left parting with Minnie.

"Where is Minnie?" said two of her schoolmates, who observed that Carrie had come home alone.

"Oh," said she, "one of the strangest things I ever heard of happened!"

"Well, what was it?" said the girls; and by this time they had joined another group of girls.

"Why this morning, Minnie and I walked out shopping, and just as I came out of Carruthers' I met an old friend of mother's, and stopped to speak with her, and I said 'Minnie, just wait a minute.'"

"She passed on, and left me talking with Mrs. Jackson. When I joined her, I found a colored woman talking to her, and she was trembling from head to foot, and just as pale as a ghost; and I said, 'Why, Minnie, what is the matter?'"

"She gasped for breath, and I thought she was going to faint, and I got real scared. And what do you think Minnie said?"

"Why," she said, "Carrie, this woman says she's my mother!"

"Her mother!" cried a half dozen voices. "Why you said she was colored!"

"Well, so she was. She was quite light, but I knew she was colored."

"How did you know? Maybe she was only a very dark-complexioned white woman."

"Oh no, she wasn't, I know white people from colored, I've seen enough of them."

"A colored woman! well that is very strange; but do tell us what Minnie said."

"She asked her where she came from, and where she lived. She said she came in yesterday with the Union soldiers, and that she had come from Louisiana, and then Minnie told her to come with her, and she would find a place for her to stop."

"And did she leave you in the street to walk with a Nigger?" said a coarse, rough-looking girl.

"Yes, and so I left her. I wasn't going to walk down the street with them!"

"Well, did I ever?" said a pale and interesting-looking girl.

"That is just as strange as a romance I have been reading!"

"Well, they say truth is stranger than fiction. A deceitful thing to try to pass for white when she is colored! If she comes back to this school I shan't stay!" said the coarse rough girl, twirling her gold pencil. "I ain't a going to sit alongside of niggers."

"How you talk! I don't see that if the woman is Minnie's mother, and *is* colored, it makes any difference in her. I am sure it does not to me," said one of Minnie's friends.

"Well, it does to me," said another; "you may put yourself on an equality with niggers, but I won't." "And I neither," chimed in another voice. "There are plenty of colored schools; let her go to them."

"Oh, girls, I think it real cruel the way you talk!"

"How would you like any one to treat you so?" "Can't help it, I ain't a coming to school with a nigger." "She is just as good as you are, Mary Patuck, and a great deal smarter." "I don't care, she's a nigger, and that's enough for me."

And so the sentiment of the school was divided. Some were in favor of treating her just as well as usual, and others felt like complaining to their parents that a Negro was in school.

At last the news reached the teacher, and he, poor, weak, and vacillating man, had not manhood enough to defend her, but acted according to the prejudices of society, and wrote Thomas a note telling him that circumstances made it desirable that she should not again come to school.

In the meantime the news had reached their quiet little village, and of course it offered food for gossip; it was discussed over tea-tables and in the sewing circle. Some concluded that Thomas should have brought her up among the colored people, and others that he did perfectly right.

Still there was a change in Minnie's social relations. Some were just as kind as ever. Others grew distant, and some avoided having anything to say to her, and stopped visiting the house. Anna and Thomas, although superior people, were human, and could not help feeling the difference, but some business of importance connected with the death of a relative called Thomas abroad, and he made up his mind that he would take Anna and Minnie with him, hoping that the voyage and change of scene would be beneficial to his little girl, as he still called Minnie, and so on a bright and beautiful morning in the spring of '62 he left the country for a journey to England and the Continent.

Let us now return to Louis Le Croix, whom we left disappointed and wounded by Minnie's refusal. After he left her he entered his room, and sat for a long time in silent thought; at last he rose, and walked to the window and stood with his hands clenched, and his finely chiseled lips firmly set as if he had bound his whole soul to some great resolve—a resolve which he would accomplish, let it cost what it might.

And so he had; for he had made up in his mind within the last two hours that he would join the Confederacy. "That live or die, sink or swim, survive or perish," he would unite his fortunes to her destiny.

His next step then was to plan how he could reach Louisiana; he felt confident that if he could get as far as Louisville he could manage to get into Tennessee, and from thence to Louisiana.

And so nothing daunted by difficulties and dangers, he set out on his journey, and being aided by rebels on his way in a few weeks he reached the old plantation on Red River; he found his sister and Miriam there both glad to see him.

Camilla's husband was in Charleston, some of the slaves had deserted to the Union ranks, but the greater portion she still retained with her.

Miriam was delighted to see Louis, and seemed never weary of admiring his handsome face and manly form. And Louis, who had never known any other mother seemed really gratified by her little kindnesses and attention; but of course the pleasant and quiet monotony of home did not suit the restless and disquieted spirit of Louis. All the young men around here were in the army or deeply interested in its success.

There was a call for more volunteers, and a new company was to be raised in that locality. Louis immediately joined, and turned his trained intellect to the study of military tactics; day and night he was absorbed in this occupation, and soon, although Minnie was not forgotten, the enthusiasm of his young life gathered around the Confederate cause.

He did not give himself much time to reflect. Thought was painful to him, and he continued to live in a whirl of excitement.

News of battle, tidings of victory and defeats, the situation of the armies, and the hopes and fears that clustered around those fearful days of struggle made the staple of conversation.

Louis rapidly rose in favor with the young volunteers, and was chosen captain of a company who were permitted to drill and stay from the front as a reserve corps, ready to be summoned at any moment.

Chapter XIII

Miriam and Camilla watched with anguish Louis' devotion to the Confederation, and many sorrowful conversations they had about it.

At last one day Miriam said, "Miss Camilla, I can stand it no longer;—that boy is going to lift his hand agin his own people, and I can't stand it no longer; I'se got to tell him all about it. I just think I'd bust in two if I didn't tell him."

"Well, Mammy," said Camilla, "I'd rather he should know it

than that he should go against his country and raise his hand against the dear old flag."

"It's not the flag nor the country I care for," said Miriam, "but it is that one of my own flesh and blood should jine with these secesh agin his own people."

"Well, Miriam, if you get a chance you can tell him."

"Get a chance, Miss Camilla, I'se bound to get that."

Louis was somewhat reticent about his plans; for he knew that Camilla was a strong Union woman; that she not only loved the flag, but she had taught her two boys to do the same; but he understood from headquarters that his company was to march in a week, and although on that subject there was no common sympathy between them, yet he felt that he must acquaint her with his plans, and bid her and Miriam good-bye.

So one morning he came in looking somewhat flushed and excited, and said: "Sister, we have got our marching orders; we leave on Thursday, and I have only three days to be with you. I am sorry that I have seen so little of you, but my country calls me, and when she is in danger it is no time for me to seek for either ease or pleasure."

"Your country! Louis," said Miriam, her face paling and flushing by turns. "Where is your country?"

"Here," said he, somewhat angrily, "in Louisiana."

"My country," said Camilla,[7] "is the whole Union. Yes, Louis," said she, "your country is in danger, but not from the Abolitionists in the North, but from the rebels and traitors in the South."

"Rebels and traitors!" said Louis, in a tone like one who felt the harsh grating of the words.

"Whom do you mean?"

"I mean," said she, "the ambitious, reckless men who have brought about this state of things. The men who are stabbing their country in their madness and folly; who are crowding our graves and darkening our homes; who are dragging our young men, men like you, who should be the pride and hope of our country, into the jaws of ruin and death."

Louis looked surprised and angry; he had never seen Camilla under such deep excitement. Her words had touched his pride and roused his anger; but suppressing his feelings he answered her coolly, "Camilla, I am old enough to do my own thinking. We had better drop this subject; it is not pleasant to either of us."

"Louis," said she, her whole manner changing from deep excitement to profound grief, "Oh, Louis, it will never do for you to go! Oh, no, you must not!"

"And why not?"

"Because,"—and she hesitated. Just then Miriam took up the unfinished sentence, "—because to join the secesh is to raise your hands agin your own race."

"My own race?" and Louis laughed scornfully. "I think you are talking more wildly than Camilla. What do you mean, Miriam?"

"I mean," said she, stung by his scornful words, "I mean that you, Louis Le Croix, white as you look, are colored, and that you are my own daughter's child, and if it had not been for Miss Camilla, who's been such an angel to you, that you would have been a slave to-day, and then you wouldn't have been a Confederate."

At these words a look of horror and anguish passed over the face of Le Croix, and he turned to Camilla, but she was deadly pale, and trembling like an aspen leaf; but her eyes were dry and tearless.

"Camilla," said he, turning fiercely to his adopted sister, "Tell me, is there any truth in these words? You are as pale as death, and trembling like a leaf, —tell me if there is any truth in these words," turning and fixing his eyes on Miriam, who stood like some ancient prophetess, her lips pronouncing some fearful doom, while she watched in breathless anguish the effect upon the fated victim.

"Yes, Louis," said Camilla, in a voice almost choked by emotion. "Yes, Louis, it is all true."

"But how is this that I never heard it before? Before I believe this tale I must have some proof, clear as daylight. Bring me proofs."

"Here they are," said Miriam, drawing from her pocket the free papers she had been carrying about her person for several days.

Louis grasped them nervously, hastily read them, and then more slowly, like one who might read a sentence of death to see if there was one word or sentence on which he might hang a hope of reprieve.

Camilla watched him anxiously, but silently, and when he had finished, he covered his bowed face with his hands as he said with a deep groan, "It is true, too true. I see it all. I can never raise my hand against my mother's race."

He arose like one in a dream, walked slowly to the door and left the room.

"It was a painful task," said Camilla, with a sigh of relief, as if a burden had fallen from her soul.

"Yes," said Miriam, "but not so bad as to see him fighting agin his own color. I'd rather follow him to his grave than see him join that miserable secesh crew."

"Yes," said Camilla, "It was better than letting him go."

When Louis left the room a thousand conflicting thoughts passed through his mind. He felt as a mariner at midnight on a moonless sea, who suddenly, when the storm is brewing, finds that he has lost his compass and his chart.

Chapter XIV

Where was he steering; and now, the course of his life was changed, what kind of future must he make for himself?

Had it been in time of peace, he could have easily decided, as he had a large amount of money in the North, which his father left him when he came of age.

He would have no difficulty as to choosing the means of living; for he was well supplied, as far as that was concerned; but here was a most unpleasant dilemma in which he had placed himself.

Convinced that he was allied to the Negro race, his whole soul rose up against the idea of laying one straw in its way; if he belonged to the race he would not join its oppressors. And yet his whole sympathy had been so completely with them, that he felt that he had no feeling in common with the North.

And as to the colored people, of course it never entered his mind to join their ranks, and ally himself to them; he had always regarded them as inferior; and this sudden and unwelcome revelation had not changed the whole tenor of his thoughts and opinions.

But what he had to do must be done quickly; for in less than three days his company would start for the front. To desert was to face death; to remain was to wed dishonor. He surveyed the situation calmly and bravely, and then resolved that he would face the perils of re-capture rather than the contempt of his own soul.

While he was deciding, he heard Camilla's step in the passage; he opened the door, and beckoned her to a seat, and said, very calmly, "I have been weighing the whole matter in my mind, and I have concluded to leave the South."

"How can you do it?" said Camilla. "I tremble lest you should be discovered. Oh slavery! what a curse. Our fathers sowed the wind, and we are reaping the whirlwind! What," continued she, as if speaking to herself, "What are your plans? Have you any?"

"None, except to disguise myself and escape."

"When?"

"As soon as possible."

"Suppose I call Miriam. She can help you. Shall I?"

"Yes."

Camilla called Miriam, and after a few moments consultation it was decided that Louis should escape that night, and that Miriam should prepare whatever was needed for his hasty flight.

"Don't trust your secret to any white person," said Miriam, "but if you meet any of the colored people, just tell them that you is for the Linkum soldiers, and it will be all right; we don't know all about this war, but we feels somehow we's all mixed up in it."

And so with many prayers and blessings from Miriam, and sad farewells from Camilla, he left his home to enter upon that perilous flight, the whole current of his life changed.

It was in the early part of Winter; but the air was just as pleasant as early Spring in that climate. Louis walked all that night, guiding himself northward at night by the light of the stars and a little pocket compass, Camilla had just given him before starting, and avoiding the public roads during the day.

And thus he travelled for two days, when his lunch was exhausted, his lips parched with thirst, and his strength began to fail.

Just in this hour of extremity he saw seated by the corner of a fence a very black and homely-looking woman; there was something so gloomy and sullen in her countenance that he felt repelled by its morose expression. Still he needed food, and was very weary, and drawing near he asked her if she would give him anything to eat.

"Ain't got nothing. De sojers done been here, and eat all up."

Louis drew near and whispered a few words in her ear, and immediately a change passed over her whole countenance. The sullen expression turned to a look of tenderness and concern. The harsh tones of her voice actually grew mellow, and rising up in haste she almost sprang over the fence, and said, "I'se been looking for you, if you's Northman you's mighty welcome," and she set before him her humble store of provisions.

"Do you know," said Louis, "where I will find the Lincoln soldiers, or where the secesh are encamped?"

"No," said she "but my old man's mighty smart, and he'll find out; you come wid me."

Nothing doubting he went, and found the husband ready to do anything in his power to help him.

"You's better not go any furder to-day. I'll get you a place to hide where nobody can't find you, and then I'll pump Massa 'bout the sojers."

True to his word, he contrived to find out whether the soldiers were near.

"Massa," said he, scratching his head, and looking quite sober, "Massa, hadn't I better hide the mules? Oh I's 'fraid the Linkum sojers will come take 'em, cause dey gobbles up ebery ting dey lays dere hans on, jis like geese. I yerd dey was coming; mus' I hide de mules?"

"No, Sam, the scalawags are more than a hundred miles away; they are near Natchez."

"Well, maybe, t'was our own Fedrate soldiers."

"No, Sam, our nearest soldiers are at Baton Rouge."

"All right Massa. I don't want to lose all dem fine mules."

As soon as it was convenient Sam gave Louis the desired information. "Here," said Sam, when Louis was ready to start again, "is something to break your fast, and if you goes dis way you musn't let de white folks know what you's up to, but you trust dis," said he, laying his hand on his own dark skin.

His new friend went with him several miles, and pointing him out the way left him to pursue his journey onward. The next person he met with was a colored man, who bowed and smiled, and took off his hat.

Louis returned the bow, and was passing on when he said, "Massa, 'scuse me for speakin' to you, but dem secesh been hunting all day for a 'serter, him captin dey say."

Louis turned pale, but bracing his nerves he said, "Where are they?"

"Dey's in the house; is you he?"

"I am a Union man," Louis said, "and am trying to reach the Lincoln soldiers."

"Den," said the man, "if dat am de fac I's got a place for you; come with me," and Louis having learned to trust the colored people followed him to a place of safety.

Soon it was noised abroad that another deserter had been seen in that neighborhood, but the colored man would not reveal the whereabouts of Louis. His master beat him severely, but he would let neither threats nor torture wring the secret from his lips.

Louis saw the faithfulness of that man, and he thought with shame of his former position to the race from whom such unswerving devotion could spring. The hunt proving ineffectual, Louis after the search and excitement had subsided resumed his journey Northward, meeting with first one act of kindness and then another.

One day he had a narrow escape from the bloodhounds. He had trusted his secret to a colored man who, faithful like the rest, was directing him on his way when deep ominous sounds fell on their ears. The colored man knew that sound too well; he knew something of the nature of bloodhounds, and how to throw them off the track.

So hastily opening his pen-knife he cut his own feet so that the blood from them might deepen the scent on one track, and throw them off from Louis's path.

It was a brave deed, and nobly done, and Louis began to feel that he had never known them, and then how vividly came into his mind the words of Dr. Channing: "After all we may be trampling on one of the best branches of the human race." Here were men and women too who had been trampled on for ages ready to break to him their bread, aye share with him their scanty store.

One had taken the shoes from his feet and almost forced him to take them. What was it impelled these people? What was the

Union to them, and who were Lincoln's soldiers that they should be so ready to gravitate to the Union army and bring the most reliable information to the American General?

Was it not the hope of freedom which they were binding as amulets around their hearts? They as a race had lived in a measure upon an idea; it was the hope of a deliverance yet to come. Faith in God had underlain the life of the race, and was it strange if when even some of our politicians did not or could not read the signs of the times aright these people with deeper intuitions understood the war better than they did.

But at last Louis got beyond the borders of the confederacy, and stood once more on free soil, appreciating that section as he had never done before.

Chapter XV

[Text missing.]

Chapter XVI

"And I," said Minnie, "will help you pay it."

And so their young hearts had met at last, and with the approval and hearty consent of Anna, Minnie and Louis were married.

It was decided that Minnie should spend the winter in Southern France, and then in the spring they returned to America. On their arrival they found the war still raging, and Louis was ready and anxious to benefit that race to whom he felt he owed his life, and with whom he was connected by lineage.

He had plenty of money, a liberal education, and could have chosen a life of ease, but he was too ardent in his temperament, too decided in his character, not to feel an interest in the great events which were then transpiring in the country.

He made the acquaintance of some Anti-Slavery friends, and listened with avidity to their doctrines; he attended a number of war meetings, and caught the enthusiasm which inspired the young men who were coming from valley, hill, and plain to fill up the broken ranks of the Union army.

Minnie, educated in peace principles, could not conscientiously encourage him, and yet when she saw how the liberty of a whole race was trembling in the balance she could not help wishing [success?] to the army, nor find it in her heart to dissuade him from going.

Others had given their loved and cherished ones to camp and field. The son of a dear friend had said to his mother, "I know I shall be killed, but I go to free the slave." His presentiment had been met, for he had been brought home in his shroud.

Another dear friend had said, "I have drawn my sword, and it shall never sleep in its scabbard till the nation is free!" And she had heard that summer of '64 how bravely the colored soldiers had stood at Fort Wagner, when the storms of death were sweeping through the darkened sky. How they summoned the world to see the grandeur of their courage and the daring of their prowess.

How Corny had held with unyielding hand the nation's flag, and even when he was wounded still held it in his grasp, and crawling from the scene of action exclaimed, "I only did my duty, the old flag, I didn't let it trail on the ground."

And she felt on reading it with tearful eyes, that if she belonged to that race they had not shamed her by their want of courage; and so when Louis came to her and told her his intention, she would not attempt to oppose him, and when he was ready to depart, with many prayers, and sad farewells, she gave him up to fight the battles of freedom, for such it was to him, who went with every nerve in his right arm tingling to strike a blow for liberty.

Hitherto Louis had known the race by their tenderness and compassion, but the war gave him an opportunity to become acquainted with men brave to do, brave to dare, and brave to die.

A colored man was the hero of one of the most tender, touching, and tragic incidents of the war. A number of soldiers were in a boat exposed to the fire of the rebels; on board was a colored man who had not enrolled as a soldier, though his soul was full of sublime valor. The bullets hissed and split the water, and the rowers tried to get out of their reach, but all their efforts were in vain; the treacherous mud had caught the boat, and some one must peril life and limb to shove that boat into the water. And this man, the member of a doomed, a fated race, who had been trodden down for ages, comprehending the danger, said, "Some one must die to get us out of this, and it mout's well be me as anybody; you are soldiers, and you can fight. If they kill me it is nothing."

And with these words he arose, gave the boat a push, received a number of bullets, and died within two days after.

Louis acquitted himself bravely, and rapidly rose in favor with his superior officers. To him the place of danger was the post of duty. He often received letters from Minnie, but they were always hopeful; for she had learned to look on the bright side of everything.

She tried to beguile him with the news of the neighborhood, and to inspire him with bright hopes for the future; that future in which they should clasp hands again and find their duty and their pleasure in living for the welfare and happiness of *our* race, as Minnie would often say.

A race upon whose brows God had poured the chrism of a new era—a race newly anointed with freedom.

Oh, how the enthusiasm of her young soul gathered around that work! She felt it was no mean nor common privilege to be the pioneer of a new civilization. If he who makes two blades of grass grow where only one flourished before is a benefactor of the human race, how much higher and holier must his or her work be who dispenses light, instead of darkness, knowledge, instead of ignorance, and over the ruins of the slave-pen and auction-block erects institutions of learning.

She would say in her letters to Louis that the South will never be rightly conquered until another army should take the field, and that must be an army of civilizers; the army of the pen, and not the sword. Not the destroyers of towns and cities, but the builders of machines and factories; the organizers of peaceful industry and honorable labor; and as soon as she possibly could she intended to join that great army.

Sometimes Louis would shake his head doubtfully, and tell her that the South was a very sad place to live in, and would be for years, and, while he was willing to bear toil and privation in the cause he had learned to love, yet he shrank from exposing her to the social ostracism which she must bear whether she identified herself with the colored race or not.

However, her brave young heart never failed her, but kept true to its purpose to join that noble band who left the sunshine of their homes to help build up a new South on the basis of a higher and better civilization.

Louis remained with the army till Lee had surrendered. The storm-cloud of battle had passed away, and the thunders of contending batteries no longer crashed and vibrated on the air.

And then he returned to Minnie, who still lived with Thomas Carpenter. Very tender and joyous was their greeting. Louis thought he would rest awhile and then arrange his affairs to return to the South. In this plan he was heartily seconded by Minnie.

Thomas and Anna were sorry to part with her, but they knew that life was not made for a holiday of ease and luxury, and so they had no words of discouragement for them. If duty called them to the South it was right that they should go; and so they would not throw themselves across the purpose of their souls.

Chapter XVII

Before he located, Louis concluded to visit the old homestead, and to present his beautiful young bride to his grandmother and Camilla.

He knew his adopted sister too well to fear that Minnie would fail to receive from her the warmest welcome, and so with eager heart he took passage on one of the Mississippi boats to New Orleans, intending to stop in the city a few days, and send word to Camilla; but just as he was passing from the levee to the hotel, he caught a glimpse of Camilla walking down the street, and stopping the carriage, he alighted, and spoke to her. She immediately recognized him, although his handsome face had become somewhat bronzed by exposure in camp and field.

"Do not go to the hotel," she said, "you are heartily welcome, come home with me."

"But my wife is along."

"Never mind, she's just as welcome as you are."

"But, like myself, she is colored."

"It does not matter. I should not think of your going to a hotel, while I have a home in the city."

Camilla following, wondering how she would like the young wife. She had great kindness and compassion for the race, but as far as social equality was concerned, though she had her strong personal likings, yet, except with Louis, neither custom nor education had reconciled her to the maintenance of any equal, social relations with them.

"My wife," said Louis, introducing Camilla to Minnie. Camilla immediately reached out her hand to the young wife, and gave her a cordial greeting, and they soon fell into a pleasant and animated conversation. Mutually they were attracted to each other, and when they reached their destination, Minnie had begun to feel quite at home with Camilla.

"How is Aunt Miriam, or rather, my grandmother?" said Louis.

"She is well, and often wonders what has become of her poor boy; but she always has persisted in believing that she would see you again, and I know her dear old eyes will run over with gladness. But things have changed very much since we parted. We have passed through the fire since I saw you, and our troubles are not over yet; but we are hoping for better days. But we are at home. Let us alight."

And Louis and Minnie were ushered into a home whose quiet and refined beauty were very pleasant to the eye, for Camilla had inherited from her father his aesthetic tastes; had made her home and its surroundings models of loveliness. Half a dozen varieties of the sweetest and brightest roses clambered up the walls and arrayed them with a garb of rare beauty. Jessamines breathed their fragrance on the air; magnolias reared their stately heads and gladdened the eye with the exquisite beauty of their flowers.

"This is an unexpected pleasure," said Camilla, removing Minnie's bonnet, and gazing with unfeigned admiration upon her girlish face, "but really some one must enjoy this pleasure besides myself."

Camilla rang the bell; a bright, smiling girl of about ten years appeared. "Tell Miriam," she said, "to come; that her boy Louis is here."

Miriam appeared immediately, and throwing her arms around his neck, gave vent to her feelings in a burst of joy. "I always said you'd come back. I's prayed for you night and day, and I always believed I'd see you afore I died, and now my word's come true. There's nothing like having faith."

"Here's my wife," said Louis, turning to Minnie.

"Your wife; is you married, honey? Well I hopes you'll have a good time."

Minnie came forward and gave her hand to Miriam, as Louis said, "This is my grandmother."

A look of proud satisfaction passed over the old woman's face, and a sudden joy lit up her eyes at these words of pleasant recognition.

"Ah, my child," said Miriam, "We's had a mighty heap of trouble since you left. Them miserable secesh searched the house all over for you, when you was gone, and they was mighty sassy; but we didn't mind that, so they didn't ketch you. How did you get along? We was dreadfully uneasy about you?"

Louis then told them of the kindness of the colored people, his thrilling adventures, and hair-breadth escapes, and unfolded to them his plans for the future.

Camilla listened with deep interest, and turning to Minnie, who had left the peaceful sunshine of her mother's home to dwell in the midst of that rough and rude state of society, she said, "I cannot help feeling sad to see you exposing yourself to the dangers that lay around your path. The few Southern women who have been faithful to the flag have had a sad experience since the war. We have been ostracized and abused, and often our husbands have been brutally murdered, in a number of instances when they were faithful to the dear old flag. A friend of mine, who was an angel of mercy to the Union prisoners, dressing their wounds and carrying them relief, had a dear son, who always kept a Union flag at home, which he regarded with almost religious devotion. This made him a marked boy in the community, and during the war he was so cruelly beaten, by some young rebels, that he never recovered, and colored women who would wend their way under the darkness and cover of night to aid our suffering soldiers, were in danger of being flogged, if detected, and I understand that one did receive 75 lashes for such an offence, and I heard of another who was shot down like a dog, for giving bread to a prisoner, who said, 'Mammy, I am starving.' I think, (but I have no right to dictate to you) had I been you, and my home in the North, that I would have preferred staying there, where, to say the least, you could have had pleasanter social relations. You and Louis are nearer the white race than the colored. Why should you prefer the one to the other?"

"Because," said Minnie, "the prejudices of society are so strong against the people with whom I am connected on my mother's side, that I could not associate with white people on equal terms, without concealing my origin, and that I scorned to do. The first years of my life passed without my knowing that I was connected with the colored race; but when it was revealed to me by mother, who suddenly claimed me, at first I shrank from the social ostracism to which that knowledge doomed me, and it was some time before I was reconciled to the change. Oh, there are lessons of life that we never learn in the bowers of ease. They must be learned in the fire. For months life seemed to me a dull, sad thing, and for a while I did not care whether I lived or died, the sunshine had suddenly faded from my path, and the future looked so dark and cheerless. But now, when I look back upon those days of gloom and suffering, I think they were among the most fruitful of my life, for in those days of pain and sorrow my resolution was formed to join the fortunes of my mother's race, and I resolved to brighten her old age with a joy, with a gladness she had never known in her youth. And how could I have done that had I left her unrecognized and palmed myself upon society as a white woman? And to tell you the truth, having passed most of my life in white society, I did not feel that the advantages of that society would have ever paid me for the loss of my self-respect, by passing as white, when I knew that I was colored; when I knew that any society, however cultivated, wealthy or refined, would not be a social gain to me, if my color and not my character must be my passport of admission. So, when I found out that I was colored, I made up my mind that I would neither be pitied nor patronized by my former friends; but that I would live out my own individuality and do for my race, as a colored woman, what I never could accomplish as a white woman."

"I think I understand you," said Camilla; "and although I tremble for you in the present state, yet you cannot do better than live out the earnest purpose of your life. I feel that we owe a great debt to the colored race, and I would aid and not hinder any hand that is ready to help do the needed work. I have felt for many years that slavery was wrong, and I am glad, from the bottom of my heart, that it has at last been destroyed. And what are your plans, Louis?"

"We are going to open a school, and devote our lives to the up-building of the future race. I intend entering into some plan to facilitate the freedmen in obtaining homes of their own. I want to see this newly enfranchised race adding its quota to the civilization of the land. I believe there is power and capacity, only let it have room for exercise and development. We demand no social equality, no supremacy of power. All we ask is that the American people will take their Christless, Godless prejudices out of the way, and give us a chance to grow, an opportunity to accept life, not merely as a matter of ease and indulgence, but of struggle, conquest, and achievement."

"Yes," said Camilla, "what you want and what the nation should be just enough to grant you is fair play."

"Yes, that is what we want; to be known by our character, and not by our color; to be permitted to take whatever position in society we are fitted to fill. We do not want to be bolstered and propped up on the one hand, nor to be crushed and trampled down on the other."

"Well, Louis, I think that we are coming to that. No, I cannot feel that all this baptism of fire and blood through which we have passed has been in vain. Slavery, as an institution, has been destroyed. Slavery, as an idea, still lives, but I believe that we shall outgrow this spirit of caste and proscription which still tarnishes our civilization, both North and South."

Chapter XVIII

After spending a few weeks with Camilla, Louis resolved to settle in the town of L——n, and as soon as he had chosen his home and made arrangements for the future, he sent for Ellen, and in a few days she joined her dear children, as she called Louis and Minnie. Very pleasant were the relations between Minnie and the newly freed people.

She had found her work, and they had found their friend. She did not content herself with teaching them mere knowledge of books. She felt that if the race would grow in the right direction, it must plant the roots of progress under the hearthstone. She had learned from Anna those womanly arts that give beauty, strength and grace to the fireside, and it was her earnest desire to teach them how to make their homes bright and happy.

Louis, too, with his practical turn of mind, used his influence in teaching them to be saving and industrious, and to turn their attention towards becoming land owners. He attended their political meetings, not to array class against class, nor to inflame the passions of either side. He wanted the vote of the colored people not to express the old hates and animosities of the plantation, but the new community of interests arising from freedom.

For awhile the aspect of things looked hopeful. The Reconstruction Act, by placing the vote in the hands of the colored man, had given him a new position. There was a lull in Southern violence. It was a great change from the fetters on his wrist to the ballot in his right hand, and the uniform testimony of the colored people was, "We are treated better than we were before."

Some of the rebels indulged in the hope that their former slaves would vote for them, but they were learning the power of combination, and having no political past, they were radical by position, and when Southern State after State rolled up its majorities on the radical side, then the vials of wrath were poured upon the heads of the colored people, and the courage and heroism which might have gained them recognition, perhaps, among heathens, made them more obnoxious here.

Still Louis and Minnie kept on their labors of love; their inner lives daily growing stronger and broader, for they learned to lean upon a strength greater than their own; and some of the most beautiful lessons of faith and trust they had ever learned, they were taught in the lowly cabins of these newly freed people.

Often would Minnie enter these humble homes and listen patiently to the old story of wrong and suffering. Sympathizing with their lot, she would give them counsel and help when needed. When she was leaving they would look after her wistfully, and say,

"She mighty good; we's low down, but she feels for we."

And thus day after day of that earnest life was spent in deeds and words of love and kindness.

But let us enter their pleasant home. Louis has just returned from a journey to the city, and has brought with him the latest Northern papers. He is looking rather sober, and Minnie, ready to detect the least change of his countenance, is at his side.

"What is the matter?" Minnie asked, in a tone of deep concern.

"I am really discouraged."

"What about?"

"Look here," said he, handing her the *New York Tribune*. "State after State has rolled up a majority against negro suffrage. I have been trying to persuade our people to vote the Republican ticket, but to-day, I feel like blushing for the party. They are weakening our hands and strengthening those of the rebels."

"But, Louis, they were not Republicans who gave these majorities against us."

"But, darling, if large numbers of these Republicans stayed at home, and let the election go by default, the result was just the same. Now every rebel can throw it in our teeth and say, 'See your great Republican party; they refuse to let the negro vote with them, but they force him upon us. They don't do it out of regard to the negro, but only to spite us.' I don't think, Minnie, that I am much given to gloomy forebodings, but I see from the temper and actions of these rebels, that they are encouraged and emboldened by these tidings from the North, and to-day they are turning people out of work for voting the radical ticket. A while ago they tried flattery and cajolery. You could hear it on almost every side— 'We are the best friends of the colored people.' Appeals were made to the memories of the past; how they hunted and played together, and searched for birds' nests in the rotten peach trees, and when the colored people were not to be caught by such chaff, some were trying to force them into submission by intimidation and starvation."

Just then a knock was heard at the door, and a dark man entered. There was nothing in his appearance that showed any connection with the white race. There was a tone of hopefulness in his speech, though his face wore a somewhat anxious expression.

"Good morning, Mr. Jackson," said Louis, for, in deference to their feelings he had dropped the "aunt" and "uncle" of bygone days.

"Good morning," replied the man, while a pleasant smile flitted over his countenance.

"How does the world use you?" said Louis.

"Well, times are rather bilious with me, but I am beginning to pick up a little. I get a few boots and shoes to mend. I always used to go to the mountains, and get plenty of work to do; but this year they wouldn't give me the situation because I had joined the radicals."

"What a shame," said Louis; "these men who have always had their rights of citizenship, seem to know so little of the claims of justice and humanity, that they are ready to brow-beat and intimidate these people for voting according to their best interests.

And what saddens me most is to see so many people of the North clasping hands with these rebels and traitors, and to hear it repeated that these people are too ignorant to vote."

"Ignorant as they are," said Minnie, "during the war they knew more than their masters; for they knew how to be true to their country, when their masters were false to it, and rallied around the flag, when they were trampling it under foot, and riddling it with bullets."

"Ah!" said uncle Richard, "I knows them of old. Last week some of them offered me $500 if I would desert my party; but I wasn't going to forsake my people. I have been in purty tight places this year. One night when I come home my little girl said to me, 'Daddy, dere ain't no bread in de house.' Now, that jist got me, but I begun to pray, and the next day I found a quarter of a dollar, and then some of my colored friends said it wouldn't do to let uncle Jack starve, and they made me up seventy-five cents. My wife sometimes gets out of heart, but she don't see very far off."

"I wish," said Louis, after Mr. Jackson had left, "that some of our Northern men would only see the heroism of that simple-minded man. Here he stands facing an uncertain future, no longer young in years, stripped by slavery, his wife not in full sympathy with him, and yet with what courage he refused the bribe."

"Yes," said Minnie, "$500 means a great deal for a man landless and poor, with no assured support for the future. It means a comfortable fire when the blasts of winter are roving around your home; it means bread for the little ones, and medicine for the sick child, and little start in life."

"But on the other hand," said Louis, "it meant betrayal of the interests of his race, and I honor the faithfulness which shook his hands from receiving the bribe and clasping hands politically with his life-long oppressors. And I asked myself the question while he was telling his story, which hand was the better custodian of the ballot, the white hand that offered the bribe or the black one that refused it. I think the time will come when some of the Anglo Saxon race will blush to remember that when they were trailing the banner of freedom in the dust black men were grasping it with earnest hands, bearing it aloft amid persecution, pain, and death."

"Louis" said Minnie very seriously, "I think the nation makes one great mistake in settling this question of suffrage. It seems to me that everything gets settled on a partial basis. When they are reconstructing the government why not lay the whole foundation anew, and base the right of suffrage not on the claims of service or sex, but on the broader basis of our common humanity."

"Because, Minnie, we are not prepared for it. This hour belongs to the negro."

"But, Louis, is it not the negro woman's hour also? Has she not as many rights and claims as the negro man?"

"Well, perhaps she has, but, darling, you cannot better the condition of the colored men without helping the colored women. What elevates him helps her."

"All that may be true, but I cannot recognize that the negro man is the only one who has pressing claims at this hour. To-day our government needs woman's conscience as well as man's judgment. And while I would not throw a straw in the way of the colored man, even though I know that he would vote against me as soon as he gets his vote, yet I do think that woman should have some power to defend herself from oppression, and equal laws as if she were a man."

"But, really, I should not like to see you wending your way through rough and brawling mobs to the polls."

"Because these mobs are rough and coarse I would have women vote. I would soften the asperity of the mobs, and bring into our politics a deeper and broader humanity. When I see intemperance send its floods of ruin and shame to the homes of men, and pass by the grog-shops that are constantly grinding out their fearful grist of poverty, ruin and death, I long for the hour when woman's vote will be levelled against these charnel houses; and have, I hope, the power to close them throughout the length and breadth of the land."

"Why darling," said Louis, gazing admiringly upon the earnest enthusiasm lighting up her face, "I shall begin to believe that you are a strong-minded woman."

"Surely, you would not have me a weak-minded woman in these hours of trial."

"But, darling, I did not think that you were such an advocate for women's voting."

"I think, Louis, that basing our rights on the ground of our common humanity is the only true foundation for national peace and durability. If you would have the government strong and enduring you should entrench it in the hearts of both the men and women of the land."

"I think you are right in that remark," said Louis. And thus their evenings were enlivened by pleasant and interesting conversations upon the topics of the day.

Once when a union friend was spending an evening at their home Louis entered, looking somewhat animated, and Minnie ever ready to detect his moods and feelings, wanted to know what had happened.

"Oh, I have been to a wedding since I left home."

"And pray who was married?"

"Guess."

"I don't know whom to guess. One of our friends?"

"Yes."

"Was it Mr. Welland?"

"Yes."

"And who did he marry? Is she a Northern woman, and a staunch unionist?"

"Well, I can't imagine who she can be."

"Why he married Miss Henson, who sent you those beautiful flowers."

"Why, Louis, is it possible? Why she is a colored woman."

"I know."

"But how came he to marry her?"

"For the same reason I married you, because he loved her?"

"Well," said the union man, who sat quietly listening, "I am willing to give to the colored people every right that I possess myself, but as to intermarrying with them, I am not prepared for that."

"I think," said Louis, "that marrying and social equality among the races will simply regulate itself. I do not think under the present condition of things that there will be any general intermarrying of the races, but this idea of rooted antagonism of races to me is all moonshine. I believe that what you call the instincts of race are only the prejudices which are the result of custom and education, and if there is any instinct in the matter it is rather the instinct of nature to make a Semi-tropical race in a Semi-tropical climate. Welland told me that he had met his wife when she was a slave, that he loved her then, and would have bought her had it been in his power, but now that freedom had come to her he was glad to have the privilege of making her his wife. He is an Englishman by birth and he intends taking her home with him to England when a favorable opportunity presents itself. And that is far more honorable and manly than living together after the old order of things. I think," said Louis facing the floor "that a cruel wrong was done to Minnie and myself when life was given to us under conditions that doomed us to hopeless slavery, and from which we were rescued only by good fortune. I have heard some colored persons boasting of the white blood, but I always feel like blushing for mine. Much as my father did for me he could never atone for giving me life under the conditions he did."

"Never mind," said Minnie, "it all turned out for the best."

"Yes, Darling," said Louis, growing calmer, "for it gave me you.

And that was life's compensation. But the question of the inter-mingling of the races in marriage is one that scarcely interests this question. The question that presses upon us with the most fearful distinctness is how can we make life secure in the South. I some-times feel as if the very air was busting with bayonets. There is no law here but the revolver. There must be a screw loose somewhere, and this government that taxes its men in peace and drafts them in war, ought to be wise enough to know its citizens and strong enough to protect them."

Chapter XIX

But the pleasant home-life of Louis and Minnie was destined to be rudely broken up. He began to receive threats and anony-mous letters, such as these: "Louis Lecroix, you are a doomed man. We are determined to tolerate no scalawags, nor carpetbag-gers among us. Beware, the sacred serpent has hissed."

But Louis, brave and resolute, kept on the even tenor of his way, although he never left his home without some forebodings that he tried in vain to cast off. But his young wife being less in contact with the brutal elements of society in that sin-cursed region, did not comprehend the danger as Louis did, and yet she could not help feeling anxious for her husband's safety.

They never parted without her looking after him with a sigh, and then turning to her school, or whatever work or reading she had on her hand, she would strive to suppress her heart's forebod-ings. But the storm about to burst and to darken forever the sun-shine of that home was destined to fall on that fair young head.

Imperative business called Louis from home for one night. Minnie stood at the door and said, "Louis, I hate to have you go. I have been feeling so badly here lately, as if something was going to happen. Come home as soon as you can."

"I will, darling," he said, kissing her tenderly again and again. "I do feel rather loath to leave you, but death is every where, always lurking in ambush. A man may escape from an earthquake to be strangled by a hair. So, darling, keep in good spirits till I come."

Minnie stood at the door watching him till he was out of sight, and then turning to her mother with a sigh, she said, "What a wretched state of society. When he goes I never feel easy till he returns. I do wish we had a government under which our lives would be just as safe as they were in Pennsylvania."

Ellen felt very anxious, but she tried to hide her disquietude and keep Minnie's spirits from sinking, and so she said, "This is a hard country. We colored people have seen our hard times here."

"But, mother, don't you sometimes feel bitter towards these people, who have treated you so unkindly?"

"No, Minnie; I used to, but I don't now. God says we must forgive, and if we don't forgive, He won't forgive."

"But, mother, how did you get to feeling so?"

"Why, honey, I used to suffer until my heart was almost ready to burst, but I learned to cast my burden on the Lord, and then my misery all passed away. My burden fell off at the foot of the cross, and I felt that my feet were planted on a rock."

"How wonderful," said Minnie, "is this faith! How real it is to them! How near some of these suffering people have drawn to God!"

"Yes," said Ellen, "Mrs. Sumpter had a colored woman, to whom they were real mean and cruel, and one day they whipped her and beat her on her feet to keep her from running away; but she made up her mind to leave, and so she packed up her clothes to run away. But before she started, I believe she kneeled down and prayed, and asked what she should do, and something reasoned with her and said, 'Stand still and see what I am going to do for you,' and so she unpacked her clothes and stayed, and now the best part of it was this, Milly's son had been away, and he came back and brought with him money enough to buy his mother; for he had been out begging money to buy her, and so Milly got free, and she was mighty glad that she had stayed, because when he'd come back, if she had been gone, he would not have known where to find her."

"Well, it is wonderful. Somehow these people have passed through the darkness and laid their hands on God's robe of love and light, and have been sustained. It seems to me that some things they see clearer through their tears."

"Mother," said Minnie, "As it is Saturday I will visit some of my scholars."

"Well, Minnie, I would; you look troubled, and may be you'll feel better."

"Yes, Mother, I often feel strengthened after visiting some of these good old souls, and getting glimpses into their inner life. I sometimes ask them, after listening to the story of their past wrongs, what has sustained you? What has kept you up? And the almost invariable answer has been the power of God. Some of these poor old souls, who have been turned adrift to shift for themselves, don't live by bread alone; they live by bread and faith in God. I asked one of them a few days since, Are you not afraid of starving? and the answer was, Not while God lives."

After Minnie left, she visited a number of lowly cabins. The first one she entered was the home of an industrious couple who were just making a start in life. The room in which Minnie was, had no window-lights, only an aperture that supplied them with light, but also admitted the cold.

"Why don't you have window-lights?" said Minnie.

"Oh we must crawl before we walk;" and yet even in this humble home they had taken two orphan children of their race, and were giving them food and shelter. And this kindness to the orphans of their race Minnie found to be a very praiseworthy practice among some of those people who were not poorer than themselves.

The next cabin she entered was very neat, though it bore evidences of poverty. The woman, in referring to the past, told her how her child had been taken away when it was about two years old, and how she had lost all trace of him, and would not know him if he stood in her presence.

"How did you feel?" said Minnie.

"I felt as I was going to my grave, but I thought if I wouldn't get justice here, I would get it in another world."

"My husband," said another, "asked if God is a just God, how would sich as slavery be, and something answered and said, 'sich shan't always be,' and you couldn't beat it out of my husband's head that the Spirit didn't speak to him."

And thus the morning waned away, and Minnie returned calmer than when she had left. A holy peace stole over her mind. She felt that for high and low, rich and poor, there was a common refuge. That there was no corner so dark that the light of heaven could not shine through, and that these people in their ignorance and simplicity had learned to look upon God as a friend coming near to them in their sorrows, and taking cognizance of their wants and woes.

Minnie loved to listen to these beautiful stories of faith and trust. To her they were grand inspirations to faith and duty. Sometimes Minnie would think, when listening to some dear aged saint, I can't teach these people religion, I must learn from them.

Refreshed and strengthened she returned home and began to work upon a dress for a destitute and orphaned child, and when night came she retired quite early, being somewhat wearied with her day's work.

During his absence Louis had been among the freedmen in a

new settlement where he had lately established a school, where, notwithstanding all their disadvantages, he was pleased to see evidences of growth and progress.

There was an earnestness and growing manliness that commanded his respect. They were beginning to learn the power of combination, and gave but little heed to the cajoling words, "We are your best friends."

"Don't you think," Louis said to an intelligent freedman, "that the rebels are your best friends?"

"I'll think so when I lose my senses."

"But you are ignorant," Louis said to another one. "How will you know whom to vote for?"

"Well if I don't, I know how not to vote for a rebel."

"How do you know you didn't vote for a rebel?" said Louis to another one who came from one of the most benighted districts.

"I voted for one of my own color," as if treason and a black skin were incompatible.

In the evening Louis called the people together, and talked with them, trying to keep them from being discouraged, for the times were evil, and the days were very gloomy. The impeachment had failed. State after State in the North had voted against enfranchising the colored man in their midst. The spirit of the lost cause revived, murders multiplied. The Ku Klux spread terror and death around. Every item of Northern meanness to the colored people in their midst was a message of hope to the rebel element of the South, which had only changed. Ballot and bullet had failed, but another resort was found in secret assassination. Men advocating equal rights did so at the peril of their lives, for violence and murder were rampant in the land. Oh those dark and weary days when politicians were flattering for place and murdered Union men were sleeping in their bloody shrouds. Louis' courage did not desert him, and he tried to nerve the hearts of those that were sinking with fear in those days of gloom and terror. His advice to the people was, "Defend your firesides if they are invaded, live as peaceably as you can, spare no pains to educate your children, be saving and industrious, try to get land under your feet and homes over your heads. My faith is very strong in political parties, but, as the world has outgrown other forms of wrong, I believe that it will outgrow this also. We must trust and hope for better things. What else could he say? And yet there were times when his words seemed to him almost like bitter mockery. Here was outrage upon outrage committed upon these people, and to tell them to hope and wait for better times, but seemed like speaking hollow words. Oh he longed for a central administration strong enough to put down violence and misrule in the South. If Johnson was clasping hands with rebels and traitors was there no power in Congress to give, at least, security to life? Must they wait till murder was organized into an institution, and life and property were at the mercy of the mob? And, if so, would not such a government be a farce, and such a civilization a failure?

With these reflections passing through his mind he fell asleep, but his slumber was restless and disturbed. He dreamed (but it seemed so plain to him, that he thought it was hardly a dream,) that Minnie came to his side and pressed her lips to his, but they were very pale and very cold. He reached out his hand to clasp her, but she was gone, but as she vanished he heard her say, "My husband."

Restless and uneasy he arose; there was a strange feeling around his soul, a great sinking and depression of his spirits. He could not account for his feelings. He arose and walked the floor and looked up at the heavens, but the night was very bright and beautiful, still he could not shake off his strange and sad forebodings, and as soon as it was light he started for home.

«« »»

[Installment missing.]

Chapter XX

In the afternoon when the body had been prepared for the grave, the sorrowing friends gathered around, tearfully noting the look of peace and rest which had stolen over the pale, dead face, when all traces of the death agony had passed away by the contraction of the muscles.

"That is just the way she looked yesterday," said a sad-eyed woman, whose face showed traces of a deep "and fearful sorrow."

Louis drew near, for he was eager to hear any word that told him of Minnie before death had robbed her of life, and him of peace. He came near enough to hear, but not to interrupt the conversation.

"She was at my house yesterday, trying to comfort me, when I was telling her how these Secesh used to *cruelize* us."

"I was telling her about my poor daughter Amy, and what a sprightly, pert piece she was, and how dem awful Secesh took my poor chile and hung'd her."

"Hung'd? Aunt Susan, Oh how was dat?" said half a dozen voices.

"Well, you see it was jist dis way. My darter Amy was a mighty nice chile, and Massa could truss her wid any ting. So when de Linkum Sogers had gone through dis place, Massa got her to move some of his tings over to another place. Now when Amy seed de sojers had cum'd through she was mighty glad, and she said in a kine of childish way, 'T'se so glad, I'm gwine to marry a Linkum soger, and set up house-keeping for myself.' I don't spect she wer in arnest 'bout marrying de sojer, but she did want her freedom. Well, no body couldn't blame her for dat, for freedom's a mighty good thing."

"I don't like it, I jist loves it," said one of Aunt Sue's auditors.

"And I does too, 'cause I'd rather live on bread and water than be back again in de old place, but go on, Aunt Susan."

"Well, when she said dat, dat miserable old Heston—"

"Heston, I know dat wretch, I bound de debil's waiting for him now, got his pitch fork all ready."

"Well, he had my poor girl tookened up, and poor chile, she was beat shameful, and den dey had her up before der sogers and had her tried for saying 'cendiary words, and den dey had my poor girl hung'd." And the poor old woman bowed her head and rocked her body to and fro.

"Well," she continued after a moment's pause, "I was telling dat sweet angel dere my trouble, and she was mighty sorry, and sat dere and cried, and den she said, 'Mrs. Thomas, I hope in a better world dat you'll see a joy according to all the days wherein you have seen sorrow!' Bless her sweet heart, she's got in de shining gate afore me, but I bound to meet her on de sunny banks of deliberance.

"And she was at my house yesterday," said another. "She cum'd to see if I wanted any ting, and I tell'd her I would like to hab a little flannel, 'cause I had the rheumatiz so bad, and she said I should hab it. Den she asked me if I didn't like freedom best. I told her I would rather live in a corn crib, and so I would. It is hard getting along, but I hopes for better times. And den she took down de Bible, and read wid dat sweet voice of hers, about de eagle stirring up her nest, and den she said when de old eagle wanted her young to fly she broked up de nest, and de little eagles didn't known what was de matter, but some how dey didn't feel so cumfertable, 'cause de little twigs and sticks stuck in 'em, and den dey would work dere wings, and dat was de way she said we must do; de ole nest of slavery was broke up, but she said we mus'n't get discouraged, but we must plume our wings for higher flying. Oh she did tell it so purty. I wish I could say it like she did, it did my heart so much good. Poor thing, she done gone and folded her wing in de hebenly mansion. I wish I was 'long side of her, but I'se bound to meet her, 'cause I'm gwine to set out afresh for heben and 'ternal glory."

And thus did these stricken children of sorrow unconsciously comfort the desolate and almost breaking heart of Louis Lacroix. And their words of love and hope were like rays of light shimmering amid the gloomy shadows that overhung his suddenly darkened life.

Surely, thought Louis, if the blessings and tears of the poor and needy and the prayers of him who was ready to perish would crystalize a path to the glory-land, then Minnie's exit from earth must have been over a bridge of light, above whose radiant arches hovering angels would delight to bend.

While these thoughts were passing through his mind, a knock was heard at the door, and Louis rose to open it, and then he saw a sight which shook all his gathered firmness to tears. Headed by the eldest of Minnie's scholars came a procession of children, each one bearing a bunch of fairest and brightest flowers to spread around the couch of their beloved teacher. Some kissed her, and others threw themselves beside the corpse and wept bitter, burning tears. All shared in Louis' grief, for all had lost a dear, good friend and loving instructor.

Louis summoned all the energies of his soul to bear his mournful loss. It was his task to bow to the Chastener, and let his loved one go, feeling that when he had laid her in the earth that he left her there in the hope of a better resurrection.

Life with its solemn responsibilities still met him; its earnest duties still confronted him, and, though he sometimes felt like a weary watcher at the gates of death, longing to catch a glimpse of her shining robes and the radiant light of her glorified face, yet her knew it was his work to labor and to wait.

Sorrow and danger still surrounded his way, and he felt his soul more strongly drawn out than ever to share the fortunes of the colored race. He felt there were grand possibilities stored up in their future. The name of the negro had been associated with slavery, ignorance and poverty, and he determined as far as his influence could be exerted to lift that name from the dust of the centuries and place it among the most honored names in the history of the human race.

He still remained in the South, for Minnie's grave had made the South to him a sacred place, a place in which to labor and to wait until peace like bright dew should descend where carnage had spread ruin around, and freedom and justice, like glorified angels, should reign triumphant where violence and slavery had held their fearful carnival of shame and crime for ages. Earnestly he set himself to bring around the hour when

> Peace, white-robed and pure, should move
> O'er rifts of ruin deep and wide,
> When her hands should span with lasting love
> The chasms rent by hate and pride.

And he was blessed in his labors of love and faith.

Conclusion

And now, in conclusion, may I not ask the indulgence of my readers for a few moments, simply to say that Louis and Minnie are only ideal beings, touched here and there with a coloring from real life?

But while I confess (not wishing to mis-represent the most lawless of the Ku-Klux) that Minnie has only lived and died in my imagination, may I not modestly ask that the lesson of Minnie shall have its place among the educational ideas for the advancement of our race?

The greatest want of our people, if I understand our wants

aright, is not simply wealth, nor genius, nor mere intelligence, but live men, and earnest, lovely women, whose lives shall represent not a "stagnant mass, but a living force."

We have wealth among us, but how much of it is ever spent in building up the future of the race? in encouraging talent, and developing genius? We have intelligence, but how much do we add to the reservoir of the world's thought? We have genius among us, but how much can it rely upon the colored race for support?

Take even the *Christian Recorder*, where are the graduates from colleges and high school whose pens and brains lend beauty, strength, grace and culture to its pages?

If, when their school days are over, the last composition shall have been given at the examination, will not the disused faculties revenge themselves by rusting? If I could say it without being officious and intrusive, I would say to some who are about to graduate this year, do not feel that your education is finished, when the diploma of your institution is in your hands. Look upon the knowledge you have gained only as a stepping stone to a future, which you are determined shall grandly contrast with the past.

While some of the authors of the present day have been weaving their stories about white men marrying beautiful quadroon girls, who, in so doing were lost to us socially, I conceived of one of that same class to whom I gave a higher, holier destiny; a life of lofty self-sacrifice and beautiful self-consecration, finished at the post of duty, and rounded off with the fiery crown of martyrdom, a circlet which ever changes into a diadem of glory.

The lesson of Minnie's sacrifice is this, that it is braver to suffer with one's own branch of the human race,—to feel, that the weaker and the more despised they are, the closer we will cling to them, for the sake of helping them, than to attempt to creep out of all identity with them in their feebleness, for the sake of mere personal advantages, and to do this at the expense of self-respect, and a true manhood, and a truly dignified womanhood, that with whatever gifts we possess, whether they be genius, culture, wealth or social position, we can best serve the interests of our race by a generous and loving diffusion, than by a narrow and selfish isolation which, after all, is only one type of the barbarous and anti-social state.

Notes

1. The following two paragraphs are for the most part illegible. I have reproduced below as much of the text as can be deciphered.

The whole South is in a state of excitement [. . .   ]
[   ] nurture
[   ] and re-
[.   ] high
[   ] be for
[   ] they are [   ]and only remember they are rebels [?   ].
   They [urge the   agenda?] and their brothers in their
[mistaken?] folly. Like the women of Carthage [   ] ancient
and magnificent city was [   ]
they were ready to sacrifice their [   ] and if
need be would have cut [but it have been] so
dear to their hearts [   ]

2. The original reads "Josiah."
3. The original reads "Joseph."
4. The original reads "Josiah."
5. The original reads "Josiah."
6. The original reads "Anna."
7. The original reads "Minnie."

Sowing and Reaping
A Temperance Story

Chapter I

"I hear that John Andrews has given up his saloon; and a foolish thing it was. He was doing a splendid business. What could have induced him?"

"They say that his wife was bitterly opposed to the business. I don't know, but I think it quite likely. She has never seemed happy since John has kept saloon."

"Well, I would never let any woman lead me by the nose. I would let her know that as the living comes by me, the way of getting it is my affair, not hers, as long as she is well provided for."

"All men are not alike, and I confess that I value the peace and happiness of my home more than anything else; and I would not like to engage in any business which I knew was a source of constant pain to my wife."

"But, what right has a woman to complain, if she has every thing she wants. I would let her know pretty soon who holds the reins, if I had such an unreasonable creature to deal with. I think as much of my wife as any man, but I want her to know her place, and I know mine."

"What do you call her place?"

"I call her place staying at home and attending to her own affairs. Were I a laboring man I would never want my wife to take in work. When a woman has too much on hand, something has to be neglected. Now I always furnish my wife with sufficient help and supply every want but how I get the living, and where I go, and what company I keep, is my own business, and I would not allow the best woman in the world to interfere. I have often heard women say that they did not care what their husbands did, so that they provided for them; and I think such conclusions are very sensible."

"Well, John, I do not think so. I think a woman must be very selfish, if all she cares for her husband is, to have a good provider. I think her husband's honor and welfare should be as dear to her as her own; and no true woman and wife can be indifferent to the moral welfare of her husband. Neither man nor woman can live by bread alone in the highest and best sense of the term."

"Now Paul, don't go to preaching. You have always got some moon struck theories, some wild, visionary and impracticable ideas, which would work first rate, if men were angels and earth a paradise. Now don't be so serious, old fellow; but you know on this religion business, you and I always part company. You are always up in the clouds, while I am trying to invest in a few acres, or town lots of solid *terra firma*."

"And would your hold on earthly possessions, be less firm because you looked beyond the seen to the unseen?"

"I think it would, if I let conscience interfere constantly, with every business transaction I undertook. Now last week you lost $500 fair and square, because you would not foreclose that mortgage on Smith's property. I told you that 'business is business,' and that while I pitied the poor man, I would not have risked my money that way, but you said that conscience would not let you; that while other creditors were gathering like hungry vultures around the poor man, you would not join with them, and that you did not believe in striking a man when he is down. Now Paul, as a business man, if you want to succeed, you have got to look at business in a practical, common sense way. Smith is dead, and where is your money now?"

"Apparently lost; but the time may come when I shall feel that it was one of the best investments I ever made. Stranger things than that have happened. I confess that I felt the loss and it has somewhat cramped my business. Yet if it was to do over again, I don't think that I would act differently, and when I believe that Smith's death was hurried on by anxiety and business troubles, while I regret the loss of my money, I am thankful that I did not press my claim."

"Sour grapes, but you are right to put the best face on matters."

"No, if it were to do over again, I never would push a struggling man to the wall when he was making a desperate fight for his wife and little ones."

"Well! Paul, we are both young men just commencing life, and my motto is to look out for Number 1, and you—"

"Oh! I believe in lending a helping hand."

"So do I, when I can make every corner out to my advantage. I believe in every man looking out for himself."

You will see by the dialogue, that the characters I here introduce are the antipodes of each other. They had both been pupils in the same school, and in after life, being engaged as grocers, they frequently met and renewed their acquaintance. They were both established in business, having passed the threshold of that important event, "Setting out in life." As far as their outward life was concerned, they were acquaintances; but to each other's inner life they were strangers. John Anderson has a fine robust constitution, good intellectual abilities, and superior business faculties. He is eager, keen and alert, and if there is one article of faith that moulds and colors all his life more than anything else, it is a firm and unfaltering belief in the "main chance." He has made up his mind to be rich, and his highest ideal of existence may be expressed in four words—*getting on in life*. To this object, he is ready to sacrifice time, talent, energy and every faculty, which he possesses. Nay, he will go farther; he will spend honor, conscience and manhood, in an eager search for gold. He will change his heart into a ledger on which he will write *tare* and *tret*, loss and gain, exchange and barter, and he will succeed, as worldly men count success. He will add house to house; he will encompass the means of luxury; his purse will be plethoric but, oh, how poverty stricken his soul will be. Costly viands will please his taste, but unappeased hunger will gnaw at his soul. Amid the blasts of winter he will have the warmth of Calcutta in his home; and the health of the ocean and the breezes of the mountains shall fan his brow, amid the heats of summer, but there will be a coolness in his soul that no breath of summer can ever dispel; a fever in his spirit that no frozen confection can ever allay; he shall be rich in lands and houses, but fear of loss and a sense of poverty will poison the fountains of his life; and unless he repent, he shall go out into the eternities a pauper and a bankrupt.

Paul Clifford, whom we have also introduced to you, was the only son of a widow, whose young life had been overshadowed by the curse of intemperance. Her husband, a man of splendid abilities and magnificent culture, had fallen a victim to the wine cup. With true womanly devotion she had clung to him in the darkest hours, until death had broken his hold in life, and he was laid away the wreck of his former self in a drunkard's grave. Gathering up the remains of what had been an ample fortune, she installed herself in an humble and unpretending home in the suburbs of the city of B., and there with loving solicitude she had watched over and superintended the education of her only son. He was a promising boy, full [of?] life and vivacity, having inherited much of the careless joyousness of his father's temperament; and although he was the light and joy of his home, yet his mother sometimes felt as if her heart was contracting with a spasm of agony, when she remembered that it was through that same geniality of disposition and wonderful fascination of manner, the tempter had woven his meshes for her husband, and that the qualities that made him so desirable at home, made him equally so to his jovial, careless, inexperienced companions. Fearful that the appetite for strong drink might have been transmitted to her child as a fatal legacy of sin, she sedulously endeavored to develop within him self control, feeling that the lack of it is a prolific cause of misery and crime, and she spared no pains to create within his mind a horror of intemperance, and when he was old enough to understand the nature of a vow, she knelt with him in earnest prayer, and pledging him to eternal enmity against everything that would intoxicate, whether fermented or distilled. In the morning she sowed the seed which she hoped would blossom in time, and bear fruit throughout eternity.

Chapter II
The Decision[1]

"I hear Belle," said Jeanette Roland[2] addressing her cousin Belle Gordon, "that you have refused an excellent offer of marriage."

"Who said so?"

"Aunt Emma."

"I am very sorry that Ma told you, I think such things should be kept sacred from comment, and I think the woman is wanting in refinement and delicacy of feeling who makes the rejection of a lover a theme for conversation."

"Now you dear little prude I had no idea that you would take it so seriously but Aunt Emma was so disappointed and spoke of the rejected suitor in such glowing terms, and said that you had sacrificed a splendid opportunity because of some squeamish notions on the subject of temperance, and so of course, my dear cousin, it was just like me to let my curiosity overstep the bounds of prudence, and inquire why you rejected Mr. Romaine."[3]

"Because I could not trust him."

"Couldn't trust him? Why Belle you are a greater enigma than ever. Why not?"

"Because I feel that the hands of a moderate drinker are not steady enough to hold my future happiness."

"Was that all? Why I breathe again, we girls would have to refuse almost every young man in our set, were we to take that stand."

"And suppose you were, would that be any greater misfortune than to be the wives of drunkards."

"I don't see the least danger. Ma has wine at her entertainments, and I have often handed it to young gentlemen, and I don't see the least harm in it. On last New Year's day we had more than fifty callers. Ma and I handed wine, to every one of them." "Oh I do wish people would abandon that pernicious custom of handing around wine on New Year's day. I do think it is a dangerous and reprehensible thing."

"Wherein lies the danger? Of course I do not approve of young men drinking in bar rooms and saloons, but I cannot see any harm in handing round wine at social gatherings. Not to do so would seem so odd."

"It is said Jeanette[,?] 'He is a slave who does not be, in the right with two or three.' It is better, wiser far to stand alone in our integrity than to join with the multitude in doing wrong. You say while you do not approve of young men drinking in bar rooms and saloons, that you have no objection to their drinking beneath the shadow of their homes, why do you object to their drinking in saloons, and bar rooms?"

"Because it is vulgar. Oh! I think these bar rooms are horrid places. I would walk squares out of my way to keep from passing them." "And I object to intemperance not simply because I think it is vulgar but because I know it is wicked; and Jeanette I have a young brother for whose welfare I am constantly trembling; but I am not afraid that he will take his first glass of wine in a fashionable saloon, or flashy gin palace, but I do dread his entrance into what you call 'our set.' I fear that my brother has received as an inheritance a temperament which will be easily excited by stimulants, that an appetite for liquor once a awakened will be hard to subdue, and I am so fearful, that at some social gathering, a thoughtless girl will hand him a glass of wine, and that the first glass will be like adding fuel to a smouldering fire."

"Oh Belle do stop, what a train of horrors you can conjure out of an innocent glass of wine."

"Anything can be innocent that sparkles to betray, that charms at first, but later will bite like an adder and sting like a serpent."

"Really! Belle, if you keep on at this rate you will be a monomaniac on the temperance question. However I do not think Mr. Romaine will feel highly complimented to know that you refused him because you dreaded he might become a drunkard. You surely did not tell him so."

"Yes I did, and I do not think that I would have been a true friend to him, had I not done so."

"Oh! Belle, I never could have had the courage to have told him so."

"Why not?"

"I would have dreaded hurting his feelings. Were you not afraid of offending him?"

"I certainly shrank from the pain which I knew I must inflict, but because I valued his welfare more than my own feelings, I was constrained to be faithful to him. I told him that he was drifting where he ought steer, that instead of holding the helm and rudder of his young life, he was floating down the stream, and unless he stood firmly on the side of temperance, that I never would clasp hands will him for life."

"But Belle, perhaps you have done him more harm than good; may be you could have effected his reformation by consenting to marrying him."

"Jeanette, were I the wife of a drunken man I do not think there is any depth of degradation that I would not fathom with my love and pity in trying to save him. I believe I would cling to him, if even his own mother shrank from him. But I never would consent to [marry any man?], whom I knew to be un[?]steady in his principles and a moderate drinker. If his love for me and respect for himself were not strong enough to reform him before marriage, I should despair of effecting it afterwards, and with me in such a case discretion would be the better part of valor."

"And so you have given Mr. Romaine a release?"

"Yes, he is free."

"And I think you have thrown away a splendid opportunity."

"I don't think so, the risk was too perilous. Oh Jeanette, I know by mournful and bitter experience what it means to dwell beneath the shadow of a home cursed by intemperance. I know what it is to see that shadow deepen into the darkness of a drunkard's grave, and I dare not run the fearful risk."

"And yet Belle this has cost you a great deal, I can see it in the wanness of your face, in your eyes which in spite of yourself, are filled with sudden tears, I know from the intonations of your voice that you are suffering intensely."

"Yes Jeanette, I confess, it was like tearing up the roots of my life to look at this question fairly and squarely in the face, and to say, no; but I must learn to suffer and be strong, I am deeply pained, it is true, but I do not regret the steps I have taken. The man who claims my love and allegiance, must be a victor and not a slave. The reeling brain of a drunkard is not a safe foundation on which to build up a new home."

"Well Belle, you may be right, but I think I would have risked it. I don't think because Mr. Romaine drinks occasionally that I would have given him up. Oh young men will sow their wild oats."

"And as we sow, so must we reap, and as to saying about young men sowing their wild oats, I think it is full of pernicious license. A young man has no more right to sow his wild oats than a young woman. God never made one code of ethics for a man and another for a woman. And it is the duty of all true women to demand of men the same standard of morality that they do of woman."

"Ah Belle that is very fine in theory, but you would find it rather difficult, if you tried to reduce your theory to practice."

"All that may be true, but the difficulty of a duty is not a valid excuse for its non performance."

"My dear cousin it is not my role to be a reformer. I take things as I find them and drift along the tide of circumstances."

"And is that your highest ideal of life? Why Jeanette such a life is not worth living."

"Whether it is or not, I am living it and I rather enjoy it. Your vexing problems of life never disturb me. I do not think I am called to turn this great world 'right side up with care,' and so I float along singing as I go,

> "I'd be a butterfly born in a bower
> Kissing every rose that is pleasant and sweet,
> I'd never languish for wealth or for power
> I'd never sigh to have slaves at my feet."

"Such a life would never suit me, life must mean to me more than ease, luxury and indulgence, it must mean aspiration and consecration, endeavor and achievement."

"Well, Belle, should we live twenty years longer, I would like to meet you and see by comparing notes which of us shall have gathered the most sunshine or shadow from life."

"Yes Jeanette we will meet in less than twenty years, but before then your glad light eyes will be dim with tears, and the easy path you have striven to walk will be thickly strewn with thorn; and whether you deserve it or not, life will have for you a mournful earnestness, but notwithstanding all your frivolity and flippancy there is fine gold in your character, which the fire of affliction only will reveal.

Chapter III

[Text missing.]

Chapter IV

"How is business?"

"Very dull, I am losing terribly."

"Any prospect of times brightening?"

"I don't see my way out clear; but I hope there will be a change for the better. Confidence has been greatly shaken, men of [?] business have grown exceedingly timid about investing and there is a general depression in every department of trade and business."

"Now Paul will you listen to reason and common sense? I have a proposition to make. I am about to embark in a profitable business, and I know that it will pay better than any thing else I could undertake in these times. Men will buy liquor if they have not got money for other things. I am going to open a first class saloon, and club-house, on M. Street, and if you will join with me we can make a splendid thing of it. Why just see how well off Joe Harden is since he set up in the business; and what airs he does put on! I

know when he was not worth fifty dollars, and kept a little low
groggery on the corner of L. and S. Streets, but he is out of that
now—keeps a first class *Café*, and owns a block of houses. Now
Paul, here is a splendid chance for you; business is dull, and now
accept this opening. Of course I mean to keep a first class saloon.
I don't intend to tolerate loafing, or disorderly conduct, or to sell
to drunken men. In fact, I shall put up my scale of prices so that
you need fear no annoyance from rough, low, boisterous men who
don't know how to behave themselves. What say you, Paul?"

"I say, no! I wouldn't engage in such a business, not if it paid
me a hundred thousand dollars a year. I think these first class saloons are just as great a curse to the community as the low groggeries, and I look upon them as the fountain heads of the low
groggeries. The man who begins to drink in the well lighted and
splendidly furnished saloon is in danger of finishing in the lowest
dens of vice and shame."

"As you please," said John Anderson stiffly, "I thought that as
business is dull that I would show you a chance, that would yield
you a handsome profit; but if you refuse, there is no harm done. I
know young men who would jump at the chance."

You may think it strange that knowing Paul Clifford as John
Anderson did, that he should propose to him an interest in a
drinking saloon; but John Anderson was a man who was almost
destitute of faith in human goodness. His motto was that "every
man has his price," and as business was fairly dull, and Paul was
somewhat cramped for want of capital, he thought a good business investment would be the price for Paul Clifford's conscientious scruples.

"Anderson," said Paul looking him calmly in the face, "you may
call me visionary and impracticable; but I am determined however
poor I may be, never to engage in any business on which I cannot
ask God's blessing. And John I am sorry from the bottom of my
heart, that you have concluded to give up your grocery and keep a

saloon. You cannot keep that saloon without sending a flood of demoralizing influence over the community. Your profit will be the loss of others. Young men will form in that saloon habits which will curse and overshadow all their lives. Husbands and fathers will waste their time and money, and confirm themselves in habits which will bring misery, crime, and degradation; and the fearful outcome of your business will be broken hearted wives, neglected children, outcast men, blighted characters and worse than wasted lives. No not for the wealth of the Indies, would I engage in such a ruinous business, and I am thankful today that I had a dear sainted mother who taught me that it was better to have my hands clear than to have them full. How often would she lay her dear hands upon my head, and clasp my hands in hers and say, 'Paul, I want you to live so that you can always feel that there is no eye before whose glance you will shrink, no voice from whose tones your heart will quail, because your hands are not clean, or your record not pure,' and I feel glad to-day that the precepts and example of that dear mother have given tone and coloring to my life; and though she has been in her grave for many years, her memory and her words are still to me an ever present inspiration."

"Yes Paul; I remember your mother. I wish! Oh well there is no use wishing. But if all Christians were like her, I would have more faith in their religion."

"But John the failure of others is no excuse for our own derelictions."

"Well, I suppose not. It is said, the way Jerusalem was kept clean, every man swept before his own door. And so you will not engage in the business?"

"No John, no money I would earn would be the least inducement."

"How foolish," said John Anderson to himself as they parted. "There is a young man who might succeed splendidly if he would only give up some of his old fashioned notions, and launch out into life as if he had some common sense. If business remains as it is, I think he will find out before long that he has got to shut his eyes and swallow down a great many things he don't like."

After the refusal of Paul Clifford, John soon found a young man of facile conscience who was willing to join with him in a conspiracy of sin against the peace, happiness and welfare of the community. And he spared neither pains nor expense to make his saloon attractive to what he called, "the young bloods of the city," and by these he meant young men whose parents were wealthy, and whose sons had more leisure and spending money than was good for them. He succeeded in fitting up a magnificent palace of sin. Night after night till morning flashed the orient, eager and anxious men sat over the gaming table watching the turn of a card, or the throw of a dice. Sparkling champaign, or ruby-tinted wine were served in beautiful and costly glasses. Rich divans and easy chairs invited weary men to seek repose from unnatural excitement. Occasionally women entered that saloon, but they were women not as God had made them, but as sin had debased them. Women whose costly jewels and magnificent robes were the livery of sin, the outside garnishing of moral death; the flush upon whose cheek, was not the flush of happiness, and the light in their eyes was not the sparkle of innocent joy,—women whose laughter was sadder than their tears, and who were dead while they lived. In that house were wine, and mirth, and revelry, "but the dead were there," men dead to virtue, true honor and rectitude, who walked the streets as other men, laughed, chatted, bought, sold, exchanged and bartered, but whose souls were encased in living tombs, bodies that were dead to righteousness but alive to sin. Like a spider weaving its meshes around the unwary fly, John Anderson wove his network of sin around the young men that entered his saloon. Before they entered there, it was pleasant to see the supple vigor and radiant health that were manifested in the poise of their bodies, the lightness of their eyes, the freshness of their lips and the bloom upon their cheeks. But Oh! it was so sad to see how soon the manly gait would change to the drunkard's stagger. To see eyes once bright with intelligence growing vacant and confused and giving place to the drunkard's leer. In many cases lassitude supplanted vigor, and sickness overmastered health. But the saddest thing was the fearful power that appetite had gained over its victims, and though nature lifted her signals of distress, and sent her warnings through weakened nerves and disturbed functions, and although they were wasting money, time, talents, and health, ruining their characters, and alienating their friends, and bringing untold agony to hearts that loved them and yearned over their defections, yet the fascination grew stronger and ever and anon the grave opened at their feet; and disguise it as loving friends might, the seeds of death had been nourished by the fiery waters of alcohol.

Chapter V

[Text missing.]

Chapter VI

For a few days the most engrossing topic in A. P. was what shall I wear, and what will you wear. There was an amount of shopping to be done, and dressmakers to be consulted and employed before the great event of the season came off. At length the important evening arrived and in the home of Mr. Glossop, a wealthy and retired whiskey dealer, there was a brilliant array of wealth and fashion. Could all the misery his liquor had caused been turned into blood, there would have been enough to have oozed in great drops from every marble ornament or beautiful piece of frescoe that adorned his home, for that home with its beautiful surroundings and costly furniture was the price of blood, but the glamor of his wealth was in the eyes of his guests; and they came to be amused and entertained and not to moralize on his ill-gotten wealth.

The wine flowed out in unstinted measures and some of the women so forgot themselves as to attempt to rival the men in drinking. The barrier being thrown down Charles drank freely, till his tones began to thicken, and his eye to grow muddled, and he sat down near Jeanette and tried to converse; but he was too much under the influence of liquor to hold a sensible and coherent conversation.

"Oh! Charley you naughty boy, that wine has got into your head and you don't know what you are talking about."

"Well, Miss Jenny, I b'lieve you're 'bout half-right, my head does feel funny."

"I shouldn't wonder; mine feels rather dizzy, and Miss Thomas has gone home with a sick headache, and I know what her headaches mean," said Jeanette significantly.

"My head," said Mary Gladstone, "really feels as big as a bucket."

"And I feel real dizzy," said another.

"And so do I," said another, "I feel as if I could hardly stand, I feel awful weak."

"Why girls, you! are all, all, tipsy, now just own right up, and be done with it," said Charles Romaine.

"Why Charlie you are as good as a wizard, I believe we have all got too much wine aboard: but we are not as bad as the girls of B. S., for they succeeded in out drinking the men. I heard the men drank eight bottles of wine, and that they drank sixteen."

Alas for these young people they were sporting upon the verge of a precipice, but its slippery edge was concealed by flowers. They were playing with the firebrands of death and thought they were Roman-candles and harmless rockets.

"Good morning Belle," said Jeanette Roland to her cousin Belle as she entered her cousin's sitting-room the morning after the party and found Jeanette lounging languidly upon the sofa.

"Good morning. It is a lovely day, why are you not out enjoying the fresh air? Can't you put on your things and go shopping with me? I think you have excellent taste and I often want to consult it."

"Well after all then I am of some account in your eyes."

"Of course you are; who said you were not[?]"

"Oh! nobody only I had an idea that you thought that I was as useless as a canary bird."

"I don't think that a canary bird is at all a useless thing. It charms our ears with its song, and pleases our eye with its beauty, and I am a firm believer in the utility of beauty—but can you, or rather will you not go with me?"

"Oh Belle I would, but I am as sleepy as a cat."

"What's the matter?"

"I was up so late last night at Mrs. Glossop's party; but really it was a splendid affair, everything was in the richest profusion, and their house is magnificently furnished. Oh Belle I wish you could have been there."

"I don't; there are two classes of people with whom I never wish to associate, or number as my especial friends, and they are rum sellers and slave holders."

"Oh! well, Mr. Glossop is not in the business now and what is the use of talking about the past; don't be always remembering a man's sins against him."

"Would you say the same of a successful pirate who could fare sumptuously from the effects of his piracy?"

"No I would not; but Belle the cases is not at all parallel."

"Not entirely. One commits his crime against society within

the pale of the law, the other commits his outside. They are both criminals against the welfare of humanity. One murders the body, and the other stabs the soul. If I knew that Mr. Glossop was sorry for having been a liquor dealer and was bringing forth fruits meet for repentance, I would be among the first to hail his reformation with heartfelt satisfaction; but when I hear that while he no longer sells liquor, that he constantly offers it to his guests, I feel that he should rather sit down in sackcloth and ashes than fireside at sumptuous feasts, obtained by liquor selling. When crime is sanctioned by law, and upheld by custom and fashion, it assumes its most dangerous phase; and there is often a fearful fascination in the sin that is environed by success."

"Oh! Belle do stop. I really think that you will go crazy on the subject of temperance. I think you must have written these lines that I have picked up somewhere; let me see what they are,—

> Tell me not that I hate the bowl,
> Hate is a feeble word.

"No Jeanette, I did not write them, but I have felt all the writer has so nervously expressed. In my own sorrow-darkened home, and over my poor father's grave, I learned to hate liquor in any form with all the intensity of my nature."

"Well, it was a good thing you were not at Mrs. Glossop's last night, for some of our heads were rather dizzy, and I know that Mr. Romaine was out of gear. Now Belle! don't look so shocked and pained; I am sorry I told you."

"Yes, I am very sorry. I had great hopes that Mr. Romaine had entirely given up drinking, and I was greatly pained when I saw him take a glass of wine at your solicitation. Jeanette I think Mr. Romaine feels a newly awakened interest in you, and I know that you possess great influence over him. I saw it that night when he hesitated, when you first asked him to drink, and I was so sorry to see that influence. Oh Jeanette instead of being his temptress, try and be the angel that keeps his steps. If Mr. Romaine ever becomes a drunkard and goes down to a drunkard's grave, I cannot help feeling that a large measure of the guilt will cling to your shirts."

"Oh Belle, do stop, or you will give me the horrors. Pa takes wine every day at his dinner and I don't see that he is any worse off for it. If Charles Romaine can't govern himself, I can't see how I am to blame for it."

"I think you are to blame for this Jeanette: (and pardon me if I speak plainly). When Charles Romaine was trying to abstain, you tempted him to break his resolution, and he drank to please you. I wouldn't have done so for my right hand."

"They say old coals are easily kindled, and I shall be somewhat chary about receiving attention from him, if you feel so deeply upon the subject."

"Jeanette you entirely misapprehend me. Because I have ceased to regard Mr. Romaine as a lover, does not hinder me from feeling for him as a friend. And because I am his friend and yours also, I take the liberty to remonstrate against your offering him wine at your entertainments."

"Well Belle, I can't see the harm in it, I don't believe there was another soul who refused except you and Mr. Freeman, and you are so straightlaced, and he is rather green, just fresh from the country, it won't take him long to get citified."

"Citified or countrified, I couldn't help admiring his strength of principle which stood firm in the midst of temptation and would not yield to the blandishments of the hour. And so you will not go out with me this morning?"

"Oh! No Belle, I am too tired. Won't you excuse me?"

"Certainly, but I must go. Good morning."

"What a strange creature my cousin Belle is," said Jeanette, to herself as Miss Gordon left the room. "She will never be like any one else. I don't think she will ever get over my offering Mr. Romaine that glass of wine, I wish she hadn't seen it, but I'll try and forget her and go to sleep."

But Jeanette was not destined to have the whole morning for an unbroken sleep. Soon after Bell's departure the bell rang and Charles Romaine was announced, and weary as Jeanette was, she was too much interested in his society to refuse him; and arraying herself in a very tasteful and becoming manner, she went down to receive him in the parlor.

Chapter VII

Very pleasant was the reception Jeanette Roland gave Mr. Romaine. There was no reproof upon her lips nor implied censure in her manner. True he had been disguised by liquor or to use a softer phrase, had taken too much wine. But others had done the same and treated it as a merry escapade, and why should she be so particular? Belle Gordon would have acted very differently but then she was not Belle, and in this instance she did not wish to imitate her. Belle was so odd, and had become very unpopular, and besides she wished to be very very pleasant to Mr. Romaine. He was handsome, agreeable and wealthy, and she found it more congenial to her taste to clasp hands with him and float down stream together, than help him breast the current of his wrong tendencies, and stand firmly on the rock of principle.

"You are looking very sweet, but rather pensive this morning," said Mr. Romaine, noticing a shadow on the bright and beautiful face of Jeanette, whose color had deepened by the plain remarks of her cousin Belle. "What is the matter?"

"Oh nothing much, only my cousin Belle has been here this morning, and she has been putting me on the stool of repentance."

"Why! what have you been doing that was naughty?"

"Oh! she was perfectly horror-stricken when I told her about the wine we drank and Mrs. Glossop's party. I wish I had not said a word to her about it."

"What did she say?"

"Oh she thought it was awful, the way we were going on. She made me feel that I died [*sic*] something dreadful when I offered you a glass of wine at Ma's silver wedding. I don't believe Belle ever sees a glass of wine, without thinking of murder, suicide and a drunkard's grave."

"But we are not afraid of those dreadful things, are we Jeanette?"

"Of course not, but somehow Belle always makes me feel uncomfortable, when she begins to talk on temperance. She says she is terribly in earnest, and I think she is."

"Miss Gordon and I were great friends once," said Charles Romaine, as a shadow flitted over his face, and a slight sigh escaped his lips.

"Were you? Why didn't you remain so?"

"Because she was too good for me."

"That is a very sorry reason."

"But it is true. I think Miss Gordon is an excellent young lady, but she and I wouldn't agree on the temperance question. The man who marries her has got to toe the mark. She ought to be a minister's wife."

"I expect she will be an old maid."

"I don't know, but if I were to marry her, I should prepare myself to go to Church every Sunday morning and to stay home in the afternoon and repeat my catechism."

"I would like to see you under her discipline."

"It would come hard on a fellow, but I might go farther and fare worse."

"And so you and Belle were great friends, once?"

"Yes, but as we could not agree on the total abstinence question, we parted company."

"How so? Did you part as lovers part?"

> She with a wronged and broken heart?
> And you, rejoicing you were free,
> Glad to regain you liberty?

"Not at all. She gave me the mitten and I had to take it."

"Were you very sorry?"

"Yes, till I met you."

"Oh! Mr. Romaine," said Jeanette blushing and dropping her eyes.

"Why not? I think I have found in your society an ample compensation for the loss of Miss Gordon."

"But I think Belle is better than I am. I sometimes wish I was half so good."

"You are good enough for me; Belle is very good, but somehow her goodness makes a fellow uncomfortable. She is what I call distressingly good; one doesn't want to be treated like a wild beast in a menagerie, and to be every now and then stirred up with a long stick."

"What a comparison!"

"Well it is a fact; when a fellow's been busy all day pouring over Coke and Blackstone, or casting up wearisome rows of figures, and seeks a young lady's society in the evening, he wants to enjoy himself, to bathe in the sunshine of her smiles, and not to be lectured about his shortcomings. I tell you, Jeanette, it comes hard on a fellow."

"You want some one to smooth the wrinkles out of the brow of care, and not to add fresh ones."

"Yes, and I hope it will be my fortune to have a fair soft hand like his," said Mr. Romaine, slightly pressing Jeanette's hand to perform the welcome and agreeable task.

"Belle's hand would be firmer than mine for the talk."

"It is not the strong hand, but the tender hand I want in a woman."

"But Belle is very kind; she did it all for your own good."

"Of course she did; my father used to say so when I was a boy, and he corrected me; but it didn't make me enjoy the correction."

"It is said our best friends are those who show us our faults, and teach us how to correct them."

"My best friend is a dear, sweet girl who sits by my side, who always welcomes me with a smile, and beguiles me so with her conversation, that I take no note of the hours until the striking of the clock warns me it is time to leave; and I should ask no higher happiness than to be permitted to pass all the remaining hours of my life at her side. Can I dare to hope for such a happy fortune?"

A bright flush overspread the cheek of Jeanette Roland; there was a sparkle of joy in her eyes as she seemed intently examining the flowers on her mother's carpet, and she gently referred him to Papa for an answer. In due time Mr. Roland was interviewed, his consent obtained, and Jeanette Roland and Charles Romaine were affianced lovers.

"Girls, have you heard the news?" said Miss Tabitha Jones, a pleasant and wealthy spinster, to a number of young girls who were seated at her tea table.

"No! what is it?"

"I hear Mr. Romaine is to be married next spring."

"To whom?"

"Jeanette Roland."

"Well! I do declare; I thought he was engaged to Belle Gordon."

"I thought so too, but it is said that she refused him, but I don't believe it; I don't believe that she had a chance."

"Well I do."

"Why did she refuse him?"

"Because he would occasionally take too much wine."

"But he is not a drunkard."

"But she dreads that he will be."

"Well! I think it is perfectly ridiculous. I gave Belle credit for more common sense. I think he was one of the most eligible gentlemen in our set. Wealthy, handsome and agreeable. What could have possessed Belle? I think he is perfectly splendid."

"Yes said another girl, I think Belle stood very much in her own light. She is not rich, and if she would marry him she could have everything heart could wish. What a silly girl! You wouldn't catch me throwing away such a chance."

"I think," said Miss Tabitha, "that instead of Miss Gordon's being a silly girl, that she has acted both sensibly and honorably in refusing to marry a man she could not love. No woman should give her hand where she cannot yield her heart."

"But Miss Tabitha, the strangest thing to me is, that I really believe that Belle Gordon cares more for Mr. Romaine than she does for any one else; her face was a perfect study that night at Mrs. Roland's party."

"How so?"

"They say that after Miss Gordon requested Mr. Romaine, that for a while he scrupulously abstained from taking even a glass of wine. At several entertainments, he adhered to this purpose but on the evening of Mrs. Roland's silver wedding Jeanette succeeded in persuading him to take a glass, in honor of the occasion. I watched Belle's face and it was a perfect study, every nerve seemed quivering with intense anxiety. Once I think she reached out her hand unconsciously as if to snatch away the glass, and when at last he yielded I saw the light fade from her eyes, a deadly pallor overspread her cheek, and I thought at one time she was about to faint, but she did not, and only laid her head upon her side as if to allay a sudden spasm of agony."

Chapter VIII

Paul Clifford sat at his ledger with a perplexed and anxious look. It was near two o'clock and his note was in bank. If he could not raise five hundred dollars by three o'clock, that note would be protested. Money was exceedingly hard to raise, and he was about despairing. Once he thought of applying to John Anderson, but he said to himself, "No, I will not touch his money, for it is the price of blood," for he did not wish to owe gratitude where he did not feel respect. It was now five minutes past two o'clock and in less than an hour his note would be protested unless relief came from some unexpected quarter.

"Is Mr. Clifford in?" said a full manly voice. Paul, suddenly roused from his painful reflections, answered, "Yes, come in. Good morning sir, what can I do for you this morning?"

"I have come to see you on business."

"I am at your service," said Paul.

"Do you remember," said the young man, "of having aided an unfortunate friend more than a dozen years since by lending him five hundred dollars?"

"Yes, I remember he was an old friend of mine, a school-mate of my father's, Charles Smith."

"Well I am his son, and I have come to liquidate my father's debt. Here is the money with interest for twelve years."

Paul's heart gave a sudden bound of joy. Strong man as he was a mist gathered in his eyes as he reached out his hand to receive the thrice welcome sum. He looked at the clock, it was just fifteen minutes to three.

"Will you walk with me to the bank or wait till I return?"

"I will wait," said James Smith, taking up the morning paper.

. . .

"You are just in time, Mr. Clifford," said the banker smiling and bowing as Paul entered, "I was afraid your note would be protested; but it is all right."

"Yes," said Paul, "the money market is very tight, but I think I shall weather the storm."

"I hope so, you may have to struggle hard for awhile to keep your head above the water; but you must take it for your motto that there is no such word as 'fail.'"

"Thank you, good morning."

"Well Mr. Smith," said Paul when he returned, "your father and mine were boys together. He was several years younger than my father, and a great favorite in our family among the young folks. About twelve years since when I had just commenced business, I lent him five hundred dollars, and when his business troubles became complicated I refused to foreclose a mortgage which I had on his home. An acquaintance of mine sneered at my lack of business keenness, and predicted that my money would be totally lost, when I told him perhaps it was the best investment I ever made." He smiled incredulously and said, "I would rather see it than hear of it: but I will say that in all my business career I never received any money that came so opportune as this. It reminds me of the stories that I have read in fairy books. People so often fail in paying their own debts, it seems almost a mystery to me that you should pay a debt contracted by your father when you were but a boy."

"The clue to this mystery has been the blessed influence of my sainted mother;" and a flush of satisfaction mantled his cheek as he referred to her.

"After my father's death my mother was very poor. When she looked into the drawer there were only sixty cents in money. Of course, he had some personal property, but it was not immediately available like money, but through the help of kind friends she was enabled to give him a respectable funeral. Like many other women

in her condition of life, she had been brought up in entire ignorance of managing any other business, than that which belonged to
her household. For years she had been shielded in the warm clasp of
loving arms, but now she had to bare her breast to the storm and be
father and mother both to her little ones. My father as you know
died in debt, and he was hardly in his grave when his creditors were
upon her track. I have often heard her speak in the most grateful
manner of your forbearance and kindness to her in her hour of
trouble. My mother went to see my father's principal creditor and
asked him only to give her a little time to straighten out the tangled
threads of her business, but he was inexorable, and said that he had
waited and lost by it. Very soon he had an administrator appointed
by the court, who in about two months took the business in his
hands; and my mother was left to struggle along with her little
ones, and face an uncertain future. These were dark days but we
managed to live through them. I have often heard her say that she
lived by faith and not sight, that poverty had its compensations,
that there was something very sweet in a life of simple trust, to her,
God was not some far off and unapproachable force in the universe,
the unconscious Creator of all consciousness, the unperceiving author of all perception, but a Friend and a Father coming near to her
in sorrows, taking cognizance of her grief, and gently smoothing
her path in life. But it was not only by precept that she taught us; her
life was a living epistle. One morning as the winter was advancing I
heard her say she hoped she would be able to get a nice woolen
shawl, as hers was getting worse for wear. Shortly after I went out
into the street and found a roll of money lying at my feet. Oh I remember it as well as if it had just occurred. How my heart bounded
with joy. 'Here,' I said to myself, 'is money enough to buy mother a
shawl and bonnet. Oh I am so glad,' and hurrying home I laid it in
her lap and said with boyish glee, 'Hurrah for your new shawl; look
what I found in the street.'"

"What is it my son?" she said.

"Why here is money enough to buy you a new shawl and bonnet too." It seems as if I see her now, as she looked, when she laid it aside, and said—

"But James, it is not ours?"

"Not ours, mother, why I found it in the street!"

"Still it is not ours."

"Why mother ain't you going to keep it?"

"No my son, I shall go down to the *Clarion* office and advertise it."

"But mother why not wait till it is advertised?"

"And what then?"

"If there is no owner for it, then we can keep it."

"James" she said calmly and sadly, "I am very sorry to see you so ready to use what is not your own. I should not feel that I was dealing justly, if I kept this money without endeavoring to find the owner."

"I confess that I was rather chopfallen at her decision, but in a few days after advertising we found the rightful owner. She was a very poor woman who had saved by dint of hard labor the sum of twenty dollars, and was on her way to pay the doctor who had attended her during a spell of rheumatic fever, when she lost the money and had not one dollar left to pay for advertising and being disheartened, she had given up all hope of finding it, when she happened to see it advertised in the paper. She was very grateful to my mother for restoring the money and offered her some compensation, but she refused to take it, saying she had only done her duty, and would have been ashamed of herself had she not done so. Her conduct on this occasion made an impression on my mind that has never been erased. When I grew older she explained to me about my father's affairs, and uncancelled debts, and I resolved that I would liquidate every just claim against him, and take from his memory even the shadow of a reproach. To this end I have labored late and early; to-day I have paid the last claim against him, and I am a free man."

"But how came you to find me and pay me to-day?" "I was purchasing in Jones & Brother's store, when you came in to borrow money, and I heard Jones tell his younger brother that he was so sorry that he could not help you, and feared that you would be ruined."

"Who is he?" said I, "for out West I had lost track of you."

"He is Paul Clifford, a friend of your father's. Can you help him? He is perfectly reliable. We would trust him with ten thousand dollars if we had it. Can you do anything for him? we will go his security, he is a fine fellow and we hate to see him go under."

"Yes" said I, "he was one of my father's creditors and I have often heard my mother speak of his generosity to her little ones, and I am glad that I have the privilege of helping him. I immediately went to the bank had a note cashed and I am very glad if I have been of any special service to you."

"You certainly have been, and I feel that a heavy load had been lifted from my heart."

Years ago Paul Clifford sowed the seeds of kindness and they were yielding him a harvest of satisfaction.

Chapter IX
Belle Gordon

Belle Gordon was a Christian; she had learned or tried to realize what is meant by the apostle Paul when he said, "Ye are bought with a price." To her those words meant the obligation she was under to her heavenly Father, for the goodness and mercy that had surrounded her life, for the patience that had borne with her errors and sins, and above all for the gift of his dear Son, the ever blessed Christ. Faith to her was not a rich traditional inheritance, a set of formulated opinions, received without investigation, and adopted without reflection. She could not believe because others did, and however plausible or popular a thing might be she was too conscientious to say she believed it if she did not, and when she became serious on the subject of religion it was like entering into a wilderness of doubt and distress. She had been taught to look upon God, more as the great and dreadful God, than as the tender loving Father of his human children, and so strong was the power of association, that she found it hard to believe that God is good, and yet until she could believe this there seemed to be no resting place for her soul; but in course of time the shadows were lifted from her life. Faith took the place of doubting, and in the precious promises of the Bible she felt that her soul had found a safe and sure anchorage. If others believed because they had never doubted, she believed because she had doubted and her doubts had been dispelled by the rays of heaven, and believing, she had entered into rest. Feeling that she was bought with a price, she realized that she was not her own, but the captive of Divine Love, and that her talents were not given her to hide beneath a bushel or to use for merely selfish enjoyments. That her time was not her own to be frittered away by the demands of fashion or to be spent in unavailing regrets. Every reform which had for its object the lessening of human misery, or the increase of human happiness, found in her an earnest ally. On the subject of temperance she was terribly in earnest. Every fiber of her heart responded to its onward movement. There was no hut or den where human beings congregated that she felt was too vile or too repulsive to enter, if by so doing she could help lift some fallen soul out of the depths of sin and degradation. While some doubted the soundness of her religious opinions, none doubted the orthodoxy of her life. Little children in darkened homes smiled as the sunlight of her presence came over their paths; reformed men looked upon her as a loving counsellor and faithful friend and sister; women wretched and sorrowful, dragged down from love and light, by the intemperance of their husbands, brought to her their heavy burdens, and by her sympathy and tender consideration she helped them bear them. She was not rich in this world's goods, but she was affluent in tenderness, sympathy, and love, and out of the fullness of her heart, she was a real minister of mercy among the poor and degraded. Believing that the inner life developed the outer, she considered the poor, and strove to awaken within them self-reliance, and self-control, feeling that one of the surest ways to render people helpless or dangerous is to crush out their self-respect and self-reliance. She thought it one of the greatest privileges of her life to be permitted to scatter flowers by the wayside of life. Other women might write beautiful poems; she did more. She made her life a thing of brightness and beauty.

"Do you think she will die?" said Belle Gordon, bending tenderly over a pale and fainting woman, whose face in spite of its attenuation showed traces of great beauty.

"Not if she is properly cared for; she has fainted from exhaustion brought on by overwork and want of proper food." Tears gathered in the eyes of Belle Gordon as she lifted the beautiful head upon her lap and chafed the pale hands to bring back warmth and circulation.

"Let her be removed to her home as soon as possible," said the doctor. "The air is too heavy and damp for her."

"I wonder where she lives," said Belle thoughtfully, scanning her face, as the features began to show[4] returning animation.

"Round the corner," said an urchin, "she's Joe Gough's wife. I seed her going down the street with a great big bundle, and Mam said, she looked like she was going to topple over."

"Where is her husband?"

"I don't know, I 'spec he's down to Jim Green's saloon."

"What does he do?"

"He don't do nothing, but Mam says she works awful hard. Come this way," said he with a quickness gathered by his constant contact with street life.

Up two flights of rickety stairs they carried the wasted form of Mary Gough, and laid her tenderly upon a clean but very poor bed. In spite of her extreme poverty there was an air of neatness in the desolate room. Belle looked around and found an old tea pot in which there were a few leaves. There were some dry crusts in the cupboard, while two little children crouched by the embers in the grate, and cried for the mother. Belle soon found a few coals in an old basin with which she replenished the fire, and covering up the sick woman as carefully as she could, stepped into the nearest grocery and replenished her basket with some of good the things of life.

"Is it not too heavy for you[r] might?" said Paul Clifford from whose grocery Belle had bought her supplies.

"Can I not send them home for you?"

"No I don't want them sent home. They are for a poor woman and her suffering children, who live about a square from here in Lear's Court." Paul stood thoughtfully a moment before handing her the basket, and said—"That court has a very bad reputation; had I not better accompany you? I hope you will not consider my offer as an intrusion, but I do not think it is safe for you to venture there alone."

"If you think it is not safe I will accept of your company; but I never thought of danger for myself in the presence of that fainting woman and her hungry children. Do you know her? Her name is Mrs. Gough." "I think I do. If it is the person I mean, I remember her when she was as lighthearted and happy a girl as I ever saw, but she married against her parents' consent, a worthless fellow named Joe Gough, and in a short time she disappeared from the village and I suppose she has come home, broken in health and broken in spirit."

"And I am afraid she has come home to die. Are her parents still alive?"

"Yes, but her father never forgave her. Her mother I believe would take her to her heart as readily as she ever did, but her husband has an iron will and she has got to submit to him."

"Where do they live?"

"At No 200 Rouen St. but here we are at the door." Paul carried the basket up stairs, and sat down quietly, while Belle prepared some refreshing tea and toast for the feeble mother; and some bread and milk for the hungry children.

"What shall I do?" said Belle looking tenderly upon the wan face, "I hate to leave her alone and yet I confess I do not prefer spending the night here."

"Of course not," said Paul looking thoughtfully into the flickering fire of the grate.

"Oh! I have it now; I know a very respectable woman who occasionally cleans out my store. Just wait a few moments, and I think I can find her," said Paul Clifford turning to the door. In a short time he returned bringing with him a pleasant looking woman whose face in spite of the poverty of her dress had a look of genuine refinement which comes not so much from mingling with people of culture as from the culture of her own moral and spiritual nature. She had learned to "look up and not to look down." To lend a helping hand wherever she felt it was needed. Her life was spent in humble usefulness. She was poor in this world's goods, but rich in faith and good works. No poor person who asked her for bread ever went away empty. Sometimes people would say, "I wouldn't give him a mouthful; he is not worthy," and then she would say in the tenderest and sweetest manner:

"Suppose our heavenly Father only gave to us because we are worthy; what would any of us have?" I know she once said of a miserable sot with whom she shared her scanty food, that he is a wretched creature, but I wanted to get at his heart, and the best way to it was through his stomach. I never like to preach religion to hungry people. There is something very beautiful about the charity of the poor, they give not as the rich of their abundance, but of their limited earnings, gifts which when given in a right spirit bring a blessing with them.

Chapter X
Mary Gough

"I think," said Paul Clifford to Miss Gordon, "that I have found just the person that will suit you, and if you accept I will be pleased to see you safe home." Belle thanked the young grocer, and gratefully accepted his company.

Belle returned the next day to see her protege and found her getting along comfortably although she could not help seeing it was sorrow more than disease that was sapping her life, and drying up the feeble streams of existence.

"How do you feel this morning?" said Belle laying her hand tenderly upon her forehead.

"Better, much better," she replied with an attempt at cheerfulness in her voice. "I am so glad, that Mother Graham is here. It is like letting the sunshine into these gloomy rooms to have her around. It all seems like a dream to me, I remember carrying a large bundle of work to the store, that my employer spoke harshly to me and talked of cutting down my wages. I also remember turning into the street, my eyes almost blinded with tears, and that I felt a dizziness in my head. The next I remember was seeing a lady feeding my children, and a gentleman coming in with Aunty Graham."

"Yes," said Belle, "fortunately after I had seen you, I met with Mr. Clifford who rendered me every necessary assistance. His presence was very opportune," just then Belle turned her eyes toward the door and saw Mr. Clifford standing on the threshold.

"Ah," said he smiling and advancing "this time the old adage has failed, which says that listeners never hear any good of themselves; for without intending to act the part of an eavesdropper, I heard myself pleasantly complimented."

"No more than you deserve," said Belle smiling and blushing, as she gave him her hand in a very frank and pleasant manner. "Mrs. Gough is much better this morning and is very grateful to you for your kindness."

"Mine," said Mr. Clifford "if you, will call it so, was only the result of an accident. Still I am very glad if I have been of any service, and you are perfectly welcome to make demands upon me that will add to Mrs. Gough's comfort."

"Thank you, I am very glad she has found a friend in you. It is such a blessed privilege to be able to help others less fortunate than ourselves."

"It certainly is."

"Just a moment," said Belle, as the voice of Mrs. Gough fell faintly on her ear.

"What is it, dear?" said Belle bending down to catch her words. "Who is that gentleman? His face and voice seem familiar."

"It is Mr. Clifford."

"Paul Clifford?"

"Yes. Do you know him?"

"Yes, I knew him years ago when I was young and happy; but it seems an age since. Oh, isn't it a dreadful thing, to be a drunkard's wife?"

"Yes it is, but would you like to speak to Mr. Clifford?"

"Yes! Mam, I would."

"Mr. Clifford," said Belle, "Mrs. Gough would like to speak with you."

"Do you not know me?" said Mary, looking anxiously into his face.

"I recognized you as soon as you moved into the neighborhood."

"I am very glad. I feared that I was so changed that my own dear mother would hardly recognize me. Don't you think she would pity and forgive me, if she saw what a mournful wretch I am?"

"Yes, I think she has long forgiven you and longs to take you to her heart as warmly as she ever did."

"And my father?"

"I believe he would receive you, but I don't think he would be willing to recognize your husband. You know he is very set in his ways."

"Mr. Clifford, I feel that my days are numbered and that my span of life will soon be done; but while I live I feel it my duty to cling to my demented husband, and to do all I can to turn him from the error of his ways. But I do so wish that my poor children could have my mother's care, when I am gone. If I were satisfied on that score, I would die content."

"Do not talk of dying," said Belle taking the pale thin hand in hers. "You must try and live for your children's sake. When you get strong I think I can find you some work among my friends. There is Mrs. Roberts, she often gives out work and I think I will apply to her."

"Mrs. James Roberts on St. James St. near 16th?"

"Yes! do you know her?"

"Yes," said Mrs. Gough closing her eyes wearily, "I know her and have worked for her."

"I think she is an excellent woman, I remember one morning we were talking together on religious experience, and about women speaking in class and conference meetings. I said I did not think I should like to constantly relate my experience in public, there was often such a lack of assurance of faith about me that I shrank from holding up my inner life to inspection; and she replied that she would always say that she loved Jesus, and I thought Oh, how I would like to have her experience. What rest and peace I would have if I could feel that I was always in harmony with Him."

"Miss Belle I hope you will not be offended with me, for I am very ignorant about these matters; but there was something about Mrs. Roberts dealings with us poor working people, that did seem to me not to be just what I think religion calls for. I found her a very hard person to deal with; she wanted so much work for so little money."

"But, Mrs. Gough, the times are very hard; and the rich feel it as well as the poor."

"But not so much. It curtails them in their luxuries, and us in our necessities; perhaps I shouldn't mention, but after my husband had become a confirmed drunkard, and all hope had died out of my heart, I hadn't time to sit down and brood helplessly over my misery. I had to struggle for my children and if possible keep the wolf from the door; and besides food and clothing, I wanted to keep my children in a respectable neighborhood, and my whole soul rose up in revolt against the idea of bringing them up where their eyes and ears would be constantly smitten by improper sights and sounds. While I was worrying over my situation and feeling that my health was failing under the terrible pressure of care and overwork, Mrs. Roberts brought me work; 'What will you do this for,' she said, displaying one of the articles she wanted made. I replied, 'One dollar and twenty-five cents,' and I knew the work well worth it. 'I can get it done for one dollar,' she replied, 'and I am not willing to give any more.' What could I do? I was out of work, my health was poor, and my children clutching at my heart strings for bread; and so I took it at her price. It was very unprofitable, but it was better than nothing."

"Why that is very strange. I know she pays her dressmaker handsomely."

"That is because her dressmaker is in a situation to dictate her own terms; but while she would pay her a large sum for dressmaking, she would screw and pinch a five-cent piece from one who hadn't power to resist her demands. I have seen people save twenty-five or fifty cents in dealing with poor people, who would squander ten times as much on some luxury of the table or wardrobe. I[?] often find that meanness and extravagance go hand in hand."

"Yes, that is true, still Mrs. Gough, I think people often act like Mrs. Roberts more from want of thought than want of heart. It was an old charge brought against the Israelite, 'My people doth not consider.'"

"What is the matter, my dear?" said Belle a few mornings after this conversation as she approached the bedside of Mary Gough, "I thought you were getting along so nicely, and that with proper care you would be on your feet in a few days, but this morning you look so feeble, and seem so nervous and depressed. Do tell me what has happened and what has become of your beautiful hair; oh you had such a wealth of tresses, I really loved to toy with them. Was your head so painful that the doctor ordered them to be cut?"

"Oh, no," she said burying her face in the pillow and breaking into a paroxysm of tears. "Oh, Miss Belle, how can I tell you," she replied recovering from her sudden outburst of sorrow.

"Why, what is it darling? I am at a loss to know what has become of your beautiful hair."

With gentle womanly tact Belle saw that the loss of her hair was a subject replete with bitter anguish, and turning to the children she took them in her lap and interested and amused them by telling beautiful fairy stories. In a short time Mary's composure returned, and she said, "Miss Belle, I can now tell you how I lost my hair. Last night my husband, or the wreck of what was once my husband, came home. His eyes were wild and bloodshot; his face was pale and haggard, his gait uneven, and his hand trembling. I have seen him suffering from *Manipaotu* and dreaded lest he should have a returning of it. Mrs. Graham had just stepped out, and there was no one here but myself and children. He held in his hand a pair of shears, and approached my bedside. I was ready to faint with terror, when he exclaimed, 'Mary I must have liquor or I shall go wild,' he caught my hair in his hand; I was too feeble to resist, and in a few minutes he had cut every lock from my head, and left it just as you see it."

"Oh, what a pity, and what a shame."

"Oh, Miss Gordon do you think the men who make our laws ever stop to consider the misery, crime and destruction that flow out of the liquor traffic? I have done all I could to induce him to abstain, and he has abstained several months at a time and then suddenly like a flash of lightning the temptation returns and all his resolutions are scattered like chaff before the wind. I have been blamed for living with him, but Miss Belle were you to see him in his moments of remorse, and hear his bitter self reproach, and his earnest resolutions to reform, you would as soon leave a drowning man to struggle alone in the water as to forsake him in his weakness when every one else has turned against him, and if I can be the means of saving him, the joy for his redemption will counterbalance all that I have suffered as a drunkard's wife."

Chapter XI

[Text missing.]

Chapter XII

[Text missing.]

Chapter XIII
John Anderson's Saloon

"The end of these things is death."

"Why do you mix that liquor with such care and give it to that child? You know he is not going to pay you for it?"

"I am making an investment."

"How so?"

"Why you see that boy's parents are very rich, and in course of time he will be one of my customers."

"Well! John Anderson as old a sinner as I am, I wouldn't do such a thing for my right hand."

"What's the harm? You are one of my best customers, did liquor ever harm you?"

"Yes it does harm me, and when I see young men beginning to drink, I feel like crying out, 'Young man you are in danger, don't put your feet in the terrible flood, for ten to one you will be swamped.'"

"Well! this is the best joke of the season: Tom Cary preaching temperance. When do you expect to join the Crusade? But, Oh! talk is cheap."

"Cheap or dear, John Anderson, when I saw you giving liquor to that innocent boy, I couldn't help thinking of my poor Charley. He was just such a bright child as that, with beautiful brown eyes, and a fine forehead. Ah that boy had a mind; he was always ahead in his studies. But once when he was about twelve years old, I let him go on a travelling tour with his uncle. He was so agreeable and wide awake, his uncle liked to have him for company; but it was a dear trip to my poor Charley. During this journey they stopped at a hotel, and my brother gave him a glass of wine. Better for my dear boy had he given him a glass of strychnine. That one glass awakened within him a dreadful craving. It raged like a hungry fire. I talked to him, his mother pled with him, but it was no use, liquor was his master, and when he couldn't get liquor I've known him to break into his pantry to get our burning fluid to assuage his thirst. Sometimes he would be sober for several weeks at a time, and then our hopes would brighten that Charley would be himself again, and then in an hour all our hopes would be dashed to the ground. It seemed as if a spell was upon him. He married a dear good girl, who was as true as steel, but all her entreaties for him to give up drinking were like beating the air. He drank, and drank, until he drank himself into the grave."

By this time two or three loungers had gathered around John Anderson and Thomas Cary, and one of them said, "Mr. Cary you have had sad experience, why don't you give up drinking yourself?"

"Give it up! because I can't. To-day I would give one half of my farm if I could pass by this saloon and not feel that I wanted to come in. No, I feel that I am a slave. There was a time when I could have broken my chain, but it is too late now, and I say young men take warning by me and don't make slaves and fools of yourselves."

"Now, Tom Cary," said John Anderson, "it is time for you to dry up, we have had enough of this foolishness, if you can't govern yourself, the more's the pity for you."

Just then the newsboy came along crying: "*Evening Mail. All about the dreadful murder! John Coots and James Loraine. Last edition. Buy a paper, Sir! Here's your last edition, all 'bout the dreadful murder.*"

"John Coots," said several voices all at once, "Why he's been here a half dozen times today."

"I've drank with him," said one, "at that bar twice since noon. He had a strange look out of his eyes; and I heard him mutter something to himself."

"Yes," said another, "I heard him say he was going to kill somebody, 'one or the other's got to die,' what does the paper say?"

"LOVE, JEALOUSY, AND MURDER."

"The old story," said Anderson, looking somewhat relieved, "A woman's at the bottom of it."

"And liquor," said Tom Cary, "is at the top of it."

"I wish you would keep a civil tongue in your head," said Anderson, scowling at Cary.

"Oh! never mind; Tom, will have his say. He's got a knack of speaking out in meeting."

"And a very disagreeable knack it is."

"Oh never mind about Tom, read about the murder, and tend to Tom some other time."

Eagerly and excitedly they read the dreadful news. A woman, frail and vicious, was at the bottom; a woman that neither of those men would have married as a gracious gift, was the guilty cause of one murder, and when the law would take its course, two deaths would lie at her door. Oh, the folly of some men, who, instead of striving to make home a thing of beauty, strength and grace, wander into forbidden pastures, and reap for themselves harvests of misery and disgrace. And all for what? Because of the allurements of some idle, vain and sinful woman who has armed herself against the peace, the purity and the progress of the fireside. Such women are the dry rot in the social fabric; they dig in the dark beneath the foundation stones of the home. Young men enter their houses, and over the mirror of their lives, comes the shadow of pollution. Companionship with them unprepares them for the pure, simple joys of a happy and virtuous home; a place which should be the best school for the affections; one of the fairest spots on earth and one of the brightest types of heaven. Such a home as this, may exist without wealth, luxury or display; but it cannot exist without the essential elements of purity, love and truth.

The story was read, and then came the various comments.

"Oh, it was dreadful," said one. "Mr. Loraine belongs to one of the first families in the town; and what a cut it will be to them, not simply that he has been murdered, but murdered where he was—in the house of Lizzie Wilson. I knew her before she left husband and took to evil courses."

"Oh, what a pity, I expect it will almost kill his wife, poor thing, I pity her from the bottom of my heart."

"Why what's the matter Harry Richards? You look as white as a sheet, and you are all of a tremor."

"I've just come from the coroner's inquest, had to be one of the witnesses. I am afraid it will go hard with Coots."

"Why? What was the verdict of the jury?"

"They brought in a verdict of death by killing at the hands of John Coots."

"Were you present at the murder?"

"Yes."

"How did it happen?"

"Why you see John had been spending his money very freely on Lizzie Wilson, and he took it into his head because Loraine had made her some costly presents, that she had treated him rather coolly and wanted to ship him, and so he got dreadfully put out with Loraine and made some bitter threats against him. But I don't believe he would have done the deed if he had been sober, but he's been on a spree for several days and he was half crazy when he did it. Oh it was heartrending to see Loraine's wife when they brought him home a corpse. She gave an awful shriek and fell to the floor, stiff as a poker; and his poor little children, it made my heart bleed to look at them; and his poor old mother. I am afraid it will be the death of her."

In a large city with its varied interests, one event rapidly chases the other. Life-boats are stranded on the shores of time, pitiful wrecks of humanity are dashed amid the rocks and reefs of existence. Old faces disappear and new ones take their places and the stream of life ever hurries on to empty where death's waters meet.

At the next sitting of the Court John Coots was arraigned, tried, and convicted of murder in the first degree. His lawyer tried to bring in a plea of emotional insanity but failed. If insane he was insane through the influence of strong drink. It was proven that he had made fierce threats against the life of Loraine, and the liquor in which he had so freely indulged had served to fire his brain and nerve his hand to carry out his wicked intent; and so the jury brought in its verdict, and he was sentenced to be executed, which sentence was duly performed and that closed another act of the sad drama. Intemperance and Sensuality had clasped hands together, and beneath their cruel fostering the gallows had borne its dreadful fruit of death. The light of one home had been quenched in gloom and guilt. A husband had broken over the barriers that God placed around the path of marital love, and his sun had gone down at mid-day. The sun which should have gilded the horizon of life and lent it additional charms, had gone down in darkness, yes, set behind the shadow of a thousand clouds. Innocent and unoffending childhood was robbed of a father's care, and a once happy wife, and joyful mother sat down in her widow's weeds with the mantle of a gloomier sorrow around her heart. And all for what? Oh who will justify the ways of God to man? Who will impress upon the mind of youth with its impulsiveness that it is a privilege as well as a duty to present the body to God, as a living sacrifice holy and acceptable in his sight. That God gives man no law that is not for his best advantage, and that the interests of humanity, and the laws of purity and self-denial all lie in the same direction, and the man who does not take care of his body must fail to take the best care of his soul; for the body should be temple for God's holy spirit and the instrument to do his work, and we have no right to defile the one or blunt the other and thus render ourselves unfit for the Master's service.

Chapter XIV

Belle Gordon's indignation was thoroughly aroused by hearing Mary Gough's story about the loss of her hair, and she made up her mind that when she saw Joe Gough she would give him a very plain talking.

"I would like to see your husband; I would just like to tell him what I think about his conduct."

"Oh," said Mary, her pale cheek growing whiter with apprehension; "That's his footsteps now, Miss Belle don't say anything to him, Joe's as good and kind a man as I ever saw when he is sober, but sometimes he is really ugly when he has been drinking."

Just then the door was opened, and Joe Gough entered, or rather all that remained of the once witty, talented and handsome Josiah Gough. His face was pale and haggard, and growing premature by age, his wealth of raven hair was unkempt and hung in tangled locks over his forehead, his hand was unsteady and trembling from extreme nervousness, but he was sober enough to comprehend the situation, and to feel a deep sense of remorse and shame, when he gazed upon the weary head from whence he had bereft its magnificent covering.

"Here Mary," said he approaching the bed, "I've brought you a present; I only had four cents, and I thought this would please you, I know you women are so fond of jew-gaws," and he handed [her] a pair of sleeve buttons.

"Thank you," said she, as a faint smile illuminated her pallid cheek. "This," she said turning to Miss Gordon, "is my husband, Josiah Gough."

"Good morning, Mr. Gough," said Belle bowing politely and extending her hand. Joe returned the salutation very courteously and very quietly, sitting down by the bedside, made some remarks about the dampness of the weather. Mary lay very quiet, looking pitifully upon the mour[n]ful wretch at her side, who seemed to regard her and her friend with intense interest. It seemed from his countenance that remorse and shame were rousing up his better nature. Once he rose as if to go—stood irresolutely for a moment, and then sitting down by the bedside, clasped her thin pale hand in his with a caressing motion, and said, "Mary you've had a hard time, but I hope there are better days in store for us, don't get out of heart," and there was a moisture in his eyes in which for a moment beamed a tender, loving light. Belle immediately felt her indignation changing to pity. Surely she thought within herself, this man is worth saving—There is still love and tenderness within him, notwithstanding all his self-ruin, he reminds me of an expression I have picked up somewhere about "Old Oak," holding the young fibres at its heart, I will appeal to that better nature, I will use it as a lever to lift him from the depths into which he has fallen. While she was thinking of the best way to approach him, and how to reach that heart into whose hidden depths she had so unexpectedly glanced, he arose and bending over his wife imprinted upon her lips a kiss in which remorse and shame seemed struggling for expression, and left the room.

"Mother Graham," said Belle, "a happy thought has just struck me, Couldn't we induce Mr. Gough to attend the meeting of the Reform Club? Mr. R. N. speaks tonight and he has been meeting with glorious success as a Temperance Reformer, hundreds of men, many of them confirmed drunkards, have joined, and he is doing a remarkable work, he does not wait for the drunkards to come to him, he goes to them, and wins them by his personal sympathy, and it is wonderful the good he has done, I do wish he would go."

"I wish so too," said Martha Graham.

"If he should not return while I am here will you invite him to attend? Perhaps Mrs. Gough can spare you an hour or two this evening to accompany him."

"That I would gladly do, I think it would do me more good than all the medicines you could give me, to see my poor husband himself once more. Before he took to drinking, I was so happy, but it seems as if since then I have suffered sorrow by the spoonful. Oh the misery that this drink causes. I do hope these reform clubs will be the means of shutting up every saloon in the place, for just as long as one of them is open he is in danger."

"Yes," said Belle, "what we need is not simply to stop the men from drinking, but to keep the temptation out of their way."

"Joe," said Mary, "belongs to a good family, he has a first-rate education, is a fine penman, and a good bookkeeper, but this dreadful drink has thrown him out of some of the best situations in the town where we were living."

"Oh what a pity, I heard Mr. Clifford say that his business was increasing so that he wanted a good clerk and salesman to help him, that he was overworked and crippled for want of sufficient help. Maybe if your husband would sign the pledge, Mr. Clifford would give him a trial, but it is growing late and I must go. I would liked to have seen your husband before I left, and have given him a personal invitation, but you and Mother Graham can invite him for me, so good bye, keep up a good heart, you know where to cast your burden."

Just as Miss Gordon reached the landing, she saw Joe Gough standing at the outer door and laying her hand gently upon his shoulder, exclaimed, "Oh Mr. Gough, I am so glad to see you again, I wanted to invite you to attend a temperance meeting to-night at Amory Hall. Will you go?"

"Well I don't like to promise," he replied, looking down upon his seedy coat and dilapidated shoes.

"Never mind your wardrobe," said Miss Gordon divining his thoughts. "The soul is more than raiment, 'the world has room for another man and I want you to fill the place.'"

"Well," said he, "I'll come."

"Very well, I expect to be there and will look for you. Come early and bring Mother Graham."

"Mrs. Gough can spare her an hour or two this evening, I think your wife is suffering more from exhaustion and debility than anything else."

"Yes poor Mary has had a hard time, but it shan't be always so. As soon as I get work I mean to take her out of this," said he looking disdainfully at the wretched tenement house, with its broken shutters and look of general decay.

"Why Mother Graham is [the] meeting over? You must have had a fine time, you just look delighted. Did Joe go in with you, and where is he now?"

"Yes, he went with me, listened to the speeches, and joined the club, I saw him do it with my own eyes, Oh, we had a glorious time!"

"Oh I am so glad," said Mary, her eyes filling with sudden tears. "I do hope he will keep his pledge!"

"I hope so too, and I hope he will get something to do. Mr. Clifford was there when he signed, and Miss Belle was saying today that he wanted a clerk that would be a first r[at]e place for Joe, if he will only keep his pledge. Mr. Clifford is an active temperance man, and I believe would help to keep Joe straight."

"I hope he'll get the place, but Mother Graham, tell me all about the meeting, you don't know how happy I am."

"Don't I deary? Have I been through it all, but it seems as if I had passed through suffering into peace, but never mind Mother Graham's past troubles, let me tell you about the meeting."

"At these meetings quite a number of people speak, just as we went in one of the speakers was telling his experience, and what a terrible struggle he had to overcome the power of appetite. Now when he felt the fearful craving coming over him he would walk the carpet till he had actually worn it threadbare; but that he had been converted and found grace to help him in time of need, and how he had gone out and tried to reform others and had seen the work prosper in his hand. I watched Joe's face, it seemed lit up with earnestness and hope, as if that man had brought him a message of deliverance; then after the meeting came the signing of the pledge and joining the reform club, and it would have done you good to see the men that joined."

"Do you remember Thomas Allison?"

"Yes, poor fellow, and I think if any man ever inherited drunkenness, he did, for his father and his mother were drunkards before him."

"Well, he joined and they have made him president of the club."

"Well did I ever! But tell me all about Joe."

"When the speaking was over, Joe sat still and thoughtful as if making up his mind, when Miss Gordon came to him and asked him to join, he stopped a minute to button his coat and went right straight up and had his name put down, but oh how the people did clap and shout. Well as Joe was one of the last to sign, the red ribbons they use for badges was all gone and Joe looked so sorry, he said he wanted to take a piece of ribbon home to let his wife know that he belonged to the Reform Club, Miss Gordon heard him, and she had a piece of black lace and red ribbon twisted together around her throat and she separated the lace from the ribbon and tied it in his button-hole, so his Mary would see it. Oh Miss Belle did look so sweet and Mr. Clifford never took his eyes off her. I think he admires her very much."

"I don't see how he can help it, she is one of the dearest—sweetest, ladies I ever saw, she never seemed to say by her actions, 'I am doing so much for you poor people' and you can't be too thankful."

"Not she, and between you and I, and the gate-post, I think that will be a match."

"I think it would make a splendid one, but hush, I hear some persons coming."

The door opened and Paul Clifford, Joe Gough, and Belle Gordon entered.

"Here Mrs. Gough," said Paul Clifford, "as we children used to say. Here's your husband safe and sound, and I will add, a member of our reformed club and we have come to congratulate you upon the event."

"My dear friends, I am very thankful to you for your great kindness, I don't think I shall ever be able to repay you."

"Don't be uneasy darling," said Belle, "we are getting our pay as we go along, we don't think the cause of humanity owes us anything." "Yes," said Joe seating himself by the bed side with an air of intense gratification. "Here is my badge, I did not want to leave the meeting without having this to show you."

"This evening," said Mrs. Gough smiling through her tears, "reminds me of a little temperance song I learned when a child, I think it commenced with these words:

> And are you sure the news is true?
> Are you sure my John has joined?
> I can't believe the happy news,
> And leave my fears behind,
> If John has joined and drinks no more,
> The happiest wife am I
> That ever swept a cabin floor,
> Or sung a lullaby.

"That's just the way I feel to-night, I haven't been so happy before for years."

"And I hope," said Mr. Clifford, "that you will have many happy days and nights in the future."

"And I hope so too," said Joe, shaking hands with Paul and Belle as they rose to go.

Mr. Clifford accompanied Belle to her door, and as they parted she said, "This is a glorious work in which it is our privilege to clasp hands."

"It is and I hope," but as the words rose to his lips, he looked into the face of Belle, and it was so radiant with intelligent tenderness and joy, that she seemed to him almost like a glorified saint, a being too precious high and good for common household uses, and so the remainder of the sentence died upon his lips and he held his peace.

Chapter XV

"I have resolved to dissolve partnership with Charles," said Augustine Romaine to his wife, the next morning after his son's return from the Champaign supper at John Anderson's.

"Oh! no you are not in earnest, are you? You seem suddenly to have lost all patience with Charlie."

"Yes I have, and I have made up my mind that I am not going to let him hang like a millstone on our business. No, if he will go down, I am determined he shall not drag me down with him. See what a hurt it would be to us, to have it said, 'Don't trust your case with the Romaine's for the Junior member of that firm is a confirmed drunkard.'"

"Well, Augustine you ought to know best, but it seems like casting him off, to dissolve partnership with him."

"I can't help it, if he persists in his downward course he must take the consequences. Charles has had every advantage; when other young lawyers have had to battle year after year with obscurity and poverty, he entered into a business that was already established and flourishing. What other men were struggling for, he found ready made to his hand, and if he chooses to throw away every advantage and make a complete wreck of himself, I can't help it."

"Oh! it does seem so dreadful, I wonder what will become of my poor boy?"

"Now, mother I want you to look at this thing in the light of reason and common sense. I am not turning Charles out of the house. He is not poor, though the way he is going on he will be. You know his grandfather has left him a large estate out West, which is constantly increasing in value. Now what I mean to do is to give Charles a chance to set up for himself as attorney, wherever he pleases. Throwing him on his own resources, with a sense of responsibility, may be the best thing for him; but in the present state of things I do not think it advisable to continue our business relations together. For more than twenty-five years our firm has stood foremost at the bar. Ever since my brother and I commenced business together our reputation has been unspotted and I mean to keep it so, if I have to cut off my right hand."

Mrs. Romaine gazed upon the stern sad face of her husband, and felt by the determination of his manner that it was useless to entreat or reason with him to change his purpose; and so with a heavy heart, and eyes drooping with unshed tears, she left the room.

"John," said Mr. Romaine to the waiter, "tell Charles I wish to see him before I go down to the office." Just then Charles entered the room and bade good morning to his father.

"Good morning," replied his father, rather coldly, and for a moment there was an awkward silence.

"Charles," said Mr. Romaine, "after having witnessed the scene of last night, I have come to the conclusion to dissolve the partnership between us."

"Just as you please," said Charles in a tone of cold indifference that irritated his father; but he maintained his self-control.

"I am sorry that you will persist in your downward course; but if you are determined to throw yourself away I have made up my mind to cut loose from you. I noticed last week when you were getting out the briefs in that Sumpter case, you were not yourself, and several times lately you have made me hang my head in the court room. I am sorry, very sorry," and a touch of deep emotion gave a tone of tenderness to the closing sentence. There was a slight huskiness in Charles' voice, as he replied, "Whenever the articles of dissolution are made out I am ready to sign."

"They shall be ready by to-morrow."

"All right, I will sign them."

"And what then?"

"Set up for myself, the world is wide enough for us both."

After Mr. Romaine had left the room, Charles sat, burying his head in his hands and indulging bitter thoughts toward his father. "To-day," he said to himself, "he resolved to cut loose from me apparently forgetting that it was from his hands, and at his table I received my first glass of wine. He prides himself on his power of self-control, and after all what does it amount to? It simply means this, that he has an iron constitution, and can drink five times as much as I can without showing its effects, and to-day if Mr. R. N. would ask him to sign the total-abstinence pledge, he wouldn't hear to it. Yes I am ready to sign any articles he will bring, even if it is to sign never to enter this house, or see his face; but my mother—poor mother, I am sorry for her sake."

Just then his mother entered the room.

"My son."

"Mother."

"Just what I feared has come to pass. I have dreaded more than anything else this collision with your father."

"Now mother don't be so serious about this matter. Father's

law office does not take in the whole world. I shall either set up for myself in A. P., or go West."

"Oh! don't talk of going away, I think I should die of anxiety if you were away."

"Well, as I passed down the street yesterday I saw there was an office to let in Frazier's new block, and I think I will engage it and put out my sign. How will that suit you?"

"Anything, or anywhere, Charlie, so you are near me. And Charlie don't be too stout with your father, he was very much out of temper when you came home last night, but be calm; it will blow over in a few days, don't add fuel to the fire. And you know that you and Miss Roland are to be married in two weeks, and I do wish that things might remain as they are, at least till after the wedding. Separation just now might give rise to some very unpleasant talk, and I would rather if you and your father can put off this dissolution, that you will consent to let things remain as they are for a few weeks longer. When your father comes home I will put the case to him, and have the thing delayed. Just now Charles I dread the consequences of a separation."

"Well, Mother, just as you please; perhaps the publication of the articles of dissolution in the paper might complicate matters."

When Mr. Romaine returned home, his wrath was somewhat mollified, and Mrs. Romaine having taken care to prepare his favorite dishes for dinner, took the opportunity when he had dined to entreat him to delay the intended separation till after the wedding, to which he very graciously consented.

Again there was a merry gathering at the home of Jeanette Roland. It was her wedding night, and she was about to clasp hands for life with Charles Romaine. True to her idea of taking things as she found them, she had consented to be his wife without demanding of him any reformation from the habit which was growing so fearfully upon him. His wealth and position in society like charity covered a multitude of sins. At times Jeanette felt misgivings about the step she was about to take, but she put back the thoughts like unwelcome intruders, and like the Ostrich, hiding her head in the sand, instead of avoiding the danger, she shut her eyes to its fearful reality. That night the wine flowed out like a purple flood; but the men and women who drank were people of culture, wealth and position, and did not seem to think it was just as disgraceful or more so to drink in excess in magnificently furnished parlors, as it was in low Barrooms or miserable dens where vice and poverty are huddled together. And if the weary children of hunger and hard toil instead of seeking sleep as nature's sweet restorer, sought to stimulate their flagging energies in the enticing cup, they with the advantages of wealth, culture and refinement could not plead the excuses of extreme wretchedness, or hard and unremitting drudgery.

"How beautiful, very beautiful," fell like a pleasant ripple upon the ear of Jeanette Roland, as she approached the altar, beneath her wreath of orange blossoms, while her bridal veil floated like a cloud of lovely mist from her fair young head. The vows were spoken, the bridal ring placed upon her finger, and amid a train of congratulating friends, she returned home where a sumptuous feast awaited them.

"Don't talk so loud, but I think Belle Gordon acted wisely when she refused Mr. Romaine," said Mrs. Gladstone, one of the guests.

"Do you, indeed? Why Charles Romaine, is the only son of Mr. Romaine, and besides being the heir he has lately received a large legacy from his grandfather's estate. I think Jeanette has made a splendid match. I hope my girls will do as well."

"I hope on the other hand that my girls will never marry unless they do better."

"Why how you talk! What's the matter with Mr. Romaine?"

"Look at him now," said Mrs. Fallard joining in the conversation. "This is his wedding night and yet you can plainly see he is under the influence of wine. Look at those eyes, don't you know how beautiful and clear they are when he is sober, and how very interesting he is in conversation. Now look at him, see how muddled his eye is—but he is approaching—listen to his utterance, don't you notice how thick it is? Now if on his wedding night, he can not abstain, I have very grave fears for Jeanette's future."

"Perhaps you are both right, but I never looked at things in that light before, and I know that a magnificent fortune can melt like snow in the hands of a drunken man."

"I wish you much joy," rang out a dozen voices, as Jeanette approached them. "Oh Jeanette, you just look splendid! and Mr. Romaine, oh he is so handsome." "Oh Jeanette what's to hinder you from being so happy?" "But where is Mr. Romaine? we have missed him for some time." "I don't know, let me seek my husband." "Isn't that a mouthful?" said Jeanette laughingly disengaging herself from the merry group, as an undefined sense of apprehension swept over her. Was it a presentiment of coming danger? An unspoken prophecy to be verified by bitter tears, and lonely fear that seemed for a moment to turn life's sweetness into bitterness and gall. In the midst of a noisy group, in the dining room, she found Charles drinking the wine as it gave its color aright in the cup. She saw the deep flush upon his cheek, and the cloudiness of his eye, and for the first time upon that bridal night she felt a shiver of fear as the veil was suddenly lifted before her unwilling eye; and half reluctantly she said to herself, "Suppose after all my cousin Belle was right."

Chapter XVI

"Good morning! Mr. Clifford," said Joe Gough, entering the store of Paul Clifford, the next day after he joined the Reform

Club. "I have heard that you wanted some one to help you, and I am ready to do anything to make an honest living."

"I am very sorry," said Paul, "but I have just engaged a young man belonging to our Club to come this morning."

Joe looked sad, but not discouraged, and said, "Mr. Clifford, I want to turn over a new leaf in my life, but everyone does not know that. Do you know of any situation I can get? I have been a book-keeper and a salesman in the town of C., where I once lived, but I am willing to begin almost anywhere on the ladder of life, and make it a stepping-stone to something better."

There was a tone of earnestness in his voice, and an air of determination, in his manner that favorably impressed Paul Clifford and he replied,—

"I was thinking of a friend of mine who wants a helping hand; but it may not be, after all, the kind of work you prefer. He wants a porter, but as you say you want to make your position a stepping-stone to something better, if you make up your mind to do your level best, the way may open before you in some more congenial and unexpected quarter. Wait a few minutes, and I will give you a line to him. No! I can do better than that; he is a member of our Club, and I will see him myself; but before you do, had we better not go to the barber's?"

"I would like to," said Joe, "but I haven't—"

"Haven't the money?"

"Yes, Mr. Clifford, that's the fact, I am not able to pay even for a shave. Oh! what a fool I have been."

"Oh! well never mind, let the dead past, bury its dead. The future is before you, try and redeem that. If you accept it, I will lend you a few dollars. I believe in lending a helping hand. So come with me to the barber's and I'll make it all right, you can pay me when you are able, but here we are at the door, let us go in."

They entered, and in a few moments Joe's face was under the manipulating care of the barber.

"Fix this so," said Joe to the barber, giving him directions how to cut his mustache.

Paul was somewhat amused, and yet in that simple act, he saw a return of self-respect, and was glad to see its slightest manifestations, and it was pleasant to witness the satisfaction with which Joe beheld himself in the glass, as he exclaimed, "Why Mary would hardly know me!"

"Suppose now, we go to the tailor's and get some new rigging?"

"Mr. Clifford," said Joe hesitatingly, "you are very kind, but I don't know when I shall be able to pay you, and—"

"Oh! never mind, when you are able I will send my bill. It will help you in looking for a place to go decently dressed. So let us go into the store and get a new suit."

They entered a clothing store and in a few moments Joe was dressed in a new suit which made him look almost like another person.

"Now, we are ready," said Paul, "appearances are not so much against you."

"Good morning Mr. Tennant," said Paul to the proprietor of a large store. "I heard last night that you wanted help in your store and I have brought you Mr. Gough, who is willing to take any situation you will give him, and I will add, he is a member of our Reform Club."

Mr. Tennant looked thoughtfully a moment, and replied, "I have only one vacancy, and I do not think it would suit your friend. My porter died yesterday and that is the only situation which I can offer him at present."

"I will accept it," said Joe, "if you will give it to me, I am willing to do anything to make an honest living for my family."

"Well you can come to-morrow, or stop now and begin."

"All right," said Joe with a promptness that pleased his employer, and Joe was installed in the first day's regular work he had had for months.

. . .

"What! sitting up sewing?" said Belle Gordon entering the neat room where Mrs. Gough was rejuvenating a dress for her older daughter. "Why you look like another woman, your cheeks are getting plump, your eyes are brightening, and you look so happy."

"I feel just like I look, Miss Gordon. Joe has grown so steady, he gets constant work, and he is providing so well for us all, and he won't hear to me taking again that slop-shop work. He says all he wants me to do, is to get well, and take care of the home and children. But you look rather pale, have you been sick?"

"Yes, I have been rather unwell for several weeks, and the doctor has ordered among other things that I should have a plentiful supply of fresh air, so to-morrow as there is to be a free excursion, and I am on the Committee, I think if nothing prevents, I shall go. Perhaps you would like to go?"

"Yes, if Joe will consent, but—"

"But, what?"

"Well Joe has pretty high notions, and I think he may object, because it is receiving charity. I can't blame him for it, but Joe has a right smart of pride that way."

"No! I don't blame him, I rather admire his spirit of self-reliance, and I wouldn't lay the weight of my smallest finger upon his self-respect to repress it; still I would like to see your Mamy, and Hatty, have a chance to get out into the woods, and have what I call a good time. I think I can have it so arranged that you can go with me, and serve as one of the Committee on refreshments, and your services would be an ample compensation for your entertainment."

"Well if you put it in that light, I think Joe would be willing for me to go."

"I will leave the matter there, and when your husband comes home you can consult him and send me word. And so you are getting along nicely?"

"Oh! yes indeed, splendidly. Just look here, this is Joe's present," and Mary held up with both hands a beautifully embossed and illustrated Bible. "This was my birth-day present. Oh! Miss Belle, Joe seems to me like another man. Last night we went to a conference and prayer-meeting, and Joe spoke. Did you know he had joined the church?"

"No! when did that happen?"

"Last week."

"Has he become religious?"

"Well I think Joe's trying to do the best he can. He said last night in meeting that he felt like a new man, and if they didn't believe he had religion to ask his wife."

"And suppose they had asked you, what would you have said?"

"I would have said I believe Joe's a changed man, and I hope he will hold out faithful. And Miss Belle I want to be a Christian, but there are some things about religion I can't understand. People often used to talk to me about getting religion, and getting ready to die. Religion somehow got associated in my mind with sorrow and death, but it seems to me since I have known you and Mr. Clifford the thing looks different. I got it associated with something else besides the pall, the hearse, and weeping mourners. You have made me feel that it is as beautiful and valuable for life as it is necessary for death. And yet there are some things I can't understand. Miss Belle will you be shocked if I tell you something which has often puzzled me?"

"I don't know, I hope you have nothing very shocking to tell me."

"Well perhaps it is, and maybe I had better not say it."

"But you have raised my curiosity, and woman like I want to hear it."

"Now don't be shocked, but let me ask you, if you really believe that God is good?"

"Yes I do, and to doubt it would be to unmoor my soul from

love, from peace, and rest. It seems to me to believe that must be the first resting place for my soul, and I feel that with me

> To doubt would be disloyalty
> To falter would be sin.

But my dear I have been puzzled just as you have, and can say,—

> I have wandered in mazes dark and distressing
> I've had not a cheering ray my spirit to bless,
> Cheerless unbelief held my laboring soul in grief

"And what then?"

> I then turned to the Gospel that taught me to pray
> And trust in the living word from folly away.

"And it was here my spirit found a resting place, and I feel that in believing I have entered into rest."

"Ah!" said Mary to herself when Belle was gone, "there is something so restful and yet inspiring in her words. I wish I had her faith."

Chapter XVII

"I am sorry, very sorry," said Belle Gordon, as a shadow of deep distress flitted over her pale sad face. She was usually cheerful and serene in her manner; but now it seemed as if the very depths of her soul had been stirred by some mournful and bitter memory. "Your question was so unexpected and—"

"And what!" said Paul in a tone of sad expectancy, "so unwelcome?"

"It was so sudden, I was not prepared for it."

"I do not," said Paul, "ask an immediate reply. Give yourself ample time for consideration."

"Mr. Clifford," said Belle, her voice gathering firmness as she proceeded, "while all the relations of life demand that there should be entire truthfulness between us and our fellow creatures, I think we should be especially sincere and candid in our dealings with each other on this question of marriage, a question not only as affecting our own welfare but that of[5] others, a relation which may throw its sunshine or shadow over the track of unborn ages. Permit me now to say to you, that there is no gentleman of my acquaintance whom I esteem more highly than yourself; but when you ask me for my heart and hand, I almost feel as if I had no heart to give; and you know it would be wrong to give my hand where I could not place my heart."

"But would it be impossible for you to return my affection?" "I don't know, but I am only living out my [vow] of truthfulness when I say to you, I feel as if I had been undone for love. You tell that in offering your hand that you bring me a heart unhackneyed in the arts of love, that my heart is the first and only shrine on which you have ever laid the wealth of your affections. I cannot say the same in reply. I have had my bright and beautiful day dream, but it has faded, and I have learned what is the hardest of all lessons for a woman to learn. I have learned to live without love."

"Oh no," said Paul, "not to live without love. In darkened homes how many grateful hearts rejoice to hear your footsteps on the threshold. I have seen the eyes of young Arabs of the street grow brighter as you approached and say, 'That's my lady, she comes to see my mam when she's sick.' And I have seen little girls in the street quicken their face to catch a loving smile from their dear Sunday school teacher. Oh Miss Belle instead of living without love, I think you are surrounded with a cordon of loving hearts."

"Yes, and I appreciate them—but this is not the love to which I refer. I mean a love which is mine, as anything else on earth is mine, a love precious, enduring and strong, which brings hope and joy and sunshine over one's path in life. A love which commands my allegiance and demands my respect. This is the love I have learned to do without, and perhaps the poor and needy had learned to love me less, had this love surrounded me more."

"Miss Belle, perhaps I was presumptuous, to have asked a return of the earnest affection I have for you; but I had hoped that you would give the question some consideration; and may I not hope that you will think kindly of my proposal? Oh Miss Gordon, ever since the death of my sainted mother, I have had in my mind's eye the ideal of a woman nobly planned, beautiful, intellectual, true and affectionate, and you have filled out that ideal in all its loveliest proportions, and I hope that my desire will not be like reaching out to some bright particular star and wishing to win it. It seems to me," he said with increasing earnestness, "whatever obstacle may be in the way, I would go through fire and water to remove it."

"I am sorry," said Belle as if speaking to herself, and her face had an absent look about it, as if instead of being interested in the living present she was grouping amid the ashes of the dead past. At length she said, "Mr. Clifford, permit me to say in the first place, let there be truth between us. If my heart seems callous and indifferent to your love, believe me it is warm to esteem and value you as a friend, I might almost say as a brother, for in sympathy of feeling and congeniality of disposition you are nearer to me than my own brother; but I do not think were I so inclined that it would be advisable for me to accept your hand without letting you know something of my past history. I told you a few moments since that I had my day dream. Permit me to tell you, for I think you are entitled to my confidence. The object of that day dream was Charles Romaine."

"Charles Romaine!" and there was a tone of wonder in the voice, and a puzzled look on the face of Paul Clifford.

"Yes! Charles Romaine, not as you know him now, with the

marks of dissipation on his once handsome face, but Charles Romaine, as I knew him when he stood upon the threshold of early manhood, the very incarnation of beauty, strength and grace. Not Charles Romaine with the blurred and bloated countenance, the staggering gait, the confused and vacant eye; but Charles Romaine as a young, handsome and talented lawyer, the pride of our village, the hope of his father and the joy of his mother; before whom the future was opening full of rich and rare promises. Need I tell you that when he sought my hand in preference to all the other girls in our village, that I gave him what I never can give to another, the first, deep love of my girlish heart. For nearly a whole year I wore his betrothal ring upon my finger, when I saw to my utter anguish and dismay that he was fast becoming a drunkard. Oh! Mr. Clifford if I could have saved him I would have taken blood from every vein and strength from every nerve. We met frequently at entertainments. I noticed time after time, the effects of the wine he had imbibed, upon his manner and conversation. At first I shrank from remonstrating with him, until the burden lay so heavy on my heart that I felt I must speak out, let the consequences be what they might. And so one evening I told him plainly and seriously my fears about his future. He laughed lightly and said my fears were unfounded; that I was nervous and giving away to idle fancies; that his father always had wine at the table, and that he had never seen him under the influence of liquor. Silenced, but not convinced, I watched his course with painful solicitude. All remonstrances on my part seemed thrown away; he always had the precedent of his father to plead in reply to my earnest entreaties. At last when remonstrances and entreaties seemed to be all in vain, I resolved to break the engagement. It may have been a harsh and hard alternative, but I would not give my hand where my respect could not follow. It may be that I thought too much of my own happiness, but I felt that marriage must be for me positive misery or positive happiness, and I feared that if I married a man so lacking in self-control as to become a common drunkard, that when I ceased to love and respect him, I should be constantly tempted to hate and despise him. I think one of the saddest fates that can befall a woman is to be tied for life to a miserable bloated wreck of humanity. There may be some women with broad generous hearts, and great charity, strong enough to lift such men out of the depths, but I had no such faith in my strength and so I gave him back his ring. He accepted it, but we parted as friends. For awhile after our engagement was broken, we occasionally met at the houses of our mutual friends in social gatherings and I noticed with intense satisfaction that whenever wine was offered he scrupulously abstained from ever tasting a drop, though I think at times his self-control was severely tested. Oh! what hope revived in my heart. Here I said to myself is compensation for all I have suffered, if by it he shall be restored to manhood usefulness and society, and learn to make his life not a thing of careless ease and sensuous indulgence, but of noble struggle and high and holy endeavor. But while I was picturing out for him a magnificent future, imagining the lofty triumphs of his intellect—an intellect grand in its achievements and glorious in its possibilities, my beautiful daydream was rudely broken up, and vanished away like the rays of sunset mingling with the shadows of night. My Aunt Mrs. Roland, celebrated her silver-wedding and my cousin's birth-day by giving a large entertainment; and among other things she had a plentiful supply of wine. Mr. Romaine had lately made the acquaintance of my cousin Jeanette Roland. She was both beautiful in person and fascinating in her manners, and thoughtlessly she held a glass of wine in her hand and asked Mr. Romaine if he would not honor the occasion, by drinking her mother's health. For a moment he hesitated, his cheek paled and flushed alternately, he looked irresolute. While I watched him in silent anguish it seemed as if the agony of years was compressed in a few moments. I tried to catch his eye but failed, and with a slight tremor in his hand he lifted the glass to his lips and drank. I do not think I would have felt greater anguish had I seen him suddenly drowned in sight of land. Oh! Mr. Clifford that night comes before me so vividly, it seems as if I am living it all over again. I do not think Mr. Romaine has ever recovered from the reawakening of his appetite. He has since married Jeanette. I meet her occasionally. She has a beautiful home, dresses magnificently, and has a retinue of servants; and yet I fancy she is not happy. That somewhere hidden out of sight there is a worm eating at the core of her life. She has a way of dropping her eyes and an absent look about her that I do not fully understand, but it seems to me that I miss the old elasticity of her spirits, the merry ring of her voice, the pleasant thrills of girlish laughter, and though she never confesses it to me I doubt that Jeanette is happy. And with this sad experience in the past can you blame me if I am slow, very slow to let the broken tendrils of my heart entwine again?"

"Miss Belle," said Paul Clifford catching eagerly at the smallest straw of hope, "if you can not give me the first love of a fresh young life, I am content with the rich [aftermath?] of your maturer years, and ask from life no higher prize; may I not hope for that?"

"I will think on it but for the present let us change the subject."

《《》》

"Do you think Jeanette is happy? She seems so different from what she used to be," said Miss Tabitha Jones to several friends who were spending the evening with her.

"Happy!" replied Mary Gladstone, "don't see what's to hinder her from being happy. She has everything that heart can wish. I was down to her house yesterday, and she has just moved in her new home. It has all the modern improvements, and everything is in excellent taste. Her furniture is of the latest style, and I think it is really superb."

"Yes," said her sister, "and she dresses magnificently. Last week she showed me a most beautiful set of jewelry, and a camel's hair shawl, and I believe it is real camel's hair. I think you could almost run it through a ring. If I had all she has, I think I should be as happy as the days are long. I don't believe I would let a wave of trouble roll across my peaceful breast."

"Oh! Annette," said Mrs. Gladstone, "don't speak so extravagantly, and I don't like to hear you quote those lines for such an occasion."

"Why not mother? Where's the harm?"

"That hymn has been associated in my mind with my earliest religious impressions and experience, and I don't like to see you lift it out of its sacred associations, for such a trifling occasion."

"Oh mother you are so strict. I shall never be able to keep time with you, but I do think, if I was off as Jeanette, that I would be as blithe and happy as a lark, and instead of that she seems to be constantly drooping and fading."

"Annette," said Mrs. Gladstone, "I knew a woman who possesses more than Jeanette does, and yet she died of starvation."

"Died of starvation! Why, when, and where did that happen? and what became of her husband?"

"He is in society, caressed and [ed?] on by the young girls of his set and I have seen a number of managing mammas to whom I have imagined he would not be an objectionable son-in-law."

"Do I know him mother?"

"No! and I hope you never will."

"Well mother I would like to know how he starved his wife to death and yet escaped the law."

"The law helped him."

"Oh mother!" said both girls opening their eyes in genuine astonishment.

"I thought," said Mary Gladstone, "it was the province of the law to protect women, I was just telling Miss Basanquet yesterday, when she was talking about woman's suffrage that I had as many rights as I wanted and that I was willing to let my father and brothers do all the voting for me."

"Forgetting my dear, that there are millions of women who haven't such fathers and brothers as you have. No my dear, when you examine the matter, a little more closely, you will find there are some painful inequalities in the law for women."

"But mother, I do think it would be a dreadful thing for women to vote Oh! just think of women being hustled and crowded at the polls by rude men, their breaths reeking with whiskey and tobacco, the very air heavy with their oaths. And then they have the polls at public houses. Oh mother, I never want to see the day when women vote."

"Well I do, because we have one of the kindest and best fathers and husbands and good brothers, who would not permit the winds of heaven to visit us too roughly, there is no reason we should throw ourselves between the sunshine and our less fortunate sisters who shiver in the blast."

"But mother, I don't see how voting would help us, I am sure we have influence I have often heard papa say that you were the first to awaken him to a sense of the enormity of slavery. Now mother if we women would use our influence with our fathers, brothers, husbands, and sons, could we not have everything we want."

"No, my dear we could not, with all our influence we never could have the same sense of responsibility which flows from the possession of power. I want women to possess power as well as influence, I want every Christian woman as she passes by a grog-shop or liquor saloon, to feel that she has on her heart a burden of responsibility for its existence, I hold my dear that a nation as well as an individual should have a conscience, and on this liquor question there is room for woman's conscience not merely as a persuasive influence but as an enlightened and aggressive power."

"Well Ma I think you would make a first class stump speaker. I expect when women vote we shall be constantly having calls, for the gifted, and talented Mrs. Gladstone to speak on the duties and perils of the hour."

"And I would do it, I would go among my sister women and try to persuade them to use their vote as a moral lever, not to make home less happy, but society more holy. I would have good and sensible women, grave in manner, and cultured in intellect, attend the primary meetings and bring their moral influence and political power to frown down corruption, chicanery, and low cunning."

"But mother just think if women went to the polls how many vicious ones would go?"

"I hope and believe for the honor of our sex that the vicious women of the community are never in the majority, that for one woman whose feet turn aside from the paths of rectitude that there are thousands of feet that never stray into forbidden paths, and to-day I believe there is virtue enough in society to confront its vice, and intelligence enough to grapple with its ignorance."[6]

Chapter XVIII

"Why Mrs. Gladstone," said Miss Tabitha, "you are as zealous as a new convert to the cause of woman suffrage. We single women who are constantly taxed without being represented, know what it is to see ignorance and corruption striking hands together and voting away our money for whatever purposes they choose. I pay as large a tax as many of the men in A. P., and yet cannot say who shall assess my property for a single year."

"And there is another thing," said Mrs. Gladstone, "ought to be brought to the consideration of the men, and it is this. They refuse to let us vote and yet fail to protect our homes from the ravages of rum. My young friend, whom I said died of starvation; foolishly married a dissipated man who happened to be rich and handsome. She was gentle, loving, sensitive to a fault. He was querulous, fault-finding and irritable, because his nervous system was constantly unstrung by liquor. She lacked tenderness, sympathy and heart support, and at last faded and died, not starvation of the body, but a trophy of the soul, and when I say the law helped, I mean it licensed the places that kept the temptation ever in his way. And I fear, that is the secret of Jeanette's faded looks, and unhappy bearing."

No Jeanette was not happy. Night after night would she pace the floor of her splendidly furnished chamber waiting and watching for her husband's footsteps. She and his friends had hoped that her influence would be strong enough to win him away from his boon companions, that his home and beautiful bride would present superior attractions to Anderson's saloon, his gambling pool, and champaign suppers, and for a while they did, but soon the novelty wore off, and Jeanette found out to her great grief that her power to bind him to the simple attractions of home were as futile as a role of cobwebs to moor a ship to the shore, when it has drifted out and is dashing among the breakers. He had learned to live an element of excitement, and to depend upon artificial stimulation, until it seemed as if the very blood in his veins grew sluggish fictitious excitement was removed. His father, hopeless of his future, had dissolved partnership with him, and for months there had been no communication between them; and Jeanette saw with agony and dismay that his life was being wrecked upon the broad sea of sin and shame.

"Where is his father? The child can't live. It is one of the worst cases of croup I have had this year, why didn't you send for me sooner? Where is his father? It is now just twelve o'clock, time for all respectable men to be in the house," said the bluff but kind hearted family doctor looking tenderly upon Jeanette's little boy who lay gasping for breath in the last stages of croup.

"Oh! I don't know," said Jeanette her face crimsoning beneath the doctor's searching glance. "I suppose he is down to Anderson's."

"Anderson's!" said the doctor in a tone of hearty indignation, "what business has he there, and his child dying here?"

"But doctor, he didn't know, the child had fever when he went out, but neither of us thought much of it till I was awakened by his strange and unnatural breathing. I sent for you as soon as I could rouse the servants." "Well rouse them again, and tell them to go down to Anderson's and tell your husband that his child is dying."

"Oh! no not dying doctor, you surely don't mean it." "Yes Jeanette," said the old family doctor, tenderly and sadly, "I can do nothing for him, let me take him in my arms and rest you. Dear little darling, he will be saved from the evils to come."

Just as his life was trembling on its frailest chords, and its delicate machinery almost wound up, Charles Romaine returned, sober enough to take in the situation. He strode up to the dying child, took the clammy hands in his, and said in a tone of bitter anguish, "Charlie, don't you know papa? Wouldn't you speak one little word to papa?" But it was too late, the shadows that never deceive flitted over the pale beauty of the marble brow, the waxen lid closed over the once bright and laughing eye, and the cold grave for its rest had won the child.

Chapter XIX

[Text missing.]

Chapter XX

If riches could bring happiness, John Anderson should be a happy man; and yet he is far from being happy. He has succeeded in making money, but failed in every thing else. But let us enter his home. As you open the parlor door your feet sink in the rich and beautiful carpet. Exquisite statuary, and superbly framed pictures greet your eye and you are ready to exclaim, "Oh! how lovely." Here are the beautiful conceptions of painters' art and sculptors' skill. It is a home of wealth, luxury and display, but not of love, refinement and culture. Years since, before John Anderson came to live in the city of A. P. he had formed an attachment for an excellent young lady who taught school in his native village, and they were engaged to be married; but after coming to the city and forming new associations, visions of wealth dazzled his brain, and unsettled his mind, till the idea of love in a cottage grew distasteful to him. He had seen men with no more ability than himself who had come to the city almost pennyless, and who had grown rich in a few years, and he made up his mind that if possible he would do two things, acquire wealth and live an easy life, and he thought the easiest way to accomplish both ends was to open up a gorgeous palace of sin and entice into his meshes the unwary, the inexperienced, and the misguided slaves of appetite. For awhile after he left his native village, he wrote almost constantly to his betrothed; but as new objects and interests engaged his attention, his letters became colder and less frequent, until they finally ceased and the engagement was broken. At first the blow fell heavily upon the heart of his affianced, but she was too sensible to fade away and die the victim of unrequited love, and in after years when she had thrown her whole soul into the temperance cause, and consecrated her life to the work of uplifting fallen humanity, she learned to be thankful that it was not her lot to be united to a man who stood as a barrier across the path of human progress and would have been a weight to her instead of wings. Released from his engagement, he entered into an alliance (for that is the better name for a marriage) which was not a union of hearts, or intercommunion of kindred souls; but only an affair of convenience; in a word he married for money a woman, who was no longer young in years, nor beautiful in person, nor amiable in temper. But she was rich, and her money like charity covered a multitude of faults, and as soon as he saw the golden bait he caught at it, and they were married, for he was willing to do almost any thing for money, except work hard for it. It was a marriage however that brought no happiness to either party. Mrs. Anderson was an illy educated, self willed, narrow minded [woman], full of airs and pretensions, the only daughter of a man who had laid the foundation of his wealth by keeping a low groggery, and dying had left her his only heir. John Anderson was selfish and grasping. He loved money, and she loved display, and their home was often the scene of the most pitiful contentions about money matters. Harsh words and bitter recriminations were almost common household usages. The children brought up in this unhealthy atmosphere naturally took sides with their mother and their home was literally a house divided against itself. The foolish conduct of the mother inspired the children with disrespect for their father, who failed to support the authority of his wife as the mother and mistress of the home. As her sons grew older they often sought attractions in questionable places, away from the sombre influences of their fireside, and the daughters as soon as they stood upon the verge of early womanhood learned to look upon marriage as an escape valve from domestic discomforts; and in that beautiful home with all its costly surroundings, and sumptuous furniture, there was always something wanting, there was always a lack of tenderness, sympathy and mutual esteem.

"I can't afford it," said John Anderson, to his wife who had been asking for money for a trip to a fashionable watering place. "You will have to spend the summer elsewhere."

"Can't afford it! What nonsense; is not it as much to your interest as mine to carry the girls around and give them a chance?"

"A chance for what?"

"Why to see something of the world. You don't know what may happen. That English Earl was very attentive last night to Sophronia at Mrs. Jessap's ball."

"An English Count? who is he? and where did he spring from?"

"Why he's from England, and is said to be the only son and heir of a very rich nobleman."

"I don't believe it, I don't believe he is an Earl any more than I am."

"That's just like you, always throw cold water on every thing I say."

"It is no such thing, but I don't believe in picking up strangers and putting them into my bosom; it is not all gold that glitters."

"I know that, but how soon can you let me have some money? I want to go out this afternoon and do some shopping and engage the semptress."

"I tell you, Annette, I have not the money to spare; the money market is very tight, and I have very heavy bills to meet this month."

"The money market tight! why it has been tight ever since I have been married."

"Well you may believe it or not, just as you choose, but I tell you this crusading has made quite a hole in my business."

"Now John Anderson, tell that to somebody that don't know. I don't believe this crusading has laid a finger's weight upon your business."

"Yes it has, and if you read the papers you would find that it has even affected the revenue of the state and you will have to retrench somewhere."

"Well, I'll retrench somewhere. I think we are paying our servants too high wages any how. Mrs. Shenflint gets twice as much work done for the same money. I'll retrench, John Anderson, but I want you to remember that I did not marry you empty handed."

"I don't think I shall be apt to forget it in a hurry while I have such a gentle reminder at hand," he replied sarcastically.

"And I suppose you would not have married me if I had had no money."

"No, I would not," said John Anderson thoroughly exasperated, "and I would have been a fool if I had."

These bitter words spoken in a heat of passion were calculated to work disastrously in that sin darkened home.

For some time she had been suspecting that her money had been the chief inducement which led him to seek her hand, and now her worse suspicions were confirmed, and the last thread of confidence was severed.

"I should not have said it," said Anderson to himself, "but the woman is so provoking and unreasonable. I suppose she will have a fit of sulks for a month and never be done brooding over those foolish words"; and Anderson sighed as if he were an ill used man. He had married for money, and he had got what he bargained for; love, confidence, and mutual esteem were not sought in the contract and these do not necessarily come of themselves.

"Well, the best I can do is to give her what money she wants and be done with it."

"Is not in her room?"

"No sir and her bed has not been rumpled."

"Where in the world can she be?"

"I don't know, but here is a note she left."

"What does she say? read it Annette."

"She says she feels that you were unjust to the Earl and that she hopes you will forgive her the steps she has taken, but by the time the letter reaches you she expects to be the Countess of Clarendon."

"Poor foolish girl, you see what comes of taking a stranger to your bosom and making so much of him."

"That's just like you, John Anderson, every thing that goes wrong is blamed on me. I almost wish I was dead."

"I wish so too," thought Anderson but he concluded it was prudent to keep the wish to himself.

John Anderson had no faith whatever in the pretensions of his new son-in-law, but his vain and foolish wife on the other hand was elated at the dazzling prospects of her daughter, and often in her imagination visited the palatial residence of "My Son, the Earl," and was graciously received in society as the mother of the Countess of Clarendon. She was also highly gratified at the supposed effect of Sophronia's marriage upon a certain clique who had been too exclusive to admit her in their set. Should not those Gladstone girls be ready to snag themselves? and there was that Mary Talbot, did every thing she could to attract his attention but it was no go. My little Sophronia came along and took the rag off the bush. I guess they will almost die with envy. If he had waited for her father's consent we might have waited till the end of the chapter; but I took the responsibility on my shoulders and the thing is done. My daughter, the Countess of Clarendon. I like the ring of the words; but dear me here's the morning mail, and a letter from the Countess, but what does it mean?"

"Come to me, I am in great trouble."

In quick response to the appeal Mrs. Anderson took the first train to New York and found her daughter in great distress. The "Earl" had been arrested for forgery and stealing, and darker suspicions were hinted against him. He had been a body servant to a nobleman who had been travelling for his health and who had died by a lonely farmhouse where he had gone for fresh air and quiet, and his servant had seized upon his effects and letters of introduction, and passed himself off as the original Earl, and imitating his handwriting had obtained large remittances, for which he was arrested, tried and sent to prison, and thus ended the enchanting dream of "My daughter the Countess of Clarendon."

Chapter XXI

"I cannot ensure your life a single hour, unless you quit business. You are liable to be stricken with paralysis at any moment, if [once?] subject to the [least] excitement.[7] Can't you trust your business in the hands of your sons?"

"Doctor," said John Anderson, "I have only two boys. My oldest went West several years ago, and never writes to us unless he wants something, and as to Frank, if I would put the concern into his hands, he would drink himself into the grave in less than a month. The whole fact is this, my children are the curse of my life," and there was bitterness in the tone of John Anderson[8] as he uttered these words of fearful sorrow.

"Well," said the doctor, "you must have rest and quiet or I will not answer for the consequences."

"Rest and quiet!" said John Anderson to himself, "I don't see how I am to get it, with such a wife as I have always worrying and bothering me about something." "Mr. Anderson," said one of the servants, "Mrs. Anderson says please come, as quick as possible into Mr. Frank's room."

"What's the matter now!"

"I don't know, but Mr. Frank's acting mightily queer; he thinks there are snakes and lizards crawling over him."

"He's got the horrors, just what I expected. Tell me about rest and quiet! I'll be there in a minute. Oh what's the matter? I feel strange," said Anderson falling back on the bed suddenly stricken with paralysis. While in another room lay his younger son a victim to delirium tremens, and dying in fearful agony. The curse that John Anderson had sent to other homes had come back darkened with the shadow of death to brood over his own habitation. His son is dying, but he has no word of hope to cheer the parting spirit as it passed out into the eternity, for him the darkness of the tomb, is not gilded with the glory of the resurrection.

The best medical skill has been summoned to the aid of John Anderson, but neither art, nor skill can bind anew the broken threads of life. The chamber in which he is confined is a marvel of decoration, light streams into his home through panes of beautifully stained glass. Pillows of the softest down are placed beneath his head, beautiful cushions lie at his feet that will never take another step on the errands of sin, but no appliances of wealth can give peace to his guilty conscience. He looks back upon the past and the retrospect is a worse than wasted life; and when the future looms up before him he shrinks back from the contemplation, for the sins of the past throw their shadow over the future. He has houses, money and land, but he is a pauper in his soul, and a bankrupt in his character. In his eager selfish grasp for gold, he has shriveled his intellect and hardened and dried up his heart, and in so doing he has cut himself off from the richest sources of human enjoyment. He has wasted life's best opportunities, and there never was an angel, however bright, terrible and strong, that ever had power to roll away the stone from the grave of a dead opportunity, and what John Anderson has lost in time, he can never make up in eternity. He has formed no taste for reading, and thus has cut himself off from the glorious companionship of the good, the great, and the wise of all ages. He has been selfish, mean and grasping, and the blessing of the poor and needy never fall as benedictions on his weary head; and in that beautiful home with disease and death clutching at his heartstrings, he has wealth that he cannot enjoy, luxuries that pall upon his taste, and magnificence that can never satisfy the restless craving of his soul. His life has been a wretched failure. He neglected his children to amass the ways of iniquity, and their coldness and indifference pierce him like poisoned arrows. Marriage has brought him money, but not the sweet, tender ministrations of loving wifely care, and so he lives on starving in the midst of plenty; dying of thirst, with life's sweetest fountains eluding his grasp.

Charles Romaine is sleeping in a drunkard's grave. After the death of his boy there was a decided change in him. Night after night he tore himself away from John Anderson's saloon, and struggled with the monster that had enslaved him, and for awhile victory seemed to be perching on the banner of his resolution. Another child took the place of the first born, and the dead, and hope and joy began to blossom around Jeanette's path. His mother who had never ceased to visit the house marked the change with great satisfaction and prevailed upon his father to invite Charles and Jeanette to a New Year's dinner (only a family gathering). Jeanette being unwell excused herself from going, and Charles went alone. Jeanette felt a fearful foreboding when she saw him leaving the door, and said to herself, "I hope his father will not offer him wine. I am so afraid that something will happen to him, and yet I hated to persuade him not to go. His mother might think I was averse to his reconciliation with his father."

"It looks very natural to have Charles with us again," said Mrs. Ro[maine] looking fondly on her son.

"Yes, it seems like old times, when I always had my seat next to yours."

"And I hope," said his father, "it will never be vacant so long again."

The dinner hour passed on enlivened by social chat and pleasant reminiscences, and there was nothing to mar the harmony of the occasion. Mrs. Romaine had been careful to keep everything from the table that would be apt to awaken the old appetite for liquor, but after dinner Mr. Romaine invited Charles into the library to smoke. "Here," said he, handing him a cigar, "is one of the finest brands I have smoked lately, and by the way here is some rare old wine, more than 25 years old, which was sent to me yesterday by an old friend and college class mate of mine.[9] Let me pour you out a glass." Charles suddenly became agitated, but as his father's back was turned to him, pouring out the wine, he did not notice the sudden paling of his cheek, and the hesitation of his manner. And Charles checking back his scruples took the glass and drained it, to the bottom.

There is a fable, that a certain king once permitted the devil to kiss his shoulder, and out of those shoulders sprang[10] two serpents that in the fury of their hunger aimed at his head and tried to get at his brain. He tried to extricate himself from their terrible power. He tore at them with his fingers and found that it was his own flesh that he was lacerating. Dormant but not dead was the appetite for strong drink in Charles Romaine, and that one glass awakened the serpent coiled up in his flesh. He went out from his father's house with a newly awakened appetite clamoring and raging for strong drink. Every saloon he passed adding intensity to his craving. At last his appetite overmastered him and he almost rushed into a saloon, and waited impatiently till he was served. Every nerve seemed to be quivering with excitement, restlessness; and there was a look of wild despairing anguish on his face, as he clutched the glass to allay the terrible craving of his system. He drank till his head was giddy, and his gait was staggering, and then started for home. He entered the gate and slipped on the ice, and being too intoxicated to rise or comprehend his situation, he lay helpless in the dark and cold, until there crept over him that sleep from which there is no awakening, and when morning had broken in all its glory, Charles Romaine had drifted out of life, slain by the wine which at [last] had "bitten like an adder and stung like a serpent." Jeanette had waited and watched through the small hours of the night, till nature o'erwearied had sought repose in sleep and rising very early in the morning, she had gone to the front door to look down the street for his coming when the first object that met her gaze was the lifeless form of her husband. One wild and bitter shriek rent the air, and she fell fainting on the frozen corpse. Her friends gathered round her, all that love and tenderness could do was done for the wretched wife, but nothing could erase from her mind one agonizing sorrow, it was the memory of her fatal triumph over his good resolution years ago at her mother's silver wedding. Carelessly she had sowed the seeds of transgression whose fearful yield was a harvest of bitter misery. Mrs. Clifford came to her in her hour of trial, and tried to comfort and sustain the heart-stricken woman; who had tried to take life easy, but found it terribly hard, and she has measurably succeeded. In the home of her cousin she is trying to bear the burden of her life as well as she can. Her eye never lights up with joy. The bloom and flush have left her careworn face. Tears from her eyes long used to weeping have blenched the coloring of her life existence, and she is passing through life with the shadow of the grave upon her desolate heart.

Joe Gough has been true to his pledge, plenty and comfort have taken the place of poverty and pain. He continued his membership with the church of his choice and Mary is also striving to live a new life, and to be the ministering angel that keeps his steps, and he feels that in answer to prayer, his appetite for strong drink has been taken away.

Life with Mrs. Clifford has become a thing of brightness and beauty, and when children sprang up in her path making gladness and sunshine around her home, she was a wife and tender mother, fond but not foolish; firm in her household government, but not stern and unsympathising in her manner. The faithful friend and companion of her daughters, she won their confidence by her loving care and tender caution. She taught them to come to her in their hours of perplexity and trial and to keep no secrets from her sympathising heart. She taught her sons to be as upright in their lives and as pure in their conversation as she would have her daughters, recognizing for each only one code of morals and one law of spiritual life, and in course of time she saw her daughters ripening into such a beautiful womanhood, and her sons entering the arena of life not with the simplicity which is ignorant of danger and evil, but with the sterling integrity which baffles the darts of temptation with the panoply of principle and the armor of uprightness. Unconsciously she elevated the tone of society in which she moved by a life which was a beautiful and earnest expression of patient continuance in well doing. Paul Clifford's life has been a grand success, not in the mere accumulation of wealth, but in the enrichment of his moral and spiritual nature. He is still ever ready to lend a helping hand. He has not lived merely for wealth and enjoyment, but happiness, lasting and true springs up in his soul as naturally as a flower leaps into blossoms, and whether he is loved or hated, honored or forgotten, he constantly endeavors to make the world better by his example and gladdened by his presence feeling that if every one would be faithful to duty that even here, Eden would spring up in our path, and Paradise be around our way.

Notes

1. This installment is numbered as a second Chapter I in the original.
2. The original reads "Jeanette Romaine."
3. The original reads "Mr. Roland."
4. The original reads "to showing."
5. The phrase "that of" is repeated in the original.
6. A note from the *Christian Recorder* follows this paragraph: "[The rest of this chapter was crowded out. It will appear next week.]"
7. The original reads: "if once [or possibly "one"] subject to the lest excitement."

8. The original reads "and there was a tone of bitterness in the tone of John Anderson."

9. The original reads "by an old friend and college and class mate of mine."

10. The original reads "out of those shoulders spring two serpents."

Trial and Triumph

Chapter I

"Oh, that child! She is the very torment of my life. I have been the mother of six children, and all of them put together, never gave me as much trouble as that girl. I don't know what will ever become of her."

"What is the matter now, Aunt Susan? What has Annette been doing?"

"Doing! She is always doing something; everlastingly getting herself into trouble with some of the neighbors. She is the most mischievous and hard-headed child I ever saw."

"Well what has she been doing this morning which has so upset you?"

"Why, I sent her to the grocery to have the oil can filled, and after she came back she had not been in the house five minutes before there came such an uproar from Mrs. Larkins', my next door neighbor, that I thought her house was on fire, but—"

"Instead of that her tongue was on fire, and I know what that means."

"Yes, that's just it, and I don't wonder. That little minx sitting up there in the corner looking so innocent, stopped to pour oil on her clean steps. Now you know yourself what an aggravating thing that must have been."

"Yes, it must have been, especially as Mrs. Larkins is such a nice housekeeper and takes such pride in having everything neat and nice about her. How did you fix up matters with her."

"I have not fixed them up at all. Mrs. Larkins only knows one cure for bad children, and that is beating them, and she always blames me for spoiling Annette, but I hardly know what to do with her. I've scolded and scolded till my tongue is tired, whipping don't seem to do her a bit of good, and I hate to put her out among strangers for fear that they will not treat her right, for after all she is very near to me. She is my poor, dead Lucy's child. Sometimes when I get so angry with her that I feel as though I could almost shake the life out of her, the thought of her dying mother comes back to me and it seems to me as if I could see her eyes looking so wistfully on the child and turning so trustingly to me and saying, 'Mother, when I am gone won't you take care of Annette, and try to keep her with you?' And then all the anger dies out of me. Poor child! I don't know what is going to become of her when my head is laid low. I'm afraid she is born for trouble. Nobody will ever put up with her as I do. She has such an unhappy disposition. She is not like any of my children ever were."

"Yes. I've often noticed that she does seem different from other children. She never seems light-hearted and happy."

"Yes, that is so. She reminds me so of poor Lucy before she was born. She even moans in her sleep like she used to do. It was a dark day when Frank Miller entered my home and Lucy became so taken up with him. It seemed to me as if my poor girl just worshiped him. I did not feel that he was all right, and I tried to warn my dear child of danger, but what could an old woman like me do against him with his handsome looks and oily tongue."

"Yes," said her neighbor soothingly, "you have had a sad time, but still we cannot recall the dead past, and it is the living present with which we have to deal. Annette needs wise guidance, a firm hand and a loving heart to deal with her. To spoil her at home is only to prepare her for misery abroad."

"I am afraid that I am not equal to the task."

"If any man lack wisdom we are taught to ask it of One who giveth liberally to all men and upbraideth none. There would be so much less stumbling if we looked earnestly within for 'the light which lighteth every man that cometh into the world.'"

"Well," said Mrs. Harcourt, Annette's grandmother, "there is one thing about Annette that I like. She is very attentive to her books. If you want to keep that child out of mischief just put a book in her hand; but then she has her living to get and she can't get it by nursing her hands and reading books. She has got to work like the rest of us."

"But why not give her a good education? Doors are open to her which were closed against us. This is a day of light and knowledge. I don't know much myself, but I mean to give my girls a chance. I don't believe in saying, let my children do as I have done, when I think some of us have done poorly enough digging and delving from morning till night. I don't believe the good Lord ever sent anybody into his light and beautiful world to be nothing but a drudge, and I just think it is because some take it so easy that others, who will do, have to take it so hard."

"It always makes my blood boil," said a maiden lady who was present, "to see a great hulk of a man shambling around complaining of hard times, and that he can't get work, when his wife is just working herself down to the grave to keep up the family." I asked Mrs. Johnson, who just lives in the wash tub and is the main stay of her family, what would her husband do if she were to die? and she said, 'get another wife.' Now, I just think she has spoiled that man and if she dies first, I hope that he will never find another woman to tread in her footsteps. He ought to have me to deal with. When he got through with me he would never want to laze around another woman."

"I don't think he ever would," said Mrs. Harcourt, while a gleam of humor sparkled in her eye. Her neighbor was a maiden lady who always knew how to manage other people's husbands, but had never succeeded in getting one of her own, and not having any children herself understood perfectly well how to rate other people's.

Just then a knock was heard at the door and Mr. Thomas, Annette's former school teacher, entered the room. After an exchange of courtesies he asked, "How does Annette come on with her new teacher?"

"I have not heard any complaint," said Mrs. Harcourt. "At first Mrs. Joseph's girl did not want to sit with Annette, but she soon got over it when she saw how well the other girls treated Annette and how pleasant the teacher was to her. Mr. Scott, who has been so friendly to us, told us not to mind her; that her mother had been an ignorant servant girl, who had married a man with a little money; that she was still ignorant, loud and [dressy?] and liked to put on airs. The nearer the beggar the greater the prejudice."

"I think it is true," said Mr. Thomas. "If you apply those words, not to condition, but human souls, for none but beggarly souls would despise a man because of circumstances over which he had no control; noble, large-hearted men and women are never scornful. Contempt and ridicule are the weapons of weak souls. I am glad however, that Annette is getting on so well. I hope that she will graduate at the head of her class, with high honors."

"What's the use of giving her so much education? there are no openings for her here, and if she gets married she won't want it," and Mrs. Harcourt sighed as she finished her sentence.

Mr. Thomas looked grave for a moment and then his face relaxed into a smile. "Well, really, Mrs. Harcourt, that is not very complimentary to us young men; do we have no need of intelligent and well educated wives? I think our race needs educated mothers for the home more than we do trained teachers for the school room. Not that I would ignore or speak lightly of the value of good colored teachers nor suggest as a race, that we can well afford to do without them; but to-day, if it were left to my decision, whether the education of the race should be placed in the hands of the school teacher or the mothers and there was no other alternative, I should, by all means, decide for the education of the race through its motherhood rather than through its teachers."

"But we poor mothers had no chance. We could not teach our children."

"I think you could teach some of them more than they wish to learn; but I must go now; at some other time we will talk on this subject."

Chapter II

"Oh, Annette!" said Mrs. Harcourt, turning to her grand-daughter after Mr. Thomas had left the door; "What makes you so naughty? Why did you pour that oil on Mrs. Larkin's steps; didn't you know it was wrong?"

Annette stood silent looking like a guilty culprit.

"Why don't you answer me; what makes you behave so bad?"

"I don't know, grandma, I 'specs I did it for the devil. The preacher said the devil makes people do bad things."

"The preacher didn't say any such thing; he said the devil tempts people to be bad, but you are not to mind every thing the devil tells you to do, if you do, you will get yourself into a lot of trouble."

"Well, grandma, Mrs. Larkins is so mean and cross and she is always telling tales on me and I just did it for fun."

"Well, that is very poor fun. You deserve a good whipping, and I've a great mind to give it to you now."

"Why don't she let me alone; she is all the time trying to get you to beat me. She's a spiteful old thing anyhow. I don't like her, and I know she don't like me."

"Hush Annette, you must not talk that way of any one so much older than yourself. When I was a child I wouldn't have talked that way about any old person. Don't let me hear you talk that way again. You will never rest till I give you a good whipping."

"Yes ma'm," said Annette very demurely.

"Oh, Annette!" said her grandmother with a sudden burst of feeling. "You do give me so much trouble. You give me more worry than all my six children put together; but there is always one scabby sheep in the flock and you will be that one. Now get ready for school and don't let me hear any more complaints about you; I am not going to let you worry me to death."

Annette took up her bonnet and glided quietly out of the door, glad to receive instead of the threatened whipping a liberal amount of talk, and yet the words struck deeper than blows. Her own grandmother had prophesied evil things of her. She was to be the scabby sheep of the flock. The memory of the blows upon her body might have passed soon away after the pain and irritation of the infliction were over, but that inconsiderate prophecy struck deep into her heart and left its impress upon her unfolding life. Without intending it, Mrs. Harcourt had struck a blow at the child's self-respect; one of the things which she should have strengthened, even if it was "ready to die." Annette had entered life sadly handicapped. She was the deserted child of a selfish and un-principled man and a young mother whose giddiness and lack of self-control had caused her to trail the robes of her womanhood in the dust. With such an ante-natal history how much she needed judicious, but tender, loving guidance. In that restless, sensitive and impulsive child was the germ of a useful woman with a warm, loving heart, ready to respond to human suffering, capable of being faithful in friendship and devoted in love. Before that young life with its sad inheritance seemed to lay a future of trial, and how much, humanly speaking, seemed to depend upon the right training of that life and the development within her of self-control, self-reliance and self-respect. There was no mother's heart for her to nestle upon in her hours of discouragement and perplexity; no father's strong, loving arms to shelter and defend her; no sister to brighten her life with joyous companionship, and no brother to champion her through the early and impossible period of ripening womanhood. Her grandmother was kind to her, but not very tender and loving. Her struggle to keep the wolf from the door had absorbed her life, and although she was neither hard nor old, yet she was not demonstrative in her affections, and to her a restless child was an enigma she did not know how to solve. If the child were hungry or cold she could understand physical wants, but for the hunger of the heart she had neither sympathy nor comprehension. Fortunately Annette had found a friend who understood her better than her grandmother, and who, looking beneath the perverseness of the child, saw in her rich possibilities, and would often speak encouragingly to her. Annette early developed a love for literature and poetry and would sometimes try to make rhymes and string verses together and really Mrs. Lasette thought that she had talent or even poetic genius and ardently wished that it might be cultivated and rightly directed; but it never entered the minds of her grandmother and aunts that in their humble home was a rarely gifted soul destined to make music which would set young hearts to thrilling with higher hopes and loftier aspirations.

Mrs. Lasette had been her teacher before she married. After she became a wife and mother, instead of becoming entirely absorbed in a round of household cares and duties, the moment the crown of motherhood fell upon her, as she often said, she had poured a new interest into the welfare of her race.[1] With these feelings she soon became known as a friend and helper in the community in which she lived. Young girls learned to look to her for council and encouragement amid the different passages of their [lives?] sometimes with blushing cheeks they whispered in to her ears tender secrets they did not always bring to their near relatives, and young men about to choose their life work, often came to consult her and to all her heart was responsive. With this feeling of confidence in her judgment, Mr. Thomas had entered her home after leaving Mrs. Harcourt's, educating himself for a teacher. He had spent several years in the acquisition of knowledge and was proving himself an acceptable and conscientious teacher, when the change came which deprived him of his school, by blending his pupils in the different ward schools of the city. Public opinion which moves slowly, had advanced far enough to admit the colored children into the different schools, irrespective of color, but it was not prepared, except in a few places to admit the colored teachers as instructors in the schools. "What are you going to do next?" inquired Mrs. Lasette of Mr. Thomas as he seated himself somewhat wearily by the fire. "I hardly know, I am all at sea, but I am going to be like the runaway slave who, when asked, 'Where is your pass?' raised his fist and said 'Dem is my passes,' and if 'I don't see an opening I will make one.'"

"Why don't you go into the ministry? When Mr. Pugh failed in his examination he turned his attention to the ministry, and it is said that he is succeeding admirably."

"Mrs. Lasette, I was brought up to respect the institutions of religion, and not to lay rash hands on sacred things, and while I believe that every man should preach Christ by an upright life, and chaste conversation, yet I think one of the surest ways to injure a Church, and to make the pulpit lose its power over the rising generation, is for men without a true calling, or requisite qualifications to enter the ministry because they have failed in some other avocation and find in preaching an open door to success."

"But they often succeed."

"How?"

"Why by getting into good churches, increasing their congregations and paying off large church debts." "And is that necessarily success? We need in the Church men who can be more than financiers and who can attract large congregations. We need earnest thoughtful Christly men, who will be more anxious to create and develop moral earnestness than to excite transient emotions. Now there is Rev. Mr. Lamson who was educated in R. College. I have heard him preach to, as I thought, an honest, well meaning, but an ignorant congregation, and instead of lifting them to more rational forms of worship, he tried to imitate them and made a complete failure. He even tried to moan as they do in worship but it didn't come out natural."

"Of course it did not. These dear old people whose moaning during service, seems even now so pitiful and weird, I think learned to mourn out in prayers, thoughts and feelings wrung from their agonizing hearts, which they did not dare express when they were forced to have their meetings under the surveillance of a white man."

"It is because I consider the ministry the highest and most sacred calling, that I cannot, nay I dare not, rush into it unless I feel impelled by the strongest and holiest motives."

"You are right and I think just such men as you ought to be in the ministry."

"Are you calling me?" "I wish it were in my power." "I am glad that it is not, I think there are more in the ministry now than magnify their calling."

"But Mr. Thomas[2] are you not looking on the dark side of the question? you must judge of the sun, not by its spots, but by its brightness."

"Oh I did not mean to say that the ministry is crowded with unworthy men, who love the fleece more than the flock. I believe that there are in the ministry a large number who are the salt of the earth and whose life work bears witness to their fitness. But unfortunately there are men who seem so lacking in reverence for God, by their free handling of sacred things; now I think one of the great wants of our people is more reverence for God who is above us, and respect for the man who is beside us, and I do hope that our next minister will be a good man, of active brain, warm heart and Christly sympathies, who will be among us a living, moral, and spiritual force, and who will be willing to teach us on the Bible plan of 'line upon line, precept upon precept, here a little there a little.'"

"I hope he will be; it is said that brother Lomax our new minister is an excellent young man."

"Well I hope that we will not fail to receive him as an apostle and try to hold up his hands."

"I hope so. I think that to be called of God to be an ambassador for Christ, to help him build the kingdom of righteousness, love and peace, amid the misery, sin and strife, is the highest and most blessed position that a man can hold, and because I esteem the calling so highly I would not rush into it unless I felt divinely commissioned."

Chapter III

Mrs. Harcourt was a Southern woman by birth, who belonged to that class of colored people whose freedom consisted chiefly in not being the chattels of the dominant race—a class to whom little was given and from whom much was required. She was naturally bright and intelligent, but had come up in a day when the very book of the Christian's law was to her a sealed volume; but if she had not been educated through the aid of school books and blackboards, she had obtained that culture of manners and behavior which comes through contact with well-bred people, close observation and a sense of self-respect and self-reliance, and when deprived of her husband's help by an untimely death, she took up the burden of life bravely and always tried to keep up what she called "a stiff upper lip." Feeling the cramping of Southern life, she became restive under the privations and indignities which were heaped upon free persons of color, and at length she and her husband broke up their home and sold out at a pecuniary sacrifice to come North, where they could breathe free air and have educational privileges for their children. But while she was strong and healthy her husband, whose health was not very firm, soon succumbed to the change of climate and new modes of living and left Mrs. Harcourt a stranger and widow in a strange land with six children dependent on her for bread and shelter; but during her short sojourn in the North[3] she had enlisted the sympathy and respect of kind friends, who came to her relief and helped her to help herself, the very best assistance they could bestow upon her. Capable and efficient, she found no difficulty in getting work for herself and older children, who were able to add their quota to the support of the family by running errands, doing odd jobs for the neighbors and helping their mother between school hours. Nor did she lay all the household burdens on the shoulders of the girls and leave her boys to the mercy of the pavement; she tried to make her home happy and taught them all to have a share in adding to its sunshine. "It makes boys selfish," she would say, "to have their sisters do all the work and let the boys go scot-free. I don't believe there would be so many trifling men if the boys were trained to be more helpful at home and to feel more for their mothers and sisters." All this was very well for the peace and sunshine of that home, but as the children advanced in life the question came to her with painful emphasis—"What can I do for the future of my boys and girls?" She was not anxious to have them all professional men and school teachers and government clerks, but she wanted each one to have some trade or calling by which a respectable and comfortable living could be made; but first she consulted their tastes and inclinations. Her youngest boy was very fond of horses, but instead of keeping him in the city, where he was in danger of getting too intimate with horse jockeys and stable boys, she found a place for him with an excellent farmer, who, seeing the tastes of the boy, took great interest in teaching him how to raise stock and he became a skillful farmer. Her second son showed that he had some mechanical skill and ingenuity and she succeeded in getting him a situation with a first-class carpenter, and spared no pains to have him well instructed in all the branches of carpentry, and would often say to him, "John, don't do any sham work if you are going to be a carpenter; be thorough in every thing you do and try to be the best carpenter in A. P., and if you do your work better than others, you won't have to be all the time going around advertising yourself; somebody will find out what you can do and give you work." Her oldest son was passionately fond of books and she helped him through school till he was able to become a school teacher. But as the young man was high spirited and ambitious, he resolved that he would make his school teaching a stepping stone to a more congenial employment. He studied medicine and graduated with M.D., but as it takes a young doctor some time to gain the confidence of an old community, he continued after his graduation to teach and obtained a certificate to practice medicine. Without being forced to look to his mother for assistance, while the confidence of his community was slowly growing, he depended on the school for his living and looked to the future for his success as a physician.

For the girls, because they were colored, there were but few avenues open, but they all took in sewing and were excellent seamstresses, except Lucy, who had gone from home to teach school in a distant city as there were no openings of the kind for her at her own home.

Mrs. Harcourt was very proud of her children and had unbounded confidence in them. She was high-spirited and self-respecting and it never seemed to enter her mind that any evil might befall the children that would bring sorrow and shame to her home; but nevertheless it came and Lucy, her youngest child, the pet and pride of the household returned home with a great sorrow tugging at her heart and a shadow on her misguided life. It was the old story of woman's weakness and folly and man's perfidy and desertion. Poor child, how wretched she was till "peace bound up her bleeding heart," and even then the arrow had pierced too deep for healing. Sorrow had wasted her strength and laid the foundation of disease and an early death. Religion brought balm to the wounded spirit, but no renewed vigor to the wasted frame and in a short time she fell a victim to consumption, leaving Annette to the care of her mother. It was so pitiful to see the sorrow on the dear old face as she would nestle the wronged and disinherited child to her heart and would say so mournfully, "Oh, I never, never expected this!"

Although Annette had come into the family an unbidden and unwelcome guest, associated with the saddest experience of her grandmother's life, yet somehow the baby fingers had wound themselves around the tendrils of her heart and the child had found a shelter in the warm clasp of loving arms. To her, Annette was a new charge, an increased burden; but burden to be defended by her love and guarded by her care. All her other children had married and left her, and in her lowly home this young child with infantile sweetness, beguiled many a lonely hour. She loved Lucy and that was Lucy's child.

> But where was he who sullied
>   Her once unspotted name;
> Who lured her from life's brightness
>   To agony and shame?

Did society, which closed its doors against Lucy and left her to struggle as best she might out of the depth into which she had fallen, pour any righteous wrath upon his guilty head? Did it demand that he should at least bring forth some fruit meet for repentance by at least helping Mrs. Harcourt to raise the unfortunate child? Not so. He left that poor old grandmother to struggle with her failing strength, not only to bear her own burden, but the one he had so wickedly imposed upon her. He had left A. P. before Lucy's death and gone to the Pacific coast where he became wealthy through liquor selling, speculation, gambling and other disreputable means, and returned with gold enough to hide a multitude of sins, and then fair women permitted and even courted his society. Mothers with marriageable daughters condoned his offences against morality and said, "oh, well, young men will sow their wild oats; it is no use to be too straight laced." But there were a few thoughtful mothers old fashioned enough to believe that the law of purity is as binding upon the man as the woman, and who, under no conditions, would invite him to associate with their daughters. Women who tried to teach their sons to be worthy of the love and esteem of good women by being as chaste in their conversation and as pure in their lives as their young daughters who sat at their side sheltered in their pleasant and peaceful homes. One of the first things that Frank Miller did after he returned to A. P. was to open a large and elegantly furnished saloon and restaurant. The license to keep such a place was very high, and men said that to pay it he resorted to very questionable means, that his place was a resort for gamblers, and that he employed a young man to guard the entrance of his saloon from any sudden invasion of the police by giving a signal without if he saw any of them approaching, and other things were whispered of his saloon which showed it to be a far more dangerous place for the tempted, unwary and inexperienced feet of the young men of A. P., than any low groggery in the whole city. Young men who would have scorned to enter the lowest dens of vice, felt at home in his gilded palace of sin. Beautiful pictures adorned the walls, light streamed into the room through finely stained glass windows, women, not as God had made them, but as sin had debased them, came there to spend the evening in the mazy dance, or to sit with partners in sin and feast at luxurious tables. Politicians came there to concoct their plans for coming campaigns, to fix their slates and to devise means for grasping with eager hands the spoils of government. Young men anxious for places in the gift of the government found that winking at Frank Miller's vices and conforming to the demoralizing customs of his place were passports to political favors, and lacking moral stamina, hushed their consciences and became partakers of his sins.[4] Men talked in private of his vices, and drank his liquors and smoked his cigars in public. His place was a snare to their souls. "The dead were there but they knew it not." He built a beautiful home and furnished it magnificently, and some said that the woman who married him would do well, as if it were possible for any woman to marry well who linked her destinies to a wicked, selfish and base man, whose business was a constant menace to the peace, the purity and progress of society. I believe it was Milton who said that the purity of a man should be more splendid than the purity of a woman, basing his idea upon the declaration, "The head of the woman is the man, and the head of the man is Jesus Christ." Surely if man occupies this high rank in the creation of God he should ever be the true friend and helper of woman and not, as he too often proves, her falsest friend and basest enemy.

Chapter IV

"Annette," said Mrs. Harcourt one morning early, "I want you to stir your stumps to-day; I am going to have company this evening and I want you to help me to get everything in apple pie order."

"Who is coming, grandma?"

"Mr. Thomas and Mrs. Lasette."

"Mrs. Lasette!" Annette's eyes brightened. "I hope she will come; she is just as sweet as a peach and I do love her ever so much; and who else?"

"Brother Lomax, the minister who preached last Sunday and gave us such a good sermon."

"Is he coming, too?" Annette opened her eyes with pleased surprise. "Oh, I hope he will come, he's so nice."

"What do you know about him?"

"Why, grandmother, I understood everything that he said, and I felt that I wanted to be good just like he told us, and I went and asked aunt 'Liza how people got religion. She had been to camp-meeting and seen people getting religion, and I wanted her to tell me all about it for I wanted to get it too."

"What did she tell you?"

"She told me that people went down to the mourner's bench and prayed and then they would get up and shout and say they had religion, and that was all she knew about it."

"You went to the wrong one when you went to your aunt 'Liza. And what did you do after she told you?"

"Why, I went down in the garden and prayed and I got up and shouted, but I didn't get any religion. I guess I didn't try right."

"I guess you didn't if I judge by your actions. When you get older you will know more about it."

"But, grandma, Aunt 'Liza is older than I am, why don't she know?"

"Because she don't try; she's got her head too full of dress and dancing and nonsense."

Grandmother Harcourt did not have very much faith in what she called children's religion, and here was a human soul crying out in the darkness; but she did not understand the cry, nor look for the "perfecting of praise out of the mouths of babes and sucklings," not discerning the emotions of that young spirit, she let the opportunity slip for rightly impressing that young soul. She depended too much on the church and too little on the training of the home. For while the church can teach and the school instruct, the home is the place to train innocent and impressible childhood for useful citizenship on earth and a hope of holy companionship in heaven; and every Christian should strive to have "her one of the provinces of God's kingdom," where she can plant her strongest batteries against the ramparts of folly, sin and vice.

"Who else is coming, grandma?"

"Why, of course I must invite Mrs. Larkins; it would never do to leave her out."

Annette shrugged her shoulders, a scowl came over her face and she said:

"I hope she won't come."

"I expect she will and when she comes I want you to behave yourself and don't roll up your eyes at her and giggle at her and make ugly speeches. She told me that you made mouths at her yesterday, and that when Mr. Ross was whipping his horse you said you knew some one whom you wished was getting that beating, and she said that she just believed you meant her. How was that, Annette? If I were like you I would be all the time keeping this neighborhood in hot water."

Annette looked rather crestfallen and said, "I did make mouths at her house as I came by, but I didn't know that she saw me."

"Yes she did, and you had better mind how you cut your cards with her."

Annette finding the conversation was taking a rather disagreeable turn suddenly remembered that she had something to do in the yard and ceased to prolong the dialogue. If the truth must be confessed, Annette was not a very earnest candidate for saintship, and annoying her next door neighbor was one of her favorite amusements.

Grandma Harcourt lived in a secluded court, which was shut in on every side but one from the main streets, and her environments were not of the most pleasant and congenial kind. The neighbors, generally speaking, belonged to neither the best nor worst class of colored people. The court was too fully enclosed to be a thoroughfare of travel, but it was a place in which women could sit at their doors and talk to one another from each side of the court. Women who had no scruples about drinking as much beer, and sometimes stronger drinks, as they could absorb, and some of the men said that the women drank more than men, and under the besotting influence of beer and even stronger drinks, a fearful amount of gossiping, news-carrying and tattling went on, which often resulted in quarrels and contentions, which, while it never resulted in blood, sadly lowered the tone of social life. It was the arena of wordy strife in which angry tongues were the only weapons of warfare, and poor little Annette was fast learning their modes of battle. But there was one thing against which grandmother Harcourt set her face like flint, and that was sending children to saloons for beer, and once she flamed out with righteous indignation when one of her neighbors, in her absence, sent Annette to a saloon to buy her some beer. She told her in emphatic terms she must never do so again, that she wanted her girl to grow up a respectable woman, and that she ought to be ashamed of herself, not only to be guzzling beer like a toper, but to send anybody's child to a saloon to come in contact with the kind of men who frequented such places, and that any women who sent their children to such places were training their boys to be drunkards and their girls to be street-walkers. "I am poor," she said, "but I mean to keep my credit up and if you and I live in this neighborhood a hundred years you must never do that thing again."

Her neighbor looked dazed and tried to stammer out an apology, but she never sent Annette to a beer saloon again, and in course of time she became a good temperance woman herself, influenced by the faithfulness of grandmother Harcourt.

The court in which Mrs. Harcourt lived was not a very desirable place, but, on account of her color, eligible houses could not always be obtained, and however decent, quiet or respectable she might appear on applying for a house, she was often met with the rebuff, "We don't rent to colored people," and men who virtually assigned her race the lowest place and humblest positions could talk so glibly of the degradation of the Negro while by their Christless and inhuman prejudice they were helping add to their low social condition. In the midst of her unfavorable environments Mrs. Harcourt kept her home neat and tidy; sent Annette to school constantly and tried to keep her out of mischief, but there was moral contagion in the social atmosphere of Tennis Court and Annette too often succumbed to its influence; but Annette was young and liked the company of young girls and it seemed cruel to confine the child's whole life to the home and schoolhouse and give her no chance to be merry and playful with girls of her own age. So now and then grandmother Harcourt would let her spend a little time with some of the neighbors' girls but from the questions that Annette often asked her grandmother and the conversations she sometimes repeated Mrs. Harcourt feared that she was learning things which should only be taught by faithful mothers in hours of sacred and tender confidence, and she determined, even if it gave offence to her neighbors, that she would choose among her own friends, companions for her granddaughter and not leave all her social future to chance. In this she was heartily aided by Mrs. Lasette, who made it a point to hold in that neighborhood, mothers' meetings and try to teach mothers, who in the dark days of slavery had no bolts nor bars strong enough to keep out the invader from scattering their children like leaves in wintry weather, how to build up light and happy homes under the new dispensation of freedom. To her it was a labor of love and she found her reward in the peace and love which flowed into the soul and the improved condition of society. In lowly homes where she visited, her presence was a benediction and an inspiration. Women careless in their household and slatternly in their dress grew more careful in the keeping of their homes and the arrangement of their attire. Women of the better class of their own race, coming among them awakened their self-respect. Prejudice and pride of race had separated them from their white neighbors and the more cultured of their race had shrunk from them in their ignorance, poverty and low social condition and they were left, in a great measure, to themselves—ostracised by the whites on the one side and socially isolated from the more cultured of their race on the other hand. The law took little or no cognizance of them unless they were presented at its bar as criminals; but if they were neither criminals nor paupers they might fester in their vices and perpetuate their social condition. Who understood or cared to minister to their deepest needs or greatest wants? It was just here where the tender, thoughtful love of a warm-hearted and intelligent woman was needed. To her it was a labor of love, but it was not all fair sailing. She sometimes met with coldness and distrust where she had expected kindness and confidence; lack of sympathy where she had hoped to find ready and willing cooperation; but she knew that if her life was in harmony with God and Christly sympathy with man; for such a life there was no such word as fail.

Chapter V

By dint of energy and perseverance grandmother Harcourt had succeeded in getting everything in order when her guests began to arrive. She had just put the finishing touches upon her well-spread table and was reviewing it with an expression of pleasure and satisfaction. And now while the guests are quietly taking their seats let me introduce you to them.

Mr. Thomas came bringing with him the young minister, Rev. Mr. Lomax, whose sermon had so interested and edified Mrs. Harcourt the previous Sunday. Mrs. Lasette, looking bright and happy, came with her daughter, and Mrs. Larkins entered arrayed in her best attire, looking starched and prim, as if she had made it the great business of her life to take care of her dignity and to think about herself. Mrs. Larkins,[5] though for years a member of church, had not learned that it was unchristian to be narrow and selfish. She was strict in her attendance at church and gave freely to its support; but somehow with all her attention to the forms of religion, one missed its warm and vivifying influence from her life, and in the loving clasp of a helping hand, in the tender beam of a sympathizing glance, weary-hearted mothers and wives never came to her with their heartaches and confided to her their troubles. Little children either shrank from her or grew quiet in her presence. What was missing from her life was the magnetism of love. She had become so absorbed in herself that she forgot everybody else and thought more of her rights than her duties. The difference between Mrs. Lasette and Mrs. Larkins was this, that in passing through life one scattered sunshine and the other cast shadows over her path. Mrs. Lasette was a fine conversationalist. She regarded speech as one of heaven's best gifts, and thought that conversation should be made one of the finest arts, and used to subserve the highest and best purposes of life, and always regretted when it was permitted to degenerate into gossip and backbiting. Harsh judgment she always tried to modify, often saying in doubtful cases, "Had we not better suspend our judgments? Truly we do not like people to think the worst of us and it is not fulfilling the law of love to think the worst of them. Do you not know that if we wish to dwell in his tabernacle we are not to entertain a reproach against our neighbor, nor to back-bite with our lips and I do not think there is a sin which more easily besets society than this." "Speech," she would say, "is a gift so replete with rich and joyous possibilities," and she always tried to raise the tone of conversation at home and abroad. Of her it might be emphatically said, "She opened her mouth with wisdom and in her lips was the law of kindness."

The young minister, Rev. Mr. Lomax, was an earnest, devout and gifted young man. Born in the midst of poverty, with the shadows of slavery encircling his early life, he had pushed his way upward in the world, "toiling while others slept." His father was dead. While living he had done what he could to improve the condition of his family, and had, it was thought, overworked himself in the struggle to educate and support his children. He was a kind and indulgent father and when his son had made excellent progress in his studies, he gave him two presents so dear to his boyish heart—a gun and a watch. But the hour came when the loving hands were closed over the quiet breast, and the widowed wife found herself unable to provide the respectable funeral she desired to give him. Thomas then came bravely and tenderly to her relief. He sold his watch and gun to defray the funeral expenses of his father. He was a good son to his aged mother, and became the staff of her declining years. With an earnest purpose in his soul, and feeling that knowledge is power, he applied himself with diligence to his studies, passed through college, and feeling within his soul a commission to teach and help others to develop within themselves the love of nature, he entered the ministry, bringing into it an enthusiasm for humanity and love of Christ, which lit up his life and made him a moral and spiritual force in the community. He had several advantageous offers to labor in other parts of the country, but for the sake of being true to the heavenly vision, which showed him the needs of his people and his adaptation to their wants, he chose, not the most lucrative, but the most needed work which was offered him with

> A joy to find in every station,
> Something still to do or bear.

He had seen many things in the life of the people with whom he was identified which gave him intense pain, but instead of constantly censuring and finding fault with their inconsistencies of conscience, he strove to live so blamelessly before them that he would show them by example a more excellent way and "criticise by creation." To him religion was a reasonable service and he wished it to influence their conduct as well as sway their emotions. Believing that right thinking is connected with right living, he taught them to be conservative without being bigoted, and liberal without being morally indifferent and careless in their modes of thought. He wanted them to be able to give a reason for the faith that was in them and that faith to be rooted and grounded in love. He was young, hopeful, and enthusiastic and life was opening before him full of hope and promise.

"It has been a beautiful day," said Mrs. Lasette, seating herself beside Mrs. Larkins,[6] who always waited to be approached and was ever ready to think that some one was slighting her or ignoring her presence.

"It has been a fine day, but I think it will rain soon; I judge by my corn."

"Oh! I think the weather is just perfect. The sun set gloriously this evening and the sky was the brightest blue."

"I think the day was what I call a weather breeder. Whenever you see such days this time of year, you may look out for falling weather. I [expect?] that it will snow soon."

"How that child grows," said Mrs. Larkins, as Annette entered the room.

"Ill weeds grow apace; she has nothing else to do. That girl is going to give her grandmother a great deal of trouble."

"Oh! I do not think so."

"Well, I do, and I told her grandmother so one day, but she did not thank me for it."

"No, I suppose not."

"I didn't do it for thanks; I did it just to give her a piece of my mind about that girl. She is the most mischievous and worrisome child I ever saw. The partition between our houses is very thin and many a time when I want to finish my morning sleep or take an afternoon nap, if Mrs. Harcourt is not at home, Annette will sing and recite at the top of her voice and run up and down the stairs as if a regiment of soldiers were after her."

"Annette is quite young, full of life and brimful of mischief, and girls of that age I have heard likened to persimmons before they are ripe; if you attempt to eat them they will pucker your mouth, but if you wait till the first frost touches them they are delicious. Have patience with the child, act kindly towards her, she may be slow in developing womanly sense, but I think that Annette has within her the making of a fine woman."

"Do you know what Annette wants?"

"Yes, I know what she wants; but what do you think she wants?"

"She wants kissing."

"I'd kiss her with a switch if she were mine."

"I do not think it wise to whip a child of her age."

"I'd whip her if she were as big as a house."

"I do not find it necessary with my Laura; it is sufficient to deter her from doing anything if she knows that I do not approve of it. I have tried to establish perfect confidence between us. I do not think my daughter keeps a secret from me. I think many young persons go astray because their parents have failed to strengthen their characters and to forewarn and forearm them against the temptations and dangers that surround their paths. How goes the battle?" said Mrs. Lasette, turning to Mr. Thomas.

"I am still at sea, and the tide has not yet turned in my favor. Of course, I feel the change; it has taken my life out of its accustomed channel, but I am optimist enough to hope that even this change will result in greater good to the greatest number. I think one of our great wants is the diversification of our industries, and I do not believe it would be wise for the parents to relax their endeavors to give their children the best education in their power. We cannot tell what a race can do till it utters and expresses itself, and I know that there is an amount of brain among us which can and should be utilized in other directions than teaching school or seeking for clerkships. Mr. Clarkson had a very intelligent daughter whom he wished to fit for some other employment than that of a school teacher. He had her trained for a physician. She went to B., studied faithfully, graduated at the head of her class and received the highest medal for her attainments, thus proving herself a living argument of the capability in her race. Her friend, Miss Young, had artistic talent, and learned wood carving. She developed exquisite taste and has become a fine artist in that branch of industry. A female school teacher's work in the public schools is apt to be limited to her single life, but a woman who becomes proficient in a useful trade or business, builds up for herself a wall of defense against the invasions of want and privation whether she is married or single. I think that every woman, and man too, should be prepared for the reverses of fortune by being taught how to do some one thing thoroughly so as to be able to be a worker in the world's service, and not a pensioner upon its bounty. And for this end it does not become us as a race to despise any honest labor which lifts us above pauperism and dependence. I am pleased to see our people having industrial fairs. I believe in giving due honor to all honest labor, in covering idleness with shame, and crowning labor with respect."

Chapter VI

For awhile Mrs. Harcourt was busy in preparing the supper, to which they all did ample justice. In her white apron, faultless neck handkerchief and nicely fitting, but plain dress, Mrs. Harcourt looked the impersonation of contented happiness. Sorrow had left deep furrows upon her kindly face, but for awhile the shadows seemed to have been lifted from her life and she was the pleasant hostess, forgetting her own sorrows in contributing to the enjoyment of others. Supper being over, her guests resumed their conversation.

"You do not look upon the mixing of the schools as being necessarily disadvantageous to our people," said the minister.

"That," said Mr. Thomas, "is just in accordance to the way we adapt ourselves to the change. If we are to remain in this country as a component part of the nation, I cannot fail to regard with interest any step which tends toward our unification with all the other branches of the human race in this Western Hemisphere."

"Although," said Mrs. Lasette, "I have been educating my daughter and have felt very sorry when I have witnessed the disappointment of parents who have fitted their children for teachers and have seen door after door closed against them, I cannot help regarding the mixing of the schools as at least one step in a right direction."

"But Mrs. Lasette," said the minister, "as we are educated by other means than school books and blackboards, such as the stimulus of hope, the incentives of self-respect and the consensus of public opinion, will it not add to the depression of the race if our children are made to feel that, however well educated they may be or exemplary as pupils, the color of their skin must debar them from entering avenues which are freely opened to the young girls of every other nationality."

Mr. Thomas replied, "In considering this question, which is so much broader than a mere local question, I have tried to look beyond the life of the individual to the life of the race, and I find that it is through obstacles overcome, suffering endured and the tests of trial that strength is obtained, courage manifested and character developed. We are now passing through a crucial period in our race history and what we so much need is moral earnestness, strength of character and purpose to guide us through the rocks and shoals on which so many life barques have been stranded and wrecked."

"Yes," said Mrs. Lasette, "I believe that we are capable of being more than light-hearted children of the tropics and I want our young people to gain more persistence in their characters, perseverance in their efforts and that esprit de corps, which shall animate us with higher, nobler and holier purpose in the future than we have ever known in the past; and while I am sorry for the parents who, for their children's sake, have fought against the entailed ignorance of the ages with such humble weapons as the washboard, flat iron and scrubbing brush, and who have gathered the crumbs from the humblest departments of labor, still I feel with Mr. Thomas that the mixing of the schools is a stride in the march of the nation, only we must learn how to keep step in the progress of the centuries."

"I do not think that I fully comprehend you," Mr. Lomax replied.

"Let me explain. I live in the 19th Ward. In that Ward are not a half dozen colored children. When my husband bought the land we were more than a mile from the business part of the city, but we were poor and the land was very cheap and my husband said that paying rent was like putting money in a sinking fund; so he resolved, even if it put us to a little disadvantage, that he would buy the tract of land where we now live. Before he did so, he called together a number of his acquaintances, pointed out to them the tract of land and told them how they might join with him in planting a small hamlet for themselves; but except the few colored neighbors we now have, no one else would join with us. Some said it was too far from their work, others that they did not wish to live among many colored people, and some suspected my husband of trying either to take the advantage of them, or of agrandising himself at their expense, and I have now dear friends who might have been living comfortably in their own homes, who, to-day, are crowded in tenement houses or renting in narrow alleys and little streets."

"That's true," said Mrs. Larkins, "I am one of them. I wanted my husband to take up with your husband's offer, but he was one of those men who knew it all and he never seemed to think it possible that any colored man could see any clearer than he did. I knew your husband's head was level and I tried to persuade Mr. Larkins to take up with his offer, but he would not hear to it; said he knew his own business best, and shut me up by telling me that he was not going to let any woman rule over him; and here I am to-day, Larkins gone and his poor old widow scuffing night and day to keep soul and body together; but there are some men you couldn't beat anything into their heads, not if you took a sledge hammer. Poor fellow, he is gone now and I ought not to say anything agin him, but if he had minded me, I would have had a home over my head and some land under my feet; but it is no use to grieve over spilled milk. When he was living if I said, yes, he was always sure to say, no. One day I said to him when he was opposing me, the way we live is like the old saying, 'Pull Dick and pull devil,' and what do you think he said?"

"I don't know, I'm sure, what was it?"

"Why, he just looked at me and smiled and said, 'I am Dick.' Of course he meant that I was the other fellow."

"But," said Mrs. Lasette, "this is a digression from our subject.

What I meant to say is this, that in our Ward is an excellent school house with a half score of well equipped and efficient teachers. The former colored school house was a dingy looking building about a mile and a half away with only one young school teacher, who had, it is true, passed a creditable examination. Now, when my daughter saw that the children of all other nationalities, it mattered not how low and debasing might be their environments, could enter the school for which her father paid taxes, and that she was forced either to stay at home or to go through all weathers to an ungraded school, in a poorly ventilated and unevenly heated room, would not such public inequality burn into her soul the idea of race-inferiority? And this is why I look upon the mixed school as a right step in the right direction."

"Taking this view of the matter I see the pertinence of your position on this subject. Do you know," continued Mr. Lomax,[7] his face lighting up with a fine enthusiasm, "that I am full of hope for the future of our people?"

"That's more than I am," said Mrs. Larkins very coldly. "When you have summered and wintered them as I have, you will change your tune."

"Oh, I hope not," he replied with an accent of distress in his voice. "You may think me a dreamer and enthusiast, but with all our faults I firmly believe that the Negro belongs to one of the best branches of the human race, and that he has a high and holy mission in the great drama of life. I do not think our God is a purposeless Being, but his ways are not as our ways are, and his thoughts are not our thoughts, and I dare not say 'Had I his wisdom or he my love,' the condition of humanity would be better. I prefer thinking that in the crucible of pain and apparent disaster, that we are held by the hand of a loving Father who is doing for us all, the best he can to fit us for companionship with him in the eternities, and with John G. Whittier, I feel:

> Amid the maddening maze of things
> When tossed by storm and flood,
> To one fixed stake my spirit clings
> I know that God is good.

"I once questioned and doubted, but now I have learned to love and trust in 'Him whom the heavens must receive till the time of the restitution of all things.' By this trust I do not mean a lazy leaning on Providence to do for us what we have ability to do for ourselves. I think that our people need more to be taught how to live than to be constantly warned to get ready to die. As Brother Thomas said, we are now passing through a crucial period of our history and what we need is life—more abundant life in every fibre of our souls; life which will manifest itself in moral earnestness, vigor of purpose, strength of character and spiritual progression."

"I do hope," said Mr. Thomas, "that as you are among us, you will impart some of your earnestness and enthusiasm to our young people."

"As I am a new comer here, and it is said that the people of A. P., are very sensitive to criticism, though very critical themselves and rather set and conservative in their ways, I hope that I shall have the benefit of your experience in aiding me to do all I can to help the people among whom my lot is cast."

"You are perfectly welcome to any aid I can give you. Just now some of us are interested in getting our people out of these wretched alleys and crowded tenement houses into the larger, freer air of the country. We want our young men to help us fight the battle against poverty, ignorance, degradation, and the cold, proud scorn of society. Before our public lands are all appropriated, I want our young men and women to get homesteads, and to be willing to endure privations in order to place our means of subsistence on a less precarious basis. The land is a basis of power, and like Anteus in the myth, we will never have our full measure of material strength till we touch the earth as owners of the soil. And when we get the land we must have patience and perseverance enough to hold it."

"In one of our Western States is a city which suggests the idea of Aladdin's wonderful lamp. Where that city now stands was once the homestead of a colored man who came from Virginia and obtained it under the homestead law. That man has since been working as a servant for a man who lives on 80 acres of his former section, and who has plotted the rest for the city of C."

"How did he lose it?"

"When he came from the South the country was new and female labor in great demand. His wife could earn $1.50 a day, and instead of moving on his land, he remained about forty miles away, till he had forfeited his claim, and it fell into the hands of the present proprietor. Since then our foresight has been developing and some months since in travelling in that same State, I met a woman whose husband had taken up a piece of land and was bringing it under cultivation. She and her children remained in town where they could all get work, and transmit him help and in a few years, I expect, they will be comfortably situated in a home owned by their united efforts."

Chapter VII

What next? was the question Mr. Thomas was revolving in his mind, when a knock was heard at his door, and he saw standing on the threshold, one of his former pupils.

"Well, Charley, how does the world use you? Everything going on swimmingly?"

"Oh, no indeed. I have lost my situation."

"How is that? You were getting on so well. Mr. Hazleton

seemed to be perfectly satisfied with you, and I thought that you were quite a favorite in the establishment. How was it that you lost your place?"

"I lost it through the meanness of Mr. Mahler."

"Mr. Mahler, our Superintendent of public schools?"

"Yes, it was through him that I lost my situation."

"Why, what could you have done to offend him?"

"Nothing at all; I never had an unpleasant word with him in my life."

"Do explain yourself. I cannot see why he should have used any influence to deprive you of your situation."

"He had it in his power to do me a mean, low-life trick, and he did it, and I hope to see the day when I will be even with him," said the lad, with a flashing eye, while an angry flush mantled his cheek.

"Do any of the family deal at Mr. Hazleton's store? Perhaps you gave some of them offence through neglect or thoughtlessness in dealing with them."

"It was nothing of the kind. Mr. Mahler knew me and my mother. He knew her because she taught under him, and of course saw me often enough to know that I was her son, and so last week when he saw me in the store, I noticed that he looked very closely at me, and that in a few moments after he was in conversation with Mr. Hazleton. He asked him, 'if he employed a nigger for a cashier?' He replied, 'Of course not.' 'Well,' he said, 'you have one now.' After that they came down to the desk where I was casting up my accounts and Mr. Mahler asked, 'Is Mrs. Cooper your mother?' I answered, 'yes sir.' Of course I would not deny my mother. 'Isn't your name Charley?'[8] and again I answered, yes; I could have resorted to concealment, but I would not lie for a piece of bread, and yet for mother's sake I sorely needed the place.

"What did Mr. Hazleton say?"

"Nothing, only I thought he looked at me a little embarrassed, just as any half-decent man might when he was about to do a mean and cruel thing. But that afternoon I lost my place. Mr. Hazleton said to me when the store was about to close, that he had no further use for me. Not discouraged, I found another place; but I believe that my evil genius found me out and that through him I was again ousted from that situation and now I am at my wits end."

"But, Charley, were you not sailing under false colors?"

"I do not think so, Mr. Thompson. I saw in the window an advertisement, 'A boy wanted.' They did not say what color the boy must be and I applied for the situation and did my work as faithfully as I knew how. Mr. Hazleton seemed to be perfectly satisfied with my work and as he did not seek to know the antecedents of my family I did not see fit to thrust them gratuitously upon him. You know the hard struggle my poor mother has had to get along, how the saloon has cursed and darkened our home and I was glad to get anything to do by which I could honestly earn a dollar and help her keep the wolf from the door, and I tried to do my level best, but it made no difference; as soon as it was known that I had Negro blood in my veins door after door was closed against me; not that I was not honest, industrious, obliging and steady, but simply because of the blood in my veins."

"I admit," said Mr. Thomas, trying to repress his indignation and speak calmly, "that it was a hard thing to be treated so for a cause over which you had not the least control, but, Charley, you must try to pick up courage."

"Oh, it seems to me that my courage has all oozed out. I think that I will go away; maybe I can find work somewhere else. Had I been a convict from a prison there are Christian women here who would have been glad to have reached me out a helping hand and hailed my return to a life of honest industry as a blessed crowning of their labors of love; while I, who am neither a pauper nor felon, am turned from place after place because I belong to a race on whom christendom bestowed the curse of slavery and under whose shadow has flourished Christless and inhuman caste prejudice. So I think that I had better go and start life afresh."

"No, Charley, don't go away. I know you could pass as a white man; but, Charley, don't you know that to do so you must separate from your kindred and virtually ignore your mother? A mother, who, for your sake, would, I believe, take blood from every vein and strength from every nerve if it were necessary. If you pass into the white basis your mother can never be a guest in your home without betraying your origin; you cannot visit her openly and crown her with the respect she so well deserves without divulging the secret of your birth; and Charley, by doing so I do not think it possible that however rich or strong or influential you may be as a white man, that you can be as noble and as true a man as you will be if you stand in your lot without compromise or concealment, and feel that the feebler your mother's race is the closer you will cling to it. Charley, you have lately joined the church; your mission in the world is not to seek to be rich and strong, but because there is so much sin and misery in the world by it is to clasp the hand of Christ through faith and try to make the world better by your influence and gladder and brighter by your presence."

"Mr. Thomas I try to be, and I hope I am a Christian, but if these prejudices are consistent with Christianity then I must confess that I do not understand it, and if it is I do not want it. Are these people Christians who open the doors of charitable institutions to sinners who are white and close them against the same class who are black? I do not call such people good patriots, let alone clear-sighted Christians. Why, they act as if God had done wrong in making a man black, and that they have never forgiven him and had become reconciled to the workmanship of his hands."

"Charley, you are excited just now, and I think that you are making the same mistake that better educated men than you have done. You are putting Christianity and its abuses together. I do think, notwithstanding all its perversions, and all the rubbish which has gathered around its simplicity and beauty, that Christianity is the world's best religion. I know that Christ has been wounded in what should have been the house of his friends; that the banner of his religion which is broad enough to float over the wide world with all its sin and misery, has been drenched with the blood of persecution, trampled in the mire of slavery and stained by the dust of caste proscription; but I believe that men are beginning more fully to comprehend the claims of the gospel of Jesus Christ. I am not afraid of what men call infidelity. I hold the faith which I profess, to be too true, too sacred and precious to be disturbed by every wave of wind and doubt. Amid all the religious upheavals of the Nineteenth Century, I believe God is at the helm, that there are petrifactions of creed and dogma that are to [be] broken up, not by mere intellectual speculations, but by the greater solvent of the constraining love of Christ, and it is for this that I am praying, longing and waiting. Let schoolmen dispute and contend, the faith for which I most ardently long and earnestly contend, is a faith which works by love and purifies the soul."

"Mr. Thomas, I believe that there is something real about your religion, but some of these white Christians do puzzle me awfully. Oh, I think that I will go. I am sick and tired of the place. Everything seems to be against me."

"No, Charley; stay for your mother's sake. I know a noble and generous man who is brave enough to face a vitiated public opinion, and rich enough to afford himself the luxury of a good conscience. I shall tell him your story and try to interest him in your behalf. Will you stay?"

"I certainly will if he will give me any chance to get my living and help my mother."

"It has been said that everything has two handles, and if you take it by the wrong handle it will be too hard to hold."

"I should like to know which is the right handle to this prejudice against color."

"I do not think that there is prejudice against color in this country."

"No prejudice against color!" said Charley Cooper,[9] opening his eyes with sudden wonder. "What was it that dogged my steps and shut door after door against me? Wasn't that prejudice against color?"

"Whose color, Charley? Surely not yours, for you are whiter than several of Mr. Hazleton's clerks. Do you see in your case it was not prejudice against color?"

"What was it, then?"

"It was the information that you were connected by blood with a once enslaved and despised people on whom society had placed its ban, and to whom slavery and a low social condition had given a heritage of scorn, and as soon as he found out that you were connected with that race, he had neither the manliness nor the moral courage to say, the boy is capable and efficient. I see no cause why he should be dismissed for the crimes of his white ancestors. I heard an eminent speaker once say that some people would sing, 'I can smile at Satan's rage, and face a frowning world,' when they hadn't courage enough to face their next door neighbor on a moral question."

"I think that must be the case with Mr. Hazleton."

"I once used to despise such men. I have since learned to pity them."

"I don't see what you find to pity in Mr. Hazleton, unless it is his meanness."

"Well, I pity him for that. I think there never was slave more cowed under the whip of his master than he is under the lash of public opinion. The Negro was not the only one whom slavery subdued to the pliancy of submission. Men fettered the slave and cramped their own souls, denied him knowledge and then darkened their own spiritual insight, and the Negro, poor and despised as he was, laid his hands upon American civilization and has helped to mould its character. It is God's law. As ye sow, so shall ye reap, and men cannot sow avarice and oppression without reaping the harvest of retribution. It is a dangerous thing to gather

> The flowers of sin that blossom
> Around the borders of hell.

Chapter VIII

"I never want to go to that school again," said Annette entering Mrs. Lasette's sitting room, throwing down her books on the table and looking as if she were ready to burst into tears.

"What is the matter now, my dear child? You seem to be all out of sorts."

"I've had a fuss with that Mary Joseph."

"Mary Joseph, the saloon-keeper's daughter?"

"Yes."

"How did it happen?"

"Yesterday in changing seats, the teacher put us together according to the first letter in our last names. You know that I, comes next to J; but there wasn't a girl in the room whose name begins with I, and so as J comes next, she put Mary Joseph and myself together."

"Ireland and Africa, and they were not ready for annexation?"

"No, and never will be, I hope."

"Never is a long day, Annette, but go on with your story."

"Well, after the teacher put her in the seat next to me she began to wriggle and squirm and I asked her if anything was biting her, because if there was, I did not want it to get on me."

"Oh, Annette, what a girl you are; why did you notice her? What did she say?"

"She said if there was, it must have got there since the teacher put her on that seat, and it must have come from me."

"Well, Mary Joseph knows how to scratch as well as you do."

"Yes, she is a real scratch cat."

"And what are you, my dear; a pattern saint?"

"No," said Annette, as the ruefulness of her face relaxed into a smile, "but that isn't all; when I went to eat my lunch, she said she wasn't used to eating with niggers. Then I asked her if her mother didn't eat with the pigs in the old country, and she said that she would rather eat with them than to eat with me, and then she called me a nigger and I called her a poor white mick."

"Oh, Annette, I am so sorry; I am afraid that trouble may come out of this fuss, and then it is so wrong and unlady-like for you to be quarrelling that way. Do you know how old you are?"

"I am almost fourteen years old."

"Where was the teacher all this time? Did she know anything about it?"

"No; she was out of the room part of the time, but I don't think she likes colored people, because last week when Joe Smith was cutting up in school, she made him get up and sit alongside of me to punish him."

"She should not have done so, but I don't suppose she thought for one moment how it looked."

"I don't know, but when I told grandma about it, Mrs. Larkins was in the room, and she said if she had done a child of hers so, she would have gone there and sauced her head off; but grandma said that she would not notice it; that the easiest way is the best."

"I think that your grandmother was right; but what did Joe say?"

He said that the teacher didn't spite him; that he would as lieve sit by me as any girl in school, and that he liked girls."

"A little scamp."

"He says he likes girls because they are so jolly."

"But tell me all about Mary Joseph."

"Well, a mean old thing, she went and told her horrid old father, and just as I was coming along he took hold of my arm and said he had heard that I had called his daughter, Miss Mary Joseph, a poor white mick and that if I did it again he would give me a good thrashing, and that for two pins he would do it then."

"What next?"

"I guess I felt like Mrs. Larkins does when she says her Guinea gets up. My Guinea was up but I was afraid to show it. Oh, but I do hate these Irish. I don't like them for anything. Grandmother says that an Irishman is only a negro turned wrong side out, and I told her so yesterday morning when she was fussing with me."

"Say, rather, when we were fussing together; I don't think the fault was all on her side."

"But, Mrs. Lasette, she had no business calling me a nigger."

"Of course not; but would you have liked it [any] better if she had called you a negro?"

"No; I don't want her to call me anything of the kind, neither negro nor nigger. She shan't even call me black."

"But, Annette, are you not black?"

"I don't care if I am, she shan't call me so."

"But suppose you were to say to Miss Joseph, 'How white your face is,' do you suppose she would get angry because you said that she looked white?"

"No, of course not."

"But suppose you met her hurrying to school, and you said to her, how red and rosy you look this morning, would that make her angry?"

"I don't suppose that it would."

"But suppose she would say to you, 'Annette, how black your face is this morning,' how would you feel?"

"I should feel like slapping her."

"Why so; do you think because Miss Joseph—"

"Don't call her Miss, she is so mean and hateful."

"But that don't hinder her from being Miss Joseph; If she is rude and coarse, that is no reason why I should not have good manners."

"Oh, Mrs. Lasette you are too sweet for anything. I wish I was like you."

"Never mind my sweetness; that is not to the point. Will you listen to me, my dear?"

"Of course I will. I could listen to you all night."

"Well, if it were not for signs there's no mistaking I should think you had a lot of Irish blood in your veins, and had kissed the blarney stone."

"No I haven't and if I had I would try to let—"

"Hush, my child; how you do rattle on. Do you think because Miss Joseph is white that she is any better than you are."

"No, of course not."

"But don't you think that she can see and hear a little better than you can?"

"Why, no; what makes you ask such a funny question?"

"Never mind, just answer me a few more questions. Don't you think if you and she had got to fighting that she would have whipped you because she is white?"

"Why, of course not. Didn't she try to get the ruler out of my hand and didn't because I was stronger."

"But don't you think she is smarter than you are and gets her lessons better."

"Now you are shouting."

"Why, Annette, where in the world did you get that slang?"

"Why, Mrs. Lasette, I hear the boys saying it in the street, and the girls in Tennis Court all say it, too. Is there any harm in it?"

"It is slang, my child, and a young lady should never use slang. Don't use it in private and you will not be apt to use it in public. However humble or poor a person may be, there is no use in being coarse and unrefined."

"But what harm is there in it?"

"I don't say that there is any, but I don't think it nice for young ladies to pick up all sorts of phrases in the street and bring them into the home. The words may be innocent in themselves, but they may not have the best associations, and it is safer not to use them. But let us return to Miss Joseph. You do not think that she can see or hear any better than you can, learn her lessons any quicker than you can, and when it comes to a trial of strength that she is stronger than you are, now let me ask you one more question. Who made Miss Joseph?"

"Why, the Lord, of course."

"And who made you?"

"He made me, too."

"Are you sure that you did not make yourself?"

"Why, of course not," said Annette with an accent of wonder in her voice.

"Does God ever make any mistakes?"

"Why, no!"

"Then if any one calls you black, why should you get angry? You say it would not make Miss Joseph angry to say she looked white, or red and rosy."

"I don't know; I know I don't like it and it makes me mad."

"Now, let me explain the reason why it makes you angry to be called black. Suppose I were to burn my hand in that stove, what would I have on my hand?"

"A sore place."

"If it were your hand, what would you do?"

"I would put something on it, wrap it up to keep from getting cold into it and try to get it well as soon as I could."

"Well, that would be a very sensible way of dealing with it. In this country, Annette, color has been made a sore place; it has been associated with slavery, poverty and ignorance. You cannot change your color, but you can try to change the association connected with our complexions. Did slavery force a man to be servile and submissive? Learn to hold up your head and respect yourself. Don't notice Mary Joseph's taunts; if she says things to tease you don't you let her see that she has succeeded. Learn to act as if you realized that you were born into this world the child of the Ruler of the universe, that this is his world and that you have as much right in it as she has. I think it was Gilbert Haven, a Bishop of the Methodist Episcopal Church, a man for whose tombstone I do not think America has any marble too white or any laurel too green, who saw on his travels a statue of Cleopatra, which suggested to him this thought, 'I am black, but comely, the sun has looked down upon me, but I will make you who despise me feel that I am your superior,' and, Annette, I want you to be so noble, true and pure that if everybody should hate you, that no one could despise you. No, Annette, if Miss Joseph ever attempts to quarrel with you don't put yourself on the same level by quarreling with her. I knew her parents when they were very poor; when a half dozen of them slept in one room. He has made money by selling liquor; he is now doing business in one of the most valuable pieces of property I see in East L street. He has been a curse, and his saloon a nuisance in that street. He has gone up in property and even political influence, but oh, how many poor souls have gone down, slain by strong drink and debauchery."

Chapter IX

True to his word, Mr. Thomas applied to Mr. Hastings, the merchant, of whom he had spoken to his young friend. He went to his counting-room and asked for a private interview, which was readily granted. They had kindred intellectual and literary tastes and this established between them a free masonry of mind which took no account of racial differences.

"I have a favor to ask," said Mr. Thomas, "can you spare me a few moments?"

"I am at your service," Mr. Hasting replied, "what can I do for you?"

"I have," he said, "a young friend who is honest and industrious and competent to fill the place of clerk or cashier in your store. He has been a cashier for Hazleton & Co., and while there gave entire satisfaction."

"Why did he leave?"

"I cannot say, because he was guilty of a skin not colored like your own, but because a report was brought to Mr. Hazleton that he had Negro blood in his veins."

"And what then?"

"He summarily dismissed him."

"What a shame!"

"Yes, it was a shame, but this pride of caste dwarfs men's moral perception so that it prepares them to do a number of contemptible things which, under other circumstances, they would scorn to do."

"Yes, it is so, and I am sorry to see it."

"There are men, Mr. Hastings, who would grow hotly indignant if you would say that they are not gentlemen who would treat a Negro in a manner which would not be recognized as fair, even by ruffians of the ring, for, I believe, it is their code of honor not to strike a man when he is down; but with respect to the colored man, it seems to be a settled policy with some not only to push him down, but to strike him when he is down. But I must go; I came to ask a favor and it is not right to trespass on your time."

"No; sit still. I have a little leisure I can give you. My fall trade has not opened yet and I am not busy. I see and deplore these things of which you complain, but what can be done to help it?"

"Mr. Hastings, you see them, and I feel them, and I fear that I am growing morbid over them, and not only myself, but other educated men of my race, and that, I think, is a thing to be depre-cated. Between the white people and the colored people of this country there is a unanimity of interest and I know that our in-terests and duties all lie in one direction. Can men corrupt and in-timidate voters in the South without a reflex influence being felt in the North? Is not the depression of labor in the South a matter of interest to the North? You may protect yourself from what you call the pauper of Europe, but you will not be equally able to de-fend yourself from the depressed laborer of the new South, and as an American citizen, I dread any turn of the screw which will lower the rate of wages here; and I like to feel as an American cit-izen that whatever concerns the nation concerns me. But I feel that this prejudice against my race compresses my soul, narrows my po-litical horizon and makes me feel that I am an alien in the land of my birth. It meets me in the church, it confronts me in business and I feel its influence in almost every avenue of my life."

"I wish, Mr. Thomas, that some of the men who are writing and talking about the Negro problem would only come in contact with the thoughtful men of your race. I think it would greatly modify their views."

"Yes, you know us as your servants. The law takes cognizance of our crimes. Your charitable institutions of our poverty, but what do any of you know of our best and most thoughtful men and women? When we write how many of you ever read our books and papers or give yourselves any trouble to come near us as friends and help us? Even some of your professed Christians are trying to set us apart as if we were social lepers."

"You draw a dark picture. I confess that I feel pained at the con-dition of affairs in the South, but what can we do in the South?"

"Set the South a better example. But I am hindering you in your business."

"Not at all. I want to see things from the same standpoint that you do."

"Put yourself then in my place. You start both North and South from the premise that we are an inferior race and as such you have treated us. Has not the consensus of public opinion said for ages, 'No valor redeems our race, no social advancement nor individual development wipes off the ban which clings to us'; that our place is on the lowest round of the social ladder; that at least, in part of the country we are too low for the equal administrations of religion and the same dispensations of charity and a fair chance in the race of life?"

"You bring a heavy verdict against us. I hardly think that it can be sustained. Whatever our motives may have been, we have been able to effect in a few years a wonderful change in the condition of the Negro. He has freedom and enfranchisement and with these two great rights he must work out his social redemption and political solution. If his means of eduction have been limited, a better day is dawning upon him. Doors once closed against him in the South are now freely opened to him, and I do not think that there ever was a people who freed their slaves who have given as much for their education as we have, and my only hope is that the moral life of the race will keep pace with its intellectual growth. You tell me to put myself in your place. I think if I were a colored young man that I would develop every faculty and use every power which God had given me for the improvement and development of my race. And who among us would be so blind and foolish as to attempt to keep down an enlightened people who were determined to rise in the scale of character and condition? No, Mr. Thomas, while you blame us for our transgressions and shortcomings, do not fail to do all you can to rouse up all the latent energies of your young men to do their part worthily as American citizens and to add their quota to the strength and progress of the nation."

"I am conscious of the truth and pertinence of your remarks, but bear with me just a few moments while I give an illustration of what I mean."

"Speak on, I am all attention. The subject you bring before me is of too vital importance to be constantly ignored."

"I have a friend who is presiding elder in the A. M. E. Church and his wife, I think, is capable of being a social and intellectual accession in any neighborhood in which they might live. He rented a house in the city of L. and being of a fair complexion I suppose the lessee rented to him without having a suspicion of his race connection. When it was ascertained that he and his family were colored, he was ordered to leave, and this man, holding among the ministers of that city the position of ambassador for Christ, was ordered out of the house on account of the complexion of his family. Was there not a screw loose in the religious sentiment of that city which made such an act possible? A friend of mine who does mission work in your city, some time since, found a young woman in the slums and applied at the door of a midnight mission for fallen women, and asked if colored girls could be received, and was curtly answered, 'no.' For her in that mission there was no room. The love of Christ constrained no hand to strive to rescue her from the depths of degradation. The poor thing went from bad to worse till at last, wrecked and blighted, she went down to an early grave the victim of strong drink. That same lady found on her mission a white girl; seeing a human soul adrift, regardless of color, she went, in company with some others, to that same mission with the poor castaway; to her the door was opened without delay and ready admittance granted. But I might go on reciting such instances until you would be weary of hearing and I of relating them; but I appeal to you as a patriot and Christian, is it not fearfully unwise to keep alive in freedom the old animosities of slavery? To-day the Negro shares citizenship with you. He is not arraying himself against your social order; his hands are not dripping with dynamite, nor is he waving in your face the crimson banners of anarchy, but he is increasing in numbers and growing in intelligence, and is it not madness and folly to subject him to social and public inequalities, which are calculated to form and keep alive a hatred of race as a reaction against pride of caste?"

"Mr. Thomas, you have given me a new view of the matter. To tell you the truth, we have so long looked upon the colored man as a pliable and submissive being that we have never learned to look at any hatred on his part as an element of danger, and yet I should be sorry to know that by our Southern supineness we were thoughtlessly helping create a black Ireland in our Gulf States, that in case the fires of anarchy should ever sweep through our land, that a discontented and disaffected people in our midst might be as so much fuel to fire."

"But really I have been forgetting my errand. Have you any opening in your store for my young friend?"

"I have only one vacancy, and that is the place of a utility man."

"What are the duties of that position?"

"Almost anything that comes to hand; tying up bundles, looking after the mails, scattering advertisements. A factotum whose work lies here, there and everywhere."

"I am confident that he will accept the situation and render you faithful service."

"Well, then send him around tomorrow and if there is anything in him I may be able to do better by him when the fall trade opens."

And so Charley Cooper was fortunate enough in his hour of perplexity to find a helping hand to tide him over a difficult passage in his life. Gratefully and faithfully did he serve Mr. Hastings, who never regretted the hour when he gave the struggling boy such timely assistance. The discipline of the life through which he was passing as the main stay of his mother, matured his mind and imparted to it a thoughtfulness past his years. Instead of wasting his time in idle and pernicious pleasure, he learned how to use his surplus dollar and how to spend his leisure hours, and this knowledge told upon his life and character. He was not very popular in society. Young men with cigars in their mouths and the perfume of liquor on their breaths, shrugged their shoulders and called him a milksop because he preferred the church and Sunday school to the liquor saloon and gambling dens. The society of P. was cut up and divided into little sets and coteries; there was an amount of intelligence among them, but it ran in narrow grooves and scarcely one[10] intellect seemed to tower above the other, and if it did, no people knew better how to ignore a rising mind than the society people of A. P. If the literary aspirant did not happen to be of their set. As to talent, many of them were pleasant and brilliant conversationalists, but in the world of letters scarcely any of them were known or recognized outside of their set. They had leisure, a little money and some ability, but they lacked the perseverance and self-denial necessary to enable them to add to the great resources of natural thought. They had narrowed their minds to the dimensions of their set and were unprepared to take expansive[11] views of life and duty. They took life as a holiday and the lack of noble purposes and high and holy aims left its impress upon their souls and deprived them of that joy and strength which should have crowned their existence and given to their lives its "highest excellence and beauty."

Chapter X

Two years have elapsed since we left Annette recounting her school grievances to Mrs. Lasette. She has begun to feel the social contempt which society has heaped upon the colored people, but she has determined not to succumb to it. There is force in the character of that fiery, impetuous and impulsive girl, and her school experience is bringing it out. She has been bending all her mental energies to compete for the highest prize at the commencement of her school, from which she expects to graduate in a few weeks. The treatment of the saloon-keeper's daughter, and that of other girls of her ilk, has stung her into strength. She feels that however despised her people may be, that a monopoly of brains has not been given to the white race. Mr. Thomas has encouraged her efforts, and taught her to believe that not only is her own honor at stake as a student, but that as a representative of her branch of the human race, she is on the eve of winning, or losing, not only for herself, but for others. This view of the matter increases her determination and rouses up all the latent energies of her nature, and she labors day and night to be a living argument of the capability in her race. For other girls who will graduate in that school, there will be open doors, and unclosed avenues, while she knows that the color of her skin will bar against her the doors of workshops, factories and school rooms, and yet Mr. Thomas, knowing all the discouragements around her path, has done what he could to keep her interest in her studies from flagging. He knows that she has fine abilities, but that they must be disciplined by trial and endeavor before her life can be rounded by success and triumph. He has seen several of her early attempts at versification; pleased and even delighted with them, he has shown them to a few of his most intellectual friends. Eager and earnest for the elevation of the colored people, he has been pained at the coldness with which they have been received.

"I do not call that poetry," said one of the most intelligent women of A. P.

"Neither do I see anything remarkable about her," said another.

"I did not," said Mr. Thomas, "bring you the effusions of an acknowledged poet, but I think that the girl has fine ability, which needs encouragement and recognition."

But his friends could not see it; they were very charry of their admiration, lest their judgment should be found at fault, and then it was so much easier to criticise than it was to heartily admire; and they knew it seemed safer to show their superior intelligence by dwelling on the defects, which would necessarily have an amount of crudeness in them than to look beneath the defects for the suggestions of beauty, strength and grace which Mr. Thomas saw in these unripe, but promising effusions. It seemed perfectly absurd with the surroundings of Tennis Court to expect anything grand or beautiful [to] develop in its midst; but with Annette, poetry was a passion born in her soul, and it was as natural for her to speak in tropes and figures as it was for others to talk in plain, common prose. Mr. Thomas called her "our inveterate poet," and encouraged her, but the literary aspirants took scarcely any interest in the girl whom they left to struggle on as best she might. In her own home she was doomed to meet with lack of encouragement and appreciation from her relatives and grandmother's friends. One day her aunt, Eliza Hanson, was spending the day with her mother, and Annette showed her some of her verses and said to her, "that is one of my best pieces."

"Oh, you have a number of best pieces," said her aunt, carelessly. "Can you cook a beefsteak?"

"I suppose I could if I tried."

"Well, you had better try than to be trying to string verses together. You seem to think that there must be something very great about you. I know where you want to get. You want to get among the upper tens, but you haven't got style enough about you for that."

"That's just what I tell her," said her grandmother. "She's got too many airs for a girl in her condition. She talks about writing a book, and she is always trying to make up what she calls poetry. I expect that she will go crazy some of these days. She is all the time talking to herself, and I just think it is a sin for her to be so much taken up with her poetry."

"You had better put her to work; had she not better go out to service?"

"No, I am going to let her graduate first."

"What's the use of it? When she's through, if she wants to teach, she will have to go away."

"Yes, I know that, but Mrs. Lasette has persuaded me to let Annette graduate, and I have promised that I would do so, and besides I think to take Annette from school just now would almost break her heart."

"Well, mother, that is just like you; you will work yourself almost to death to keep Annette in school, and when she is through what good will it do her?"

"Maybe something will turn up that you don't see just now. When a good thing turns up if a person ain't ready for it they can't take hold of it."

"Well, I hope a good husband will turn up for my Alice."

"But maybe the good husband won't turn up for Annette."

"That is well said, for they tell me that Annette is not very popular, and that some of the girls are all the time making fun of her."

"Well, they had better make fun of themselves and their own bad manners. Annette is poor and has no father to stand by her, and I cannot entertain like some of their parents can, but Annette, with all her faults, is as good as any of them. Talk about the prejudice of the white people, I think there is just as much prejudice among some colored as there is among them, only we do not get the same chance to show it; we are most too mixed up and dependent on one another for that." Just then Mrs. Lasette entered the room and Mrs. Hanson, addressing her, said, "We were just discussing Annette's prospects. Mother wants to keep Annette at school till she graduates, but I think she knows enough now to teach a country school and it is no use for mother to be working as she does to keep Annette in school for the sake of letting her graduate. There are lots of girls in A. P. better off than she who have never graduated, and I don't see that mother can afford to keep Annette at school any longer."

"But, Eliza, Annette is company for me and she does help about the house."

"I don't think much of her help; always when I come home she has a book stuck under her nose."

"Annette," said Mrs. Lasette, "is a favorite of mine; I have always a warm place in my heart for her, and I really want to see the child do well. In my judgment I do not think it advisable to take her from school before she graduates. If Annette were indifferent about her lessons and showed no aptitude for improvement I should say as she does not appreciate education enough to study diligently and has not aspiration enough to keep up with her class, find out what she is best fitted for and let her be instructed in that calling for which she is best adapted."

"I think," said Mrs. Hanson, "you all do wrong in puffing up Annette with the idea that she is something extra. You think, Mrs. Lasette, that there is something wonderful about Annette, but I can't see it, and I hear a lot of people say she hasn't got good sense."

"They do not understand the child."

"They all say that she is very odd and queer and often goes out into the street as if she never saw a looking glass. Why, Mrs. Miller's daughter just laughed till she was tired at the way Annette was dressed when she went to call on an acquaintance of hers. Why, Annette just makes herself a perfect laughing stock."

"Well, I think Mary Miller might have found better employment than laughing at her company."

"Now, let me tell you, Mary Miller don't take her for company, and that very evening Annette was at my house, just next door, and when Mary Miller went to church she never asked her to go along with her, although she belongs to the same church."

"I am sorry to say it," said grandmother Harcourt, "but your Alice hardly ever comes to see Annette, and never asks her to go anywhere with her, but may be in the long run Annette will come out better than some who now look down upon her. It is a long road that has no turn and Annette is like a singed cat; she is better than she looks."

"I think," said Mrs. Lasette, "while Annette is very bright and intelligent as a pupil, she has been rather slow in developing in some other directions. She lacks tact, is straightforward to bluntness and has not any style about her and little or no idea of company manners, but she is never coarse nor rude. I never knew her to read a book whose author I would blush to name, and I never heard her engage in any conversation I would shrink to hear repeated. I don't think there is a girl of purer lips in A. P. than Annette, and I do not think your set, as you call it, has such a monopoly of either virtue or intelligence that you can afford to ridicule and depress any young soul who does not happen to come up to your social standard. Where dress and style are passports Annette may be excluded, but where brain and character count Annette will gain admittance. I fear," said Mrs. Lasette, rising to go, "that many a young girl has gone down in the very depths who might have been saved if motherly women, when they saw them unloved and lonely, had reached out to them a helping hand and encouraged them to live useful and good lives. We cry am I my sister's keeper? [I?] will not wipe the blood off our hands if through pride and selfishness we have stabbed by our neglect souls we should have helped by our kindness. I always feel for young girls who are lonely and neglected in large cities and are in danger of being ensnared by pretended sympathies and false friendship, and, to-day, no girl is more welcome at any social gathering than Annette."

"Mrs. Lasette," said Mrs. Hanson, "you are rich and you can do as you choose in A. P. You can set the fashion."

"No; I am not rich, but I hope that I will always be able to lend a hand to any lonely girl who is neglected, slighted and forgotten while she is trying to do right, who comes within my reach while I live in A. P. Good morning."

"Annette," said Mrs. Hanson,[12] "has a champion who will stand by her."

"Yes," said Mrs. Harcourt,[13] "Anna is true as steel; the kind of woman you can tie to. When my great trouble came, she was good as gold, and when my poor heart was almost breaking, she always had a kind word for me. I wish we had ten thousand like her."

"Well, mother, I must go, but if Annette does graduate don't let her go on the stage looking like a fright. General H's daughter has a beautiful new silk dress and a lovely hat which she got just a few weeks before her mother's death; as she has gone in black she wants to sell it, and if you say so, and will pay for it on installments, I can get if for Annette, and I think with a little alteration it would be splendid for her graduation dress."

"No; Eliza, I can't afford it."

"Why, mother, Annette will need something nice for the occasion, and it will not cost any more than what you intend to pay for her dress and hat. Why not take them?"

"Because Annette is not able to wear them. Suppose she had that one fine dress and hat, would she not want more to match with them? I don't want her to learn to dress in a style that she cannot honestly afford. I think this love of dress is the ruination of many a young girl. I think this straining after fine things when you are not able to get them, is perfectly ridiculous. I believe in cutting your coat according to your cloth. I saw Mrs. Hempstead's daughter last Sunday dressed up in a handsome light silk, and a beautiful spring hat, and if she or her mother would get sick to-morrow, they would, I suppose, soon be objects of public charity or dependent on her widowed sister, who is too proud to see her go to the poor house; and this is just the trouble with a lot of people; they not only have their own burdens to bear but somebody else's. You may call me an old fogy, but I would rather live cheap and dress plain than shirk my burdens because I had wasted when they had saved. You and John Hanson are both young and have got your health and strength, and instead of buying sealskins, and velvets and furbelows, you had better be laying up for a rainy day. You have no more need for a sealskin cloak than a cat has for a catechism. Now you do as you please, I have had my say."

Chapter XI

It has been quite a length of time since we left Mr. Thomas and his young friend facing an uncertain future. Since then he has not only been successful in building up a good business for himself, but in opening the gates to others. His success has not inflated him with pride. Neither has he become self-abashed and isolated from others less fortunate, who need his counsel and sympathy. Generous and noble in his character, he was conservative enough to cling to the good of the past and radical enough to give hospitality to every new idea which was calculated to benefit and make life noble and better. Mr. Thomas, in laying the foundation of his education, was thoughtful enough to enter a manual labor school, where he had the double advantage of getting an education and learning a trade, through which he was enabled to rely on himself without asking aid from any one, which in itself was an education in manliness, self-respect and self-reliance, that he could not have obtained had he been the protege of the wealthiest philanthropist in the land. As he had fine mechanical skill and ingenuity, he became an excellent carpenter. But it is one thing to have a trade and another thing to have an opportunity to exercise that trade. It was a time when a number of colored churches were being erected. To build large and even magnificent churches seemed to be a ruling passion with the colored people. Their homes might be very humble, their walls bare of pictured grace, but by united efforts they could erect large and handsome churches in which they had a common possession and it was one of the grand satisfactions of freedom that they were enabled to build their own churches and carry on their own business without being interfered with, and overlooked by a class of white ecclesiastics whose presence was a reminder of their implied inferiority. The church of which Mr. Thomas was a member was about to erect a costly edifice. The trustees would probably have willingly put the work in the hands of a colored man, had there been a sufficient number to have done the work, but they did not seem to remember that white prejudice had barred the Northern workshops against the colored man, that slavery, by degrading and monopolizing labor had been the means of educating colored men in the South to be good mechanics, and that a little pains and search on their part might have brought to light colored carpenters in the South who would have done the work as efficiently as those whom they employed, but as the trustees were not very farsighted men, they did the most available thing that came to hand; they employed a white man. Mr. Thomas' pastor applied to the master builder for a place for his parishioner.

"Can you give employment to one of my members, on our church?" Rev. Mr. Lomax asked the master builder.

"I would willingly do so, but I can not."

"Why not?"

"Because my men would all rise up against it. Now, for my part, I have no prejudice against your parishioner, but my men will not work with a colored man. I would let them all go if I could get enough colored men to suit me just as well, but such is the condition of the labor market, that a man must either submit to a number of unpalatable things or run the risk of a strike and being boycotted. I think some of these men who want so much liberty for themselves have very little idea of it for other people."

After this conversation the minister told Mr. Thomas the result of his interview with the master builder, and said,

"I am very sorry; but it is as it is, and it can't be any better."

"Do you mean by that that things are always going to remain as they are?"

"I do not see any quick way out of it. This prejudice is the outgrowth of ages; it did not come in a day, nor do I expect that it will vanish in an hour."

"Nor do I; but I do not think the best way for a people to mend their pastures is to sit down and bewail their fate."

"No; we must be up and going for ourselves. White people will—"

"White people," exclaimed Mr. Thomas somewhat impatiently. "Is there not a great deal of bosh in the estimate some of us have formed of white people. We share a common human feeling, from which the same cause produces the same effect. Why am I today a social Pariah, begging for work, and refused situation after situation? My father is a wealthy Southerner; he has several other sons who are inheritors of his name and heirs of his wealth. They are educated, cultured and occupy high social positions. Had I not as good a right to be well born as any of them? And yet, through my father's crime, I was doomed to the status of a slave with its heritage of ignorance, poverty and social debasement. Talk of the heathenism of Africa, of hostile tribes warring upon each other and selling the conquered foes into the hands of white men, but how much higher in the scale of moral progression was the white man who doomed his own child, bone of his bone, and flesh of his flesh, to a life of slavery? The heathen could plead in his defence the fortunes of war, and the hostility of an opposing tribe, but the white man who enslaved his child warred upon his hapless offspring and wrote chattel upon his condition when his hand was too feeble to hurl aside the accursed hand and recognize no other ownership but God. I once felt bitterly on this subject, and although it is impossible for my father to make full reparation for the personal wrong inflicted on me, I owe him no grudge. Hating is poor employment for any rational being, but I am not prepared to glorify him at the expense of my mother's race. She was faithful to me when he deserted me to a life of ignorance and poverty, and although three-fourths of the blood in my veins belongs to my father's face, I feel a kinship with my mother's people that I do not with his, and I will defend that race from the aspersions of the meanest Negro hater in the land. Heathenism and civilization live side by side on American soil, but all the heathenism is not on the side of the Negro. Look at slavery and kukluxism with their meanness and crimes, mormonism with its vile abominations, lynch law with its burnings and hangings, our national policy in regard to the Indians and Chinese."

"I do not think," said the minister, "that there is another civilized country in the world where men are lynched for real or supposed crimes outside of America."

"The Negro need not bow his head like a bulrush in the presence of a race whose records are as stained by crime and dishonor as theirs. Let others decry the Negro, and say hard things about him, I am not prepared to join in the chorus of depreciation."

After parting with the minister, Mr. Thomas resolved, if pluck and energy were of any avail, that he would leave no stone unturned in seeking employment. He searched the papers carefully for advertisements, walked from one workshop to the other looking for work, and was eventually met with a refusal which meant, no negro need apply. At last one day when he had tried almost every workshop in the place, he entered the establishment of Wm. C. Nell, an Englishman who had not been long enough in America to be fully saturated by its Christless and inhuman prejudices. He was willing to give Mr. Thomas work, and put tools in his hands, and while watching how deftly he handled them, he did not notice the indignant scowls on the faces of his workmen, and their murmurs of disapprobation as they uttered their dissatisfaction one to the other. At length they took off their aprons, laid down their tools and asked to be discharged from work.

"Why, what does this mean?" asked the astounded Englishman.

"It means that we will not work with a nigger."

"Why, I don't understand? what is the matter with him?"

"Why, there's nothing the matter, only he's a nigger, and we never put niggers on an equality with us, and we never will."

"But I am a stranger in this country, and I don't understand you."

"Well, he's a nigger, and we don't want niggers for nothing; would you have your daughter marry a nigger?"

"Oh, go back to your work; I never thought of such a thing. I think the Negro must be an unfortunate man, and I do not wish my daughter to marry any unfortunate man, but if you do not want to work with him I will put him by himself; there is room enough on the premises; will that suit you any better?"

"No; we won't work for a man who employs a nigger."

The builder bit his lip; he had come to America hearing that it was a land of liberty but he had found an undreamed of tyranny which had entered his workshop and controlled his choice of workmen, and as much as he deprecated the injustice, it was the dictum of a vitiated public opinion that his field of occupation should be closed against the Negro, and he felt that he was forced, either to give up his business or submit to the decree.

Mr. Thomas then thought, "my money is vanishing, school rooms and workshops are closed against me. I will not beg, and I can not resort to any questionable means for bread. I will now take any position or do any work by which I can make an honest living." Just as he was looking gloomily at the future an old school mate laid his hand upon his shoulder and said, "how do you do, old fellow? I have not seen you for a week of Sundays. What are you driving at now?"

"Oh, nothing in particular. I am looking for work."

"Well, now this is just the ticket. I have just returned from the Pacific coast and while I was there I did splendidly; everything I touched turned to gold, and now I have a good job on hand if you are not too squeamish to take it. I have just set up a tiptop restaurant and saloon, and I have some of the best merchants of the city as my customers, and I want a first rate clerk. You were always good at figures and if you will accept the place come with me right away. Since high license went into operation, I am making money hand over fist. It is just like the big fish eating up the little fish. I am doing a rushing business and I want you to do my clerking."

The first thought which rushed into Mr. Thomas' mind was, "Is thy servant a dog that he should do this thing?" but he restrained his indignation and said,

"No, Frank, I cannot accept your offer; I am a temperance man and a prohibitionist, and I would rather have my hands clean than to have them foul."

"You are a greater milksop than I gave you credit for. Here you are hunting work, and find door after door closed against you, not because you are not but because you are colored, and here am I offering you easy employment and good wages and you refuse them."

"Frank," said Mr. Thomas, "I am a poor man, but I would rather rise up early, and sit up late and eat the bread of carelessness, than to roll in wealth by keeping a liquor saloon, and I am determined that no drunkard shall ever charge me with having helped drag him down to misery, shame and death. No drunkard's wife shall ever lay the wreck of her home at my door."

"My business," said Frank Miller, "is a legitimate one; there is money in it, and I am after that. If people will drink too much and make fools of themselves I can't help it; it is none of my business, and if I don't sell to them other people will. I don't think much of a man who does not know how to govern himself, but it is no use arguing with you when you are once set in your ways; good morning."

Chapter XII

It was a gala day in Tennis Court. Annette had passed a highly successful examination, and was to graduate from the normal school, and as a matter of course, her neighbors wanted to hear Annette "speak her piece" as they called the commencement theme, and also to see how she was going to behave before all "them people." They were, generally speaking, too unaspiring to feel envious toward any one of their race who excelled them intellectually, and so there was little or no jealousy of Annette in Tennis Court; in fact some of her neighbors felt a kind of pride in the thought that Tennis Court would turn out a girl who could stand on the same platform and graduate alongside of some of their employers' daughters. If they could not stand there themselves they were proud that one of their race could.

"I feel," said one, "like the boy when some one threatened to slap off his face who said 'you can slap off my face, but I have a big brother and you can't slap off his face;'" and strange as it may appear, Annette received more encouragement from a class of honest-hearted but ignorant and well meaning people who knew her, than she did from some of the most cultured and intelligent people of A. P. Nor was it very strange; they were living too near the poverty, ignorance and social debasement of the past to have developed much race pride, and a glowing enthusiasm in its progress and development. Although they were of African descent, they were Americans whose thoughts were too much Americanized to be wholly free from imbibing the social atmosphere with which they were in constant contact in their sphere of enjoyments. The literature they read was mostly from the hands of white men who would paint them in any colors which suited their prejudices or predilections. The religious ideas they had embraced came at first thought from the same sources, though they may have undergone modifications in passing through their channels of thought, and it must be a remarkable man or woman who thinks an age ahead of the generation in which his or her lot is cast, and who plans and works for the future on the basis of that clearer vision. Nor is it to be wondered at, if under the circumstances, some of the more cultured of A. P. thought it absurd to look for anything remarkable to come out of the black Nazareth of Tennis court. Her neighbors had an idea that Annette was very smart; that she had a great "head piece," but unless she left A. P. to teach school elsewhere, they did not see what good her education was going to do her. It wasn't going to put any meal in the barrel nor any potatoes in the bin. Even Mrs. Larkins relaxed her ancient hostility to Annette and opened her heart to present her with a basket of flowers. Annette within the last year had become very much changed in her conduct and character. She had become friendly in her manner and considerate in her behavior to Mrs. Larkins since she had entered the church, during a protracted meeting. Annette was rather crude in her religious views but here again Mrs. Lasette became her faithful friend and advisor. In dealing with a young convert she thought more was needed than getting her into the church and making her feel that the moment she rose from the altar with rejoicing on her lips, that she was a full blown christian. That, to Mrs. Lasette was the initial step in the narrow way left luminous by the bleeding feet of Christ, and what the young convert needed was to be taught how to walk worthy of her high calling, and to make her life a thing of usefulness and faithfulness to God and man, a growth in grace and in the saving knowledge of our Lord Jesus Christ. Simply attired in a dress which Mrs. Lasette thought fitted for the occasion, Annette took her seat quietly on the platform and calmly waited till her turn came. Her subject was announced: "The Mission of the Negro." It was a remarkable production for a girl of her age. At first she portrayed an African family seated beneath their bamboo huts and spreading palms; the light steps of the young men and maidens tripping to music, dance and song; their pastimes suddenly broken upon by the tramp of the merchants of flesh and blood; the capture of defenceless people suddenly surprised in the midst of their sports, the cries of distress, the crackling of flames, the cruel oaths of reckless men, eager for gold though they coined it from tears and extracted it from blood; the crowding of the slaveships, the horrors of the middle passage, the landing of the ill-fated captives were vividly related, and the sad story of ages of bondage. It seemed as if the sorrow of centuries was sobbing in her voice. Then the scene changed, and like a grand triumphal march she recounted the deliverance of the Negro, and the wondrous change which had come over his condition; the slave pen exchanged for the free school, the fetters on his wrist for the ballot in his right hand. Then her voice grew musical when she began to speak of the mission of the Negro, "His mission," she said, "is grandly constructive." Some races had been "architects of destruction," but their mission was to build over the ruins of the dead past, the most valuable thing that a man or woman could possess on earth, and that is good character. That mission should be to bless and not to curse. To lift up the banner of the Christian religion from the mire and dust into which slavery and pride of caste had trailed it, and to hold it up as an ensign of hope and deliverance to other races of the world, of whom the greater portion were not white people. It seemed as if an inspiration lit up the young face; her eye glowed with unwonted fervor; it seemed as if she had fused her whole soul into the subject, which was full of earnestness and enthusiasm. Her theme was the sensation of the hour. Men grew thoughtful and attentive, women tender and sympathetic as they heard this member of a once despised people, recount the trials and triumphs of her race, and the hopes that gathered around their future. The day before Annette graduated Mr. Thomas had met a friend of his at Mrs. Lasette's, who had lately returned from an extensive tour. He had mingled with many people and had acquired a large store of information. Mr. Thomas had invited him to accompany him to the commencement. He had expected that Annette would acquit herself creditably, but she had far exceeded his most sanguine expectations. Clarence Luzerne had come because his friend Mr. Thomas had invited him and because he and Mrs. Lasette had taken such great interest in Annette's welfare, and his curiosity was excited to see how she would acquit herself and compare with the other graduates. He did not have much faith in graduating essays. He had heard a number of such compositions at commencements which had inspired him with glowing hopes for the future of the authors, which he had never seen realized, and he had come more to gratify Mr. Thomas than to please himself. But if he came through curiosity, he remained through interest, which had become more and more absorbing as she proceeded.

"Clarence," said Mr. Thomas to his friend, noticing the deep interest he was manifesting, "Are you entranced? You appear perfectly spell-bound."

"Well, I am; I am really delighted and indebted to you for a rare and unexpected pleasure. Why, that young lady gave the finest production that I have heard this morning. I hardly think she could have written it herself. It seems wonderful that a girl of her age should have done it so well. You are a great friend of hers; now own up, are not your finger marks upon it? I wouldn't tell it out of our ranks, but I don't think she wrote that all herself."

"Who do you think wrote it for her?"

"Mrs. Lasette."

"I do not think so; Mrs. Lasette is a fine writer, but that nervous, fervid and impassioned style is so unlike hers, that I do not think she wrote one line of it, though she might have overlooked it, and made some suggestions, but even if it were so that some one else wrote it, we know that no one else delivered it, and that her delivery was excellent."

"That is so; why, she excelled all the other girls. Do you know what was the difference between her and the other girls?"

No; what was it?" said Mr. Thomas.

"They wrote from their heads, she wrote from her heart. Annette has begun to think; she has been left a great deal to herself, and in her loneliness, she has developed a thoughtfulness past her years, and I think that a love for her race and a desire to serve it has become a growing passion in her soul; her heart has supplied her intellect."

"Ah, I think from what you say that I get the true clue to the power and pathos with which she spoke this morning and that accounts for her wonderful success."

"Yes," said Mr. Luzerne,[14] "it is the inner life which develops the outer life, and just such young people as Annette make me more hopeful of the future of the race."

Mrs. Lasette witnessed Annette's graduation with intense interest and pleasure. Grandmother Harcourt looked the very impersonation of satisfaction as she gathered up the floral gifts, and modestly waited while Annette received the pleasant compliments of admiring friends.

At his request Mr. Thomas introduced Mr. Luzerne to Annette, who in the most gracious and affable manner, tendered to Annette his hearty congratulations which she modestly received, and for the time being all went merry as a marriage bell.

Chapter XIII

"What a fool he is to refuse my offer," thought the saloon-keeper. "What a pity it is," said Mr. Thomas to himself, "that a man of his education and ability should be engaged in such accursed business."

After refusing the saloonkeeper's offer Mr. Thomas found a job of work. It was not a job congenial to his feelings, but his motto was, "If I do not see an opening I will make one." After he had turned from Mr. Englishman's workshop, burning with a sense of wrong which he felt powerless to overcome, he went on the levee and looked around to see if any work might be picked up by him as a day laborer. He saw a number of men singing, joking and plying their tasks with nimble feet and apparently no other care upon their minds than meeting the demands of the present hour, and for a moment he almost envied their lightheartedness, and he thought within himself, where all men are born blind, no man misses the light. These men are contented with privileges, and I who have fitted myself for a different sphere in life, am chaffing because I am denied rights. The right to sell my labor in any workshop in this city same as the men of other nationalities, and to receive with them a fair day's wages for a fair day's work. But he was strong and healthy and he was too high spirited to sit moping at home depending upon his mother to divide with him her scanty means till something should turn up. The first thing that presented itself to him was the job of helping unload a boat which had landed at the wharf, and a hand was needed to assist in unloading her. Mr. Thomas accepted the position and went to work and labored manfully at the unaccustomed task. That being finished the merchant for whom he had done the work, hired him to labor in his warehouse. He showed himself very handy in making slight repairs when needed and being ready to turn his hand to any service out of his routine of work, hammering a nail, adjusting a disordered lock and showing a general concern in his employer's interests. One day his employer had engaged a carpenter to make him a counter, but the man instead of attending to his work had been off on a drunken spree, and neglected to do the job. The merchant, vexed at the unnecessary delay, said to Mr. Thomas in a bantering manner, "I believe you can do almost anything, couldn't you make this counter?"

Mr. Thomas answered quite modestly, "I believe I could if I had my tools."

"Tools! What do you mean by tools?"

Mr. Thomas told him how he learned to be a carpenter in the South and how he had tried so unsuccessfully in the North to get an opportunity to work at his trade until discouraged with the attempt, he had made up his mind to take whatever work came to hand till he could see farther.

The merchant immediately procured the materials and set Mr. Thomas to work, who in a short time finished the counter, and showed by his workmanship that he was an excellent carpenter. The merchant pleased with his work and satisfied with his ability, entrusted him with the erection of a warehouse and, strange as it may appear, some of those men who were too proud or foolish to work with him as a fellow laborer, were humble enough to work under him as journeymen. When he was down they were ready to kick him down. When he was up they were ready to receive his helping hand. Mr. Thomas soon reached that "tide in his affairs which taken at the flood leads on to fortune." Against the odds which were against him his pluck and perseverance prevailed, and he was enabled not only to build up a good business for himself, but also to help others, and to teach them by his own experience not to be too easily discouraged, but to trust to pluck more than luck, and learn in whatever capacity they were employed to do their work heartily as unto the Lord and not unto men.

Anxious to do what she could to benefit the community in which she lived, Mrs. Lasette threw open her parlors for the gathering together of the best thinkers and workers of the race, who choose to avail themselves of the privilege of meeting to discuss any question of vital importance to the welfare of the colored people of the nation. Knowing the entail of ignorance which slavery had left them, she could not be content by shutting up herself to mere social enjoyments within the shadow of her home. And often the words would seem to ring within her soul, "my people is destroyed for lack of knowledge," and with those words would come the question, am I doing what I can to dispel the darkness which has hung for centuries around our path? I have been blessed with privileges which were denied others; I sat 'mid the light of knowledge when some of my ill-fated sisters did not know what it was to see daylight in their cabins from one week's end to the other. Sometimes when she met with coldness and indifference where she least expected it, she would grow sad but would not yield to discouragement. Her heart was in the right place. "Freely she had received and freely she would give." It was at one of Mrs. Lasette's gatherings that Mr. Thomas met Rev. Mr. Lomax on whose church he had been refused a place, and Mr. Thurman, a tradesman who also had been ousted from his position through pride of caste and who had gone into another avocation, and also Charley Cooper, of whom we have lost sight for a number of years. He is now a steady and prosperous young man, a constant visitor at Mrs. Lasette's. Rumor says that Mrs. Lasette's bright-eyed and lovely daughter is the magnet which attracts him to their pleasant home. Rev. Lomax has also been absent for several years on other charges, but when he meets Mr. Thomas, the past flows back and the incidents of their latest interviews naturally take their place in the conversation. "It has been some time since we met," said Mr. Thomas, heartily shaking the minister's hand.

"How has life used you since last we met?" said Rev. Lomax to Mr. Thomas. "Are you well?"

"Perfectly well, I have had a varied experience since I met you, but I have no reason to complain, and I think my experience has been invaluable to me, and with this larger experience and closer observation, I feel that I am more able to help others, and that, I feel, has been one of my most valued acquirements. I sometimes think of members of our people in some directions as sheep without a shepherd, and I do wish from the bottom of my heart that I knew the best way to help them."

"You do not," said the minister, somewhat anxiously, "ignore the power of the pulpit."

"No, I do not; I only wish it had tenfold force. I wish we had ten thousand ministers like Oberlin who was not ashamed to take the lead in opening a road from Bande Roche to Strasburgh, a distance of several miles to bring his parishioners in contact with the trade and business of a neighboring village. I hope the time will come when every minister in building a church which he consecrates to the worship of God will build alongside of it or under the same roof, parish buildings or rooms to be dedicated to the special wants of our people in their peculiar condition."

"I do wish, Brother Lomax, those costly buildings which you erect will cover more needs and wants of our people than some of them do now."

"What would you have in them?"

"I would have a parish building to every church, and I would have in them an evening home for boys. I would have some persons come in and teach them different handicrafts, so as at least to give them an opportunity to be more expert in learning how to use their hands. I would have that building a well warmed and well lighted room in winter, where all should be welcome to come and get a sandwich and a warm cup of tea or coffee and a hot bowl of soup, and if the grogshops were selling liquor for five cents, I would sell the soup for three or four cents, with a roll. I would have a room reserved for such ladies as Mrs. Lasette, who are so willing to help, for the purpose of holding mother's meetings. I would try to have the church the great centre of moral, spiritual and intellectual life for the young, and try to present counter attractions to the debasing influence of the low grogshops, gambling dens and houses of ill fame."

"Part of our city (ought I confine myself to saying part of the city) has not the whole city been cursed by rum? But I now refer to a special part. I have seen church after church move out of that part of the city where the nuisance and curse were so rife, but I never, to my knowledge, heard of one of those churches offering to build a reading room and evening home for boys, or to send out paid and sustained by their efforts, a single woman to go into rum-cursed homes and teach their inmates a more excellent way. I would have in that parish building the most earnest men and women to come together and consult and counsel with each other on the best means to open for ourselves, doors which are still closed against us."

"I am sure," said the minister, "I am willing to do what I can for the temporal and spiritual welfare of our people, and in this I have the example of the great Physician who did not consider it beneath him to attend to physical maladies as well as spiritual needs, and who did not consider the synagogue too holy, nor the Sabbath day too sacred to administer to the destitute and suffering."

"I was very sorry when I found out, Brother Thomas, that I could not have you employed on my church, but I do not see what else I could have done except submit."

"That was all you could have done in that stage of the work when I applied, and I do not wish to bestow the slightest censure on you or the trustees of your church, but I think, if when you were about to build had you advertised for competent master-builders in the South, that you could have gotten enough to have built the church without having employed Mr. Hoog the master-builder. Had you been able to have gone to him and said, 'we are about to build a church and it is more convenient for us to have it done by our citizens than to send abroad for laborers. We are in communication with a colored master builder in Kentucky, who is known as an efficient workman and who would be glad to get the job, and if your men refuse to work with a colored man our only alternative will be to send for colored carpenters and put the building in their hands.' Do you think he would have refused a thirty thousand dollar job just because some of his men refused to work with colored men? I think the greater portion of his workmen would have held their prejudices in abeyance rather than let a thirty thousand dollar job slip out of their hands. Now here is another thing in which I think united effort could have effected something. Now, here is my friend Mr. Thurman; he was a saddler versed in both branches of harness making. For awhile he got steady work in a saddler's shop, but the prejudice against him was so great that his employer was forced to dismiss him. He took work home, but that did not heal the dissatisfaction, and at last he gave it up and went to well-digging. Now, there were colored men in that place who could have, as I think, invested some money in buying material and helped him, not as a charity, but as a mere business operation to set up a place for himself; he had the skill; they had the money, and had they united both perhaps to-day there would be a flourishing business carried on by the man who is now digging wells for a living. I do hope that some time there will be some better modes of communication between us than we now possess; that a labor bureau will be established not as a charity among us, but as a business with capable and efficient men who will try to find out the different industries that will employ men irrespective of color and advertise and find steady and reliable colored men to fill them. Colored men in the South are largely employed in raising cotton and other produce; why should there not be more openings in the South for colored men to handle the merchandize and profit by it?"

"What hinders?" said Rev. Lomax.

"I will not say what hinders, but I will say what I think you can try to do to help. Teach our young to dedicate their young lives to the noble service of devoting them to the service of our common cause; to throw away their cigars, dash down the foaming beer and sparkling wine and strive to be more like those of whom it was said, 'I write unto you, young men, because you are strong.'"

Chapter XIV

Grandmother Harcourt was failing. Annette was rising towards life's summit. Her grandmother was sinking to death's vale.

> The hours are rifting day by day
> Strength from the walls of living clay.

Her two children who were living in A. P. wished her to break up her home and come and live with them. They had room in their hearts and homes for her, but not for Annette. There was something in Annette's temperament with which other members of the family could not harmonize. They were not considerate enough to take into account her antenatal history, and to pity where they were so ready to condemn. Had Annette been born deficient in any of her bodily organs, they could have made allowance for her, and would have deemed it cruel to have demanded that she should have performed the same amount of labor with one hand that she could have done with both. They knew nothing of heredity, except its effects, which they were not thoughtful enough to trace back to the causes over which Annette had no control, and instead of trying to counteract them as one might strive to do in a case of inherited physical tendencies, they only aggravated, and constantly strengthened all the unlovely features in Annette's character, and Annette really seemed like an anomalous contradiction. There was a duality about her nature as if the blood of two races were mingling in her veins. To some persons Annette was loving and loveable, bright, intelligent, obliging and companionable; to others, unsociable, unamiable and repelling. Her heart was like a harp which sent out its harmonious discords in accordance with the moods of the player who touched its chords. To some who swept them it gave out tender and touching melody, to others its harshest and saddest discords. Did not the Psalmist look beneath the mechanism of the body to the constitution of the soul when he said that "We are fearfully and wonderfully made?"

But the hour came when all discussion was ended as to who was to shelter the dear old grandmother in her declining years. Mrs. Harcourt was suddenly paralyzed, and in a few days Annette stood doubly orphaned. Grandmother Harcourt's children gathered around the bedside of their dying mother. She was conscious but unable to speak. Occasionally her eyes would rest lovingly upon Annette and then turn wistfully to her children. Several times she assayed to speak, but the words died upon her lips. Her eldest son entered the room just as life was trembling on its faintest chords. She recognized him, and gathering up her remaining strength she placed his hand on Annette's, and tried again to speak. He understood her and said very tenderly,

"Mother, I will look after Annette."

All the care faded from the dear old face. Amid the shadows that never deceive flitted a smile of peace and contentment. The fading eye lit up with a sudden gaze of joy and wonder. She reached out her hand as if to meet a welcome and precious friend, and then the radiant face grew deathly pale; the outstretched hands relaxed their position, and with a smile, just such a smile as might greet a welcoming angel, her spirit passed out into the eternities, and Annette felt as she had never felt before, that she was all alone. The love that had surrounded and watched over her, born with her perverseness, and sheltered her in its warm clasp, was gone; it had faded suddenly from her vision, and left in its stead a dull and heavy pain. After the funeral, Mrs. Harcourt's children returned to the house where they quietly but earnestly discussed the question what shall be done with Annette. Mrs. Hanson's house was rather small; that is, it was rather small for Annette. She would have found room in her house if she only had room in her heart for her. She had nursed her mother through her sickness, and said with unnatural coldness, "I have got rid of one trouble and I do not want another." Another sister who lived some distance from A. P., would have taken Annette, but she knew that other members of her family would object, as they would be fearful that Annette would be an apple of discord among them. At length, her uncle Thomas decided that she should go with him. He felt that his mother had died with the assurance on her mind that he would care for Annette, and he resolved to be faithful in accepting what was to him the imposition of a new burden on his shoulders. His wife was a cold and unsympathizing woman. She was comfortably situated but did not wish that comfort invaded by her husband's relations. In household matters her husband generally deferred to her judgment, but here was no other alternative than that of taking Annette under the shadow of his home, or leaving her unprotected in the wide world, and he was too merciful and honorable to desert Annette in her saddest hour of need. Having determined that Annette should share his home, he knew that it was advisable to tell his wife about his decision, and to prepare her for Annette's coming.

"Well," said Dr. Harcourt's wife after her husband's return from the funeral, "what are you going to do with Annette?"

"She is coming here," said Dr. Harcourt quietly and firmly.

"Coming here?" said Mrs. Harcourt, looking aghast. "I think at least you might have consulted me."

"That is true, my dear, I would have gladly done so had you been present when the decision was made."

"But where are her aunts, and where was your brother, John; why didn't they take her?"

"John was at home sick with the rheumatism and sister Jane did not appear to be willing to have her come."

"I guess Jane is like I am; got enough to do to look after her own family."

"And sister Eliza said she hadn't any room."

"No room; when she has eight rooms in her house and only two children? She could have made room for her had she chosen."

"May be her husband wasn't willing."

"Oh, it is no such thing. I know John Hanson[15] better than that; Liza is the head man of that house, and just leads him by the nose wherever she wants him to go, and besides, Mrs. Lord's daughter is there pretending to pay board, but I don't believe that she pays it one-half the time."

"She is company for Alice and they all seem very fond of her."

"I do get so sick of that girl, mambying and jambying about that family; calling Liza and her husband 'Ma and Pa,' I haven't a bit of faith in her."

"Well, I confess that I am not very much preposessed in her favor. She just puts me in mind of a pussy cat purring around you."

"Well, now as to Annette. You do not want her here?"

"Not if I can help it."

"But can't she help you to work?"

"She could if she knew how. If wishes were horses beggars might ride. Your mother made a great mistake in bringing Annette up. Annette has a good education, but when that is said, all is said."

"Why, my dear mother was an excellent housekeeper. Did she not teach Annette?"

"Your mother was out a great deal as a sick nurse, and when she went away from home she generally boarded Annette with a friend, who did not, as your mother paid her good board, exact any service from Annette, and while with her she never learned to make a loaf of bread or to cook a beefsteak, and when your mother was at home when she set Annette to do any work, if she did it awkwardly and clumsily she would take it out of her hand and do it herself rather than bother with her, and now I suppose I am to have all the bother and worry with her."

"Well my dear."

"Oh don't come dearing me, and bringing me all this trouble."

"Well my dear, I don't see how it could be helped. I could not leave Annette in the house all by herself. I couldn't afford to make myself the town's talk. May be things will turn out better than you expect. We've got children of our own, and we don't know when we are gone, how they will fare."

"That is true, but I never mean to bring my children up in such a way that they will be no use anywhere, and no one will want them."

"Well, I don't see any other way than bringing Annette here."

"Well, if I must, I must," she said with an air of despondency.

Dr. Harcourt rode over to his sister's where Annette was spending the day and brought the doubly orphaned girl to his home. As she entered the room, it seemed as though a chill struck to her heart when her Aunt bade her good morning. There was no warm pressure in the extended hand. No loving light in the cold unsympathizing eyes which seemed to stab her through and through. The children eyed her inquisitively, as if wishing to understand her status with their parents before they became sociable with her. After supper Annette's uncle went out and her aunt sat quietly and sewed till bed time, and then showed Annette to her room and left the lonely girl to herself and her great sorrow. Annette sat silent, tearless, and alone. Grief had benumbed her faculties. She had sometimes said when grandmother had scolded her that "she was growing cross and cold." But oh, what would she not have given to have had the death-created silence broken by that dear departed voice, to have felt the touch of a vanished hand, to have seen again the loving glance of the death darkened eye. But it was all over; no tears dimmed her eye, as she sat thinking so mournfully of her great sorrow, till she unfastened from her neck a little keepsake containing a lock of grandmother's hair, then all the floodgates of her soul were opened and she threw herself upon her bed and sobbed herself to sleep. In the morning she awoke with that sense of loss and dull agony which only they know, who have seen the grave close over all they have held dearest on earth. The beautiful home of her uncle was very different from the humble apartments; here she missed all the freedom and sunshine that she had enjoyed beneath the shelter of her grandmother's roof.

"Can you sew?" said her aunt to Annette, as she laid on the table a package of handkerchiefs.

"Yes ma'm."

"Let me see how you can do this," handing her one to hem. Annette hemmed the handkerchief nicely; her aunt examined it, put it down and gave her some others to hem, but there was no word of encouragement for her, not even a pleasant, "well done." They both relapsed into silence; between them there was no pleasant interchange of thought. Annette was tolerated and endured, but she did not feel that she was loved and welcomed. It was no place to which she could invite her young friends to spend a pleasant evening. Once she invited some of her young friends to her home, but she soon found that it was a liberty which she should be careful never to repeat. Soon after Annette came to live with her aunt her aunt's mother had a social gathering and reunion of the members of her family. All Dr. Harcourt's children were invited, from the least to the greatest, but poor Annette was left behind. Mrs. Lasette, who happened in the house the evening before the entertainment, asked, "Is not Annette going?" when Mrs. Harcourt replied, very coldly, "She is not one of the family," referring to her mother's family circle.

A shadow flitted over the face of Mrs. Lasette; she thought of her own daughter and how sad it would be to have her live in such a chilly atmosphere of social repression and neglect at a period of life when there was so much danger that false friendship might spread their lures for her inexperienced feet. I will criticize, she said to herself, by creation. I, too, have some social influence, if not among the careless, wine-bibbing, ease-loving votaries of fashion, among some of the most substantial people of A. P., and as long as Annette preserves her rectitude at my house she shall be a welcome guest and into that saddened life I will bring all the sunshine that I can."

Chapter XV

"Well mama," said Mrs. Lasette's daughter to her mother, "I cannot understand why you take so much interest in Annette. She is very unpopular. Scarcely any of the girls ever go with her, and even her cousin never calls for her to go to church or anywhere else, and I sometimes feel so sorry to see her so much by herself, and some of the girls when I went with her to the exposition, said that they wouldn't have asked her to have gone with them, that she isn't our set."

"Poor child," Mrs. Lasette replied; "I am sorry for her. I hope that you will never treat her unkindly, and I do not think if you knew the sad story connected with her life that you would ever be unkind enough to add to the burden she has been forced to bear."

"But mamma, Annette is so touchy. Her aunt says that her tear bags must lay near her eyes and that she will cry if you look at her, and that she is the strangest, oddest creature she ever saw, and I heard she did not wish her to come."

"Why, my dear child, who has been gossipping to you about your neighbors?"

"Why, Julia Thomas."

"Well, my daughter, don't talk after her; gossip is liable to degenerate into evil speaking and then I think it tends to degrade and belittle the mind to dwell on the defects and imperfections of our neighbors. Learn to dwell on the things that are just and true and of good report, but I am sorry for Annette, poor child."

"What makes her so strange, do you know?"

"Yes," said Mrs. Lasette somewhat absently.

"If you do, won't you tell me?"

Again Mrs. Lasette answered in the same absent manner.

"Why mama, what is the matter with you; you say yes to everything and yet you are not paying any attention to anything that I say. You seem like someone who hears, but does not listen; who sees, but does not look. Your face reminds me of the time when I showed you the picture of a shipwreck and you said, 'My brother's boat went down in just such a fearful storm.'"

"My dear child," said Mrs. Lasette, rousing up from a mournful reverie, "I was thinking of a wreck sadder, far sadder than the picture you showed me. It was the mournful wreck of a blighted life."

"Whose life, mama?"

"The life of Annette's [grand]mother. We were girls together and I loved her dearly," Mrs. Lasette replied as tears gathered in her eyes when she recalled one of the saddest memories of her life.

"Do tell me all about it, for I am full of curiosity."

"My child, I want this story to be more than food for your curiosity; I want it to be a lesson and a warning to you. Annette's grandmother was left to struggle as breadwinner for a half dozen children when her husband died. Then there were not as many openings for colored girls as there are now. Our chief resource was the field of domestic service, and circumstances compelled Annette's mother to live out, as we called it. In those days we did not look down upon a girl and try to ostracize her from our social life if she was forced to be a servant. If she was poor and respectable we valued her for what she was rather than for what she possessed. Of course we girls liked to dress nicely, but fine clothes was not the chief passport to our society, and yet I think on the whole that our social life would compare favorably with yours in good character, if not in intellectual attainments. Our dear old mothers were generally ignorant of books, but they did try to teach good manners and good behavior; but I do not think they saw the danger around the paths of the inexperienced with the same clearness of vision we now do. Mrs. Harcourt had unbounded confidence in her children, and as my mother thought, gave her girls too much rein in their own hands. Our mother was more strict with her daughters and when we saw Mrs. Harcourt's daughters having what we considered such good times, I used to say, 'O, I wish mother wasn't so particular!' Other girls could go unattended to excursions, moonlight drives and parties of pleasure, but we never went to any such pleasure unless we were attended by our father, brother or some trusted friend of the family. We were young and foolish then and used to chafe against her restrictions; but to-day, when I think of my own good and noble husband, my little bright and happy home, and my dear, loving daughter, I look back with gratitude to her thoughtful care and honor and bless her memory in her grave. "Poor Lucy Harcourt was not so favored; she was pretty and attractive and had quite a number of admirers. At length she became deeply interested in a young man who came as a stranger to our city. He was a fine looking man, but there was something about him from which I instinctively shrank. My mother felt the same way and warned us to be careful how we accepted any attention from him; but poor Lucy became perfectly infatuated with him and it was rumored that they were to be shortly married. Soon after the rumor he left the city and there was a big change in Lucy's manner. I could not tell what was the matter, but my mother forbade me associating with her, and for several months I scarcely saw her, but I could hear from others that she was sadly changed. Instead of being one of the most light-hearted girls, I heard that she used to sit day after day in her mother's house and wring her hands and weep and that her mother's heart was almost broken. Friends feared that Lucy was losing her mind and might do some desperate deed, but she did not. I left about that time to teach school in a distant village, and when I returned home I heard sad tidings of poor Lucy. She was a mother, but not a wife. Her brothers had grown angry with her for tarnishing their family name, of which they were so proud; her mother's head was bowed with agony and shame. The father of Lucy's child had deserted her in her hour of trial and left her to bear her burden alone with the child like a millstone around her neck. Poor Lucy; I seldom saw her after that, but one day I met her in the Park. I went up to her and kissed her, she threw her arms around me and burst into a flood of tears. I tried to restrain her from giving such vent to her feelings. It was a lack of self-control which had placed her where she was."

"'Oh Anna!' she said, 'it does me so much good to hold your hand in mine once more. I reminds me of the days when we used to be together. Oh, what would I give to recall those days.'"

"I said to her, Lucy, you can never recall the past, but you can try to redeem the future. Try to be a faithful mother. Men may build over the wreck and ruin of their young lives a better and brighter future, why should not a woman? Let the dead past bury its dead and live in the future for the sake of your child. She seemed so grateful for what I had said. Others had treated her with scorn. Her brother Thomas had refused to speak to her; her betrayer had forsaken her; all the joyousness had faded from her life and, poor girl, I was glad that I was able to say a helpful and hopeful word to her. Mother, of course, would not let us associate with her, but she always treated her kindly when she came and did what she could to lighten the burden which was pressing her down to the grave. But, poor child, she was never again the same light-hearted girl. She grew pale and thin and in the hectic flush and faltering tread I read the death sign of early decay, and I felt that my misguided young friend was slowly dying of a broken heart. Then there came a day when we were summoned to her dying bed. Her brothers and sisters were present; all their resentment against her had vanished in the presence of death. She was their dear sister about to leave them and they bent in tearful sorrow around her couch. As one of her brothers, who was a good singer, entered the room, she asked him to sing 'Vital spark of heavenly flame.' He attempted to sing, but there were tremors in his voice and he faltered in the midst of the hymn. 'Won't you sing for your dying sister.'"

"Again he essayed to sing, but [his?] voice became choked with emotion, and he ceased, and burst into tears. Her brother Thomas who had been so hard and cold, and had refused to speak to her, now wept and sobbed like a child, but Lucy smiled as she bade them good bye, and exclaimed, 'Welcome death, the end of fear. I am prepared to die.' A sweet peace settled down on her face, and Lucy had exchanged, I hope, the sorrow and pain of life for the peace and rest of heaven, and left Annette too young to know her loss. Do you wonder then my child that I feel such an interest in Annette and that knowing as I do her antenatal history that I am ever ready to pity where others condemn, and that I want to do what I can to help round out in beauty and usefulness the character of that sinned against and disinherited child, whose restlessness and sensitiveness I trace back to causes over which she had no control."

"What became of Frank Miller? You say that when he returned to A. P. that society opened its doors to him while they were closed to Annette's mother. I don't understand it. Was he not as guilty as she was?"

"Guiltier, I think. If poor Lucy failed as a woman, she tried to be faithful as a mother, while he, faithless as a man, left her to bear her burden alone. She was frail as a woman, but he was base, mean, and selfish as a man."

"How was it that society received him so readily?"

"All did not receive him so readily, but with some his money, like charity, covered a multitude of sins. But from the depths of my heart I despised him. I had not then learned to hate the sin with all my heart, and yet the sinner love. To me he was the incarnation of social meanness and vice. And just as I felt I acted. We young folks had met at a social gathering, and were engaged in a pastime in which we occasionally clasped hands together. Some of these plays I heartily disliked, especially when there was romping and promiscuous kissing. During the play Frank Miller's hand came in contact with mine and he pressed it. I can hardly describe my feelings. It seemed as if my very veins were on fire, and that every nerve was thrilling with repulsion and indignation. Had I seen him murder Lucy and then turn with blood dripping hands to grasp mine, I do not think that I should have felt more loathing than I did when his hand clasped mine. I felt that his very touch was pollution; I immediately left the play, tore off my glove, and threw it in the fire."

"Oh, mother, how could you have done so? You are so good and gentle."

Mrs. Lasette replied, "I was not always so. I do not hate his sin any less now than I did then but I think that I have learned a Christian charity which would induce me to pluck such as he out of the fire while I hated the garments spotted by his sins. I sat down trembling with emotion. I heard a murmur of disapprobation. There was a check to the gayety of the evening. Frank Miller, bold and bad as he was looked crestfallen and uneasy. Some who appeared to be more careful of the manners of society than its morals, said that I was very rude. Others said that I was too prudish, and would be an old maid, that I was looking for perfection in young men, and would not find it. That young men sow their wild oats, and that I was more nice than wise, and that I would frighten the gentlemen away from me. I told them if the young men were so easily frightened, that I did not wish to clasp hands for life with any such timid set, and that I was determined that I would have a moral husband or none; that I was not obliged to be married, but that I was obliged to be true to my conscience. That when I married I expected to lay the foundation of a new home, and that I would never trust my future happiness in the hands of a libertine, or lay its foundations over the reeling brain of a drunkard, and I determined that I would never marry a man for whose vices I must blush, and whose crimes I must condone; that while I might bend to grief I would not bow to shame; that if I brought him character and virtue, he should give me true manhood and honor in return."

"And I think mother that you got it when you married father."

"I am satisfied that I did, and the respect and appreciation my daughter has for her father is only part of my life's reward, but it was my dear mother who taught me to distinguish between the true and the false, and although she was [not?] what you call educated, she taught me that no magnificence of fortune would atone for meanness of spirit, that without character the most wealthy and talented man is a bankrupt in soul. And she taught me how to be worthy of a true man's love."

"And I think you have succeeded splendidly."

"Thank you, my darling. But mother has become used to compliments."

Chapter XVI

"I do not think she gets any more than she deserves," said Mr. Lasette, entering the room. "She is one of whom it may be said, 'Her children arise up and call her blessed, her husband also, and he praiseth her; many daughters have done virtuously but thou excellest them all.'"

"I do not think you will say that I am excelling if I do not haste about your supper; you were not home to dinner and must be hungry by this time, and it has been said that the way to a man's heart is through his stomach."

"Oh, isn't that a libel on my sex!"

"Papa," said Laura Lasette, after her mother had left the room, "did you know Frank Miller? Mother was telling me about him but she did not finish; what became of him?"

"Now, you ask me two questions in one breath; let me answer one at a time."

"Well, papa, I am all attention."

"Do I know Frank Miller, the saloon keeper? Yes; he is connected with a turning point in my life. How so? Well, just be patient a minute and I will tell you. I was almost a stranger in A. P. when I first met your mother. It was at a social where Frank Miller was a guest. I had heard some very damaging reports concerning his reputation, but from the manner in which he was received in society, I concluded that I had been misinformed. Surely, I thought, if the man is as vicious as he has been represented, good women, while they pity him, will shrink instinctively from him, but I saw to my surprise, that with a confident and unblushing manner, he moved among what was called the elite of the place, and that instead of being withheld, attentions were lavished upon him. I had lived most of my life in a small inland town, where people were old fashioned enough to believe in honor and upright conduct, and from what I had heard of Frank Miller I was led to despise his vices and detest his character, and yet here were women whom I believed to be good and virtuous, smiling in his face, and graciously receiving his attentions. I cannot help thinking that in their case,

"Evil is wrought by want of thought"
As well as want of heart.

They were not conscious of the influence they might exert by being true to their own womanhood. Men like Frank Miller are the deadliest foes of women. One of the best and strongest safe guards of the home is the integrity of its women, and he who undermines that, strikes a fearful blow at the highest and best interests of society. Society is woman's realm and I never could understand how, if a woman really loves purity for its own worth and loveliness, she can socially tolerate men whose lives are a shame, and whose conduct in society is a blasting, withering curse."

"But, papa, tell me how you came to love my mother; but I don't see how you could have helped it."

"That's just it, my daughter. I loved her because I could not help it; and respected her because I knew that she was worthy of respect. I was present at a social gathering where Frank was a guest, and was watching your mother attentively when I saw her shrink instinctively from his touch and leave the play in which she was engaged and throw her glove in the fire. Public opinion was divided about her conduct. Some censured, others commended her, but from that hour I learned to love her, and I became her defender. Other women would tolerate Frank Miller, but here was a young and gracious girl, strong enough and brave enough to pour on the head of that guilty culprit her social disapprobation and I gloried in her courage. I resolved she should be my wife if she would accept me, which she did, and I have never regretted my choice and I think that I have had as happy a life as usually falls to the lot of mortals."

Chapter XVII

"Papa," said Laura Lasette, "all the girls have had graduating parties except Annette and myself. Would it not be nice for me to have a party and lots of fun, and then my birthday comes next week; now wouldn't it be just the thing for me to have a party?"

"It might be, darling, for you, but how would it be for me who would have to foot the bill?"

"Well, papa, could you not just give me a check like you do mama sometimes?"

"But mama knows how to use it."

"But papa, don't I know how also?"

"I have my doubts on that score, but let me refer you to your mother. She is queen of this realm, and in household matters I as a loyal subject, abide by her decisions."

"Well, I guess mama is all right on this subject."

Mrs. Lasette was perfectly willing to gratify her daughter, and it was decided to have an entertainment on Laura's birthday.

The evening of Mrs. Lasette's entertainment came bringing with it into her pleasant parlors a bright and merry throng of young people. It was more than a mere pleasure party. It was here that rising talent was encouraged, no matter how humble the garb of the possessor, and Mrs. Lasette was a model hostess who would have thought her entertainment a failure had any one gone from it smarting under a sense of social neglect. Shy and easily embarrassed Annette who was very seldom invited anywhere, found herself almost alone in that gay and chattering throng. Annette was seated next to several girls who laughed and chatted incessantly with each other without deigning to notice her. Mrs. Lasette entering the room with Mr. Luzerne whom she presented to the company, and noticing the loneliness and social isolation of Annette, gave him a seat beside her, and was greatly gratified that she had found the means to relieve the tedium of Annette's position. Mrs. Lasette had known him as a light hearted boy, full of generous impulses, with laughing eyes and a buoyant step, but he had been absent a number of years, and had developed into a handsome man with a magnificent physique, elegant in his attire, polished in his manners and brilliant in conversation. Just such a man as is desirable as a companion and valuable as a friend, staunch, honorable and true, and it was rumored that he was quite wealthy. He was generally cheerful, but it seemed at times as if some sad memories came over him, dashing all the sunshine from his face and leaving in its stead, a sadness which it was touching to behold. Some mystery seemed to surround his life, but being reticent in reference to his past history, there was a dignity in his manner which repelled all intrusion into the secrecy over which he choose to cast a veil. Annette was not beautiful, but her face was full of expression and her manner winsome at times. Lacking social influence and social adaptation, she had been ignored in society, her faults of temper made prominent her most promising traits of character left unnoticed, but this treatment was not without some benefit to Annette. It threw her more entirely on her own resources. At first she read when she had leisure, to beguile her lonely hours, and fortunately for her, she was directed in her reading by Mrs. Lasette, who gave and lent her books, which appealed to all that was highest and best in her nature, and kindled within her a lofty enthusiasm to make her life a blessing to the world. With such an earnest purpose, she was not prepared to be a social favorite in any society whose chief amusement was gossip, and whose keenest weapon was ridicule.

Mr. Luzerne had gone to Mrs. Lasette's with the hope of meeting some of the best talent in A. P., and had come to the conclusion that there was more lulliancy than depth in the intellectual life with which he came in contact; he felt that it lacked earnestness, purpose and grand enthusiasms and he was astonished to see the social isolation of Annette, whose society had interested and delighted him, and after parting with her he found his mind constantly reverting to her and felt grateful to Mrs. Lasette for affording him a rare and charming pleasure. Annette sat alone in her humble room with a new light in her eyes and a sense of deep enjoyment flooding her soul. Never before had she met with such an interesting and congenial gentleman. He seemed to understand as scarcely as any one else had done or cared to do. In the eyes of other guests she had been treated as if too insignificant for notice, but he had loosened her lips and awakened within her a dawning sense of her own ability, which others had chilled and depressed. He had fingered the keys of her soul and they had vibrated in music to his touch. Do not smile, gentle reader, and say that she was very easily impressed, it may be that you have never known what it is to be hungry, not for bread, but for human sympathy, to live with those who were never interested in your joys, nor sympathized in your sorrows. To whom your coming gave no joy and your absence no pain. Since Annette had lost her grandmother, she had lived in an atmosphere of coldness and repression and was growing prematurely cold. Her heart was like a sealed fountain beneath whose covering the bright waters dashed and leaped in imprisoned boundary. Oh, blessed power of human love to lighten human suffering, well may we thank the giver of every good and perfect gift for the love which gladdens hearts, brightens homes and sets the solitary in the midst of families. Mr. Luzerne frequently saw Annette at the house of Mrs. Lasette and occasionally called at her uncle's, but there was an air of restraint in the social atmosphere which repressed and chilled him. In that home he missed the cordial freedom and genial companionship which he always found at Mrs. Lasette's but Annette's apparent loneliness and social isolation awakened his sympathy, and her bright intelligence and good character commanded his admiration and respect, which developed within him a deep interest for the lovely girl. He often spoke admiringly of her and never met her at church, or among her friends that he did not gladly avail himself of the opportunity of accompanying her home. Madame rumor soon got tidings of Mr. Luzerne's attentions to Annette and in a shout the tongues of the gossips of A. P. began to wag. Mrs. Larkins who had fallen heir to some money, moved out of Tennis court, and often gave pleasant little teas to her young friends, and as a well spread table was quite a social attraction in A. P., her gatherings were always well attended. After rumor had caught the news of Mr. Luzerne's interest in Annette, Mrs. Larkins had a social at her house to which she invited him, and a number of her young friends, but took pains to leave Annette out in the cold. Mr. Luzerne on hearing that Annette was slighted, refused to attend. At the supper table Annette's prospects were freely discussed.

"I expected that Mr. Luzerne would have been here this evening, but he sent an apology in which he declined to come."

"Did you invite Annette?" said Miss Croker.

"No, I did not. I got enough of her when I lived next door to her."

"Well that accounts for Mr. Luzerne's absence. They remind me of the Siamese twins; if you see one, you see the other."

"How did she get in with him?"

"She met him at Mrs. Lasette's party, and he seemed so taken up with her that for a while he had neither eyes nor ears for any one else."

"That girl, as quiet as she looks, is just as deep as the sea."

"It is not that she's so deep, but we are so shallow. Miss Booker and Miss Croker were sitting near Annette and not noticing her, and we girls were having a good time in the corner to ourselves, and Annette was looking so lonely and embarrassed I think Mr. Luzerne just took pity on her and took especial pains to entertain her. I just think we stepped our feet into it by slighting Annette, and of course, as soon as we saw him paying attention to her, we wouldn't change and begin to make much of her."

"I don't know what he sees in Annette with her big nose and plain face."

"My father," said Laura Lasette, "says that Annette is a credit to her race and my mother is just delighted because Mr. Luzerne is attracted to her, but, girls, had we not better be careful how we talk about her? People might say that we are jealous of her and we know that we are taught that jealousy is as cruel as the grave."

"We don't see anything to be jealous about her. She is neither pretty nor stylish."

"But my mother says she is a remarkable girl," persisted Laura.

"Your mother," said Mrs. Larkins, "always had funny notions about Annette, and saw in her what nobody else did."

"Well, for my part, I hope it will be a match."

"It is easy enough for you to say so, Laura. You think it is a sure thing between you and Charley Cooper, but don't be too sure; there's many a slip between the cup and the lip."

There was a flush on Laura's cheek as she replied, "If there are a thousand slips between the cup and the lip and Charlie and I should never marry, let me tell you that I would almost as soon court another's husband as a girl's affianced lover. I can better afford to be an old maid than to do a dishonorable thing."

"Well, Laura, you are a chip off the old block; just like your mother, always ready to take Annette's part."

"I think, Mrs. Larkins, it is the finest compliment you can pay me, to tell me that I am like my dear mother."

Chapter XVIII

"Good morning," said Mr. Luzerne, entering Mr. Thomas' office. "Are you busy?"

"Not very; I had just given some directions to my foreman concerning a job I have undertaken, and had just settled down to read the paper. Well how does your acquaintance with Miss Harcourt prosper? Have you popped the question yet?"

"No, not exactly; I had been thinking very seriously of the matter, but I have been somewhat shaken in my intention."

"How so," said Mr. Thomas, laying down his paper and becoming suddenly interested.

"You know that I have had an unhappy marriage which has overshadowed all my subsequent life, and I cannot help feeling very cautious how I risk, not only my own, but another's happiness in a second marriage. It is true that I have been thinking of proposing to Miss Harcourt and I do prefer her to any young lady I have ever known; but there is a depreciatory manner in which people speak of her, that sorely puzzles me. For instance, when I ask some young ladies if they know Annette, they shrug their shoulders, look significantly at each other and say, 'Oh, yes, we know her; but she don't care for anything but books; oh she is so self conceited and thinks she knows more than any one else.' But when I spoke to Mrs. Larkins about her, she said Annette makes a fine appearance, but all is not gold that glitters. By this time my curiosity was excited, and I asked, 'What is the matter with Miss Harcourt? I had no idea that people were so ready to pick at her.' She replied, 'No wonder; she is such a spitfire.'"

"Well," said Mr. Thomas, a little hotly, "if Annette is a spitfire, Mrs. Larkins is a lot of combustion. I think of all the women I know, she has the greatest genius for aggravation. I used to board with her, but as I did not wish to be talked to death I took refuge in flight."

"And so you showed the white feather that time."

"Yes, I did, and I could show it again. I don't wonder that people have nick-named her 'Aunty talk forever.' I have known Annette for years and I known that she is naturally quick tempered and impulsive, but she is not malicious and implacable and if I were going to marry to-morrow I would rather have a quick, hot-tempered woman than a cold, selfish one, who never thought or cared about anyone but herself. Mrs. Larkins' mouth is not a prayer-book; don't be uneasy about anything she says against Annette."

Reassured by Mr. Thomas, Clarence Luzerne decided that he would ask Dr. Harcourt's permission to visit his niece, a request which was readily granted and he determined if she would consent that she should be his wife. He was wealthy, handsome and intelligent; Annette was poor and plain, but upright in character and richly endowed in intellect, and no one imagined that he would pass by the handsome and stylish girls of A. P. to bestow his affections on plain, neglected Annette. Some of the girls who knew of his friendship for Annette, but who never dreamed of its termination in marriage would say to Annette, "Speak a good word for me to Mr. Luzerne;" but Annette kept her counsel and would smile and think: I will speak a good word for myself. Very pleasant was the growing friendship between Annette and Mr. Luzerne. Together they read and discussed books and authors and agreed with wonderful unanimity, which often expressed itself in the words:

"I think as you do." Not that there was any weak compliance for the sake of agreement, but a unison of thought and feeling between them which gave a pleasurable zest to their companionship.

"Miss Annette," said Luzerne, "do you believe that matches are made in heaven?"

"I never thought anything about it."

"But have you no theory on the subject?"

"Not the least; have you?"

"Yes; I think that every human soul has its counterpart, and is never satisfied till soul has met with soul and recognized its spiritual affinity."

"Affinity! I hate the word."

"Why?"

"Because I think it has been so wrongly used, and added to the social misery of the world."

"What do you think marriage ought to be?"

"I think it should be a blending of hearts, an intercommunion of souls, a tie that only love and truth should weave, and nothing but death should part."

Luzerne listened eagerly and said, "Why, Miss Annette, you speak as if you had either loved or were using your fine imaginative powers on the subject with good effect. Have you ever loved any one?"

Annette blushed and stammered, and said, "I hardly know, but I think I have a fine idea of what love should be. I think the love of a woman for the companion of her future life should go out to him just as naturally as the waves leap to the strand, or the fire ascends to the sun."

"And this," said Luzerne, taking her hand in his, "is the way I feel towards you. Surely our souls have met at last. Annette," said he, in a voice full of emotion, "is it not so? May I not look on your hand as a precious possession, to hold till death us do part?"

"Why, Mr. Luzerne," said Annette, recovering from her surprise, "this is so sudden, I hardly know what to say. I have enjoyed your companionship and I confess have been pleased with your attentions, but I did not dream that you had any intentions beyond the enjoyment of the hour."

"No, Annette, I never seek amusement in toying with human hearts. I should deem myself a villain if I came into your house and stole your purse, and I should think myself no better if I entered the citadel of a woman's heart to steal her affections only to waste their wealth. Her stolen money I might restore, but what reparation could I make for wasted love and blighted affections? Annette, let there be truth between us. I will give you time to think on my proposal, hoping at the same time that I shall find favor in your eyes."

After Mr. Luzerne left, Annette, sat alone by the fireside, a delicious sense of happiness filling her soul with sudden joy. Could it be that this handsome and dignified man had honored her above all the girls in A. P., by laying his heart at her feet, or was it only a dream from which would come a rude awakening? Annette looked in the glass, but no stretch of imagination could make her conceive that she was beautiful in either form or feature. She turned from the glass with a faint sigh, wishing for his sake that she was as beautiful as some of the other girls in A. P., whom he had overlooked, not thinking for one moment that in loving her for what she was in intellect and character he had paid her a far greater compliment than if she had been magnificently beautiful and he had only been attracted by an exquisite form and lovely face. In a few days after Mr. Luzerne's proposal to Annette he came for the answer, to which he looked with hope and suspense.

"I am glad," he said, "to find you at home."

"Yes; all the rest of the family are out."

"Then the coast is clear for me?" There was tenderness and decision in his voice as he said, "Now, Annette, I have come for the answer which cannot fail to influence all my future life." He clasped the little hand which lay limp and passive in his own. His dark, handsome eyes were bent eagerly upon her as if scanning every nook and corner of her soul. Her eye fell beneath his gaze, her hand trembled in his, tears of joy were springing to her eyes, but she restrained them. She withdrew her hand from his clasp; he looked pained and disappointed. "Have I been too hasty and presumptuous?"

Annette said no rather faintly, while her face was an enigma he did not know how to solve.

"Why did you release your hand and avert your eyes?"

"I felt that my will was succumbing to yours, and I want to give you an answer untrammeled and uncontrolled by your will."

Mr. Luzerne smiled, and thought what rare thoughtfulness and judgment she has evinced. How few women older than herself would have thought as quickly and as clearly, and yet she is no less womanly, although she seems so wise.

"What say you, my dear Annette, since I have released your

hand. May I not hope to hold this hand as the most precious of all my earthly possessions until death us do part?"

Annette fixed her eyes upon the floor as if she were scanning the figures on the carpet. Her heart beat quickly as she timidly repeated the words, "Until death us do part," and placed her hand again in his, while an expression of love and tender trust lit up the mobile and expressive face, and Annette felt that his love was hers; the most precious thing on earth that she could call her own. The engagement being completed, the next event in the drama was preparation for the wedding. It was intended that the engagement should not be long. Together they visited different stores in purchasing supplies for their new home. How pleasant was that word to the girl, who had spent such lonely hours in the home of her uncle. To her it meant one of the brightest spots on earth and one of the fairest types of heaven. In the evening they often took pleasant strolls together or sat and chatted in a beautiful park near their future home. One evening as they sat quietly enjoying themselves Annette said, "How happened it that you preferred me to all the other girls in A. P.? There are lots of girls more stylish and better looking; what did you see in poor, plain me?" He laughingly replied:

> "I chose you out from all the rest,
> The reason was I loved you best."

"And why did you prefer me?"
She answered quite archly:

> "The rose is red, the violet's blue,
> Sugar is sweet and so are you."

"I chose you because of your worth. When I was young, I married for beauty and I pierced my heart through with many sorrows."

"You been married?" said Annette with a tremor in her tones. "Why, I never heard of it before."

"Did not Mr. Thomas or Mrs. Lasette tell you of it? They knew it, but it is one of the saddest passages of my life, to which I scarcely ever refer. She, my wife, drifted from me, and was drowned in a freshet near Orleans."

"Oh, how dreadful, and I never knew it."

"Does it pain you?"

"No, but it astonishes me."

"Well, Annette, it is not a pleasant subject, let us talk of something else. I have not spoken of it to you before, but to-day, when it pressed so painfully upon my mind, it was a relief to me to tell you about it, but now darling dismiss it from your mind and let the dead past bury its dead."

Just then there came along where they were sitting a woman whose face bore traces of great beauty, but dimmed and impaired by lines of sorrow and disappointment. Just as she reached the seat where they were sitting, she threw up her hands in sudden anguish, gasped out, "Clarence! my long lost Clarence," and fell at his feet in a dead faint.

As Mr. Luzerne looked on the wretched woman lying at his feet, his face grew deathly pale. He trembled like an aspen and murmured in a bewildered tone, "has the grave restored its dead?"

But with Annette there was no time for delay. She chaffed, the rigid hands, unloosed the closely fitting dress, sent for a cab and had her conveyed as quickly as possible to the home for the homeless. Then turning to Luzerne, she said bitterly, "Mr. Luzerne, will you explain your encounter with that unfortunate woman?" She spoke as calmly as she could, for a fierce and bitter anguish was biting at her heartstrings. "What claim has that woman on you?"

"She has the claim of being my wife and until this hour I firmly believed she was in her grave." Annette lifted her eyes sadly to his;

he calmly met her gaze, but there was no deception in his glance; his eyes were clear and sad and she was more puzzled than ever.

"Annette," said he, "I have only one favor to ask; let this scene be a secret between us as deep as the sea. Time will explain all. Do not judge me too harshly."

"Clarence," she said, "I have faith in you, but I do not understand you; but here is the carriage, my work at present is with this poor, unfortunate woman, whose place I was about to unconsciously supplant."

Chapter XIX

And thus they parted. All their air castles and beautiful chambers of imagery, blown to the ground by one sad cyclone of fate. In the city of A. P., a resting place was found for the stranger who had suddenly dashed from their lips the scarcely tasted cup of happiness. Mr. Luzerne employed for her the best medical skill he could obtain. She was suffering from nervous prostration and brain fever. Annette was constant in her attentions to the sufferer, and day after day listened to her delirious ravings. Sometimes she would speak of a diamond necklace, and say so beseechingly, "Clarence, don't look at me so. You surely can't think that I am guilty. I will go away and hide myself from you. Clarence, you never loved me or you would not believe me guilty."

But at length a good constitution and careful nursing overmastered disease, and she showed signs of recovery. Annette watched over her when her wild ravings sounded in her ears like requiems for the loved and cherished dead. Between her and the happiness she had so fondly anticipated, stood that one blighted life, but she watched that life just as carefully as if it had been the dearest life on earth she knew.

One day, as Annette sat by her bedside, she surmised from the look on her face that the wandering reason of the sufferer had returned. Beckoning to Annette she said "Who are you and where am I?"

Annette answered, "I am your friend and you are with friends."

"Poor Clarence," she murmured to herself; "more sinned against than sinning."

"My dear friend," Annette said very tenderly, "you have been very ill, and I am afraid that if you do not be very quiet you will be very sick again." Annette gently smoothed her beautiful hair and tried to soothe her into quietness. Rest and careful nursing soon wrought a wondrous change in Marie Luzerne, but Annette thoughtfully refrained from all reference to her past history and waited for time to unravel the mystery she could not understand, and with this unsolved mystery the match between her and Luzerne was broken off. At length, one day when Marie's health was nearly restored, she asked for writing materials, and said, "I mean to advertise for my mother in a Southern paper. It seems like a horrid dream that all I knew or loved, even my husband, whom I deserted, believed that I was dead, till I came suddenly on him in the park with a young lady by his side. She looked like you. Was it you?"

"Yes," said Annette, as a sigh of relief came to her lips. If Clarence had wooed and won her he had not willfully deceived her. "Oh, how I would like to see him. I was wayward and young when I left him in anger. Oh, if I have sinned I have suffered; but I think that I could die content if I could only see him once more." Annette related the strange sad story to her physician, who decided that it was safe and desirable that there should be an interview between them. Luzerne visited his long lost wife and after a private interview, he called Annette to the room, who listened sadly while she told her story, which exonerated Luzerne from all intent to deceive Annette by a false marriage while she had a legal claim upon him.

"I was born," she said, "in New Orleans. My father was a Spaniard and my mother a French Creole. She was very beautiful and my father met her at a French ball and wished her for his companion for life, but as she was an intelligent girl and a devout Catholic she would not consent to live a life by which she would be denied the Sacrament of her Church; so while she could not contract a civil marriage, which would give her the legal claims of a wife, she could enter into an ecclesiastical marriage by which she would not forfeit her claim to the rights and privileges of the Church as a good Catholic. I was her only child, loved and petted by my father, and almost worshipped by my mother, and I never knew what it was to have a wish unfilled if it was in her power to gratify it. When I was about 16 I met Clarence Luzerne. People then said that I was very beautiful. You would scarcely think so now, but I suppose he thought so, too. In a short time we were married, and soon saw that we were utterly unfitted to each other; he was grave and I was gay; he was careful and industrious, I was careless and extravagant; he loved the quiet of his home and books; I loved the excitements of pleasure and the ball room, and yet I think he loved me, but it was as a father might love a wayward child whom he vainly tried to restrain. I had a cousin who had been absent from New Orleans a number of years, of whose antecedents I knew not scarcely anything. He was lively, handsome and dashing. My husband did not like his society, and objected to my associating with him. I did not care particularly for him, but I chafed against the restraint, and in sheer waywardness I continued the association. One day he brought me a beautiful diamond necklace which he said he had obtained in a distant land. I laid it aside intending to show it to my husband; in the meantime, a number of burglaries had been committed in the city of B., and among them was a diamond necklace. My heart stood still with sudden fear while I read of the account and while I was resolving what to do, my husband entered the house followed by two officers, who demanded the necklace. My husband interfered and with a large sum of money obtained my freedom from arrest. My husband was very proud of the honor of his family and blamed me for staining its record. From that day my husband seemed changed in his feelings towards me. He grew cold, distant and abstracted, and I felt that my presence was distasteful to him. I could not enter into his life and I saw that he had no sympathy with mine, and so in a fit of desperation I packed my trunk and took with me some money I had inherited from my father and left, as I said in a note, forever. I entered a convent and resolved that I would devote myself to the service of the poor and needy, for life had lost its charms for me. I had scarcely entered the convent before the yellow fever broke out and raged with fearful intensity. I was reckless of my life and engaged myself as a nurse. One day there came to our hospital a beautiful girl with a wealth of raven hair just like mine was before I became a nurse. I nursed her through a tedious illness and when she went out from the hospital, as I had an abundance of clothing, I supplied her from my wardrobe with all she needed, even to the dress she wore away. The clothing was all marked with my name. Soon after I saw in the paper that a young woman who was supposed from the marks on her clothing and the general description of her person to be myself was found drowned in a freshet. I was taken ill immediately afterwards and learned on recovering that I had been sick and delirious for several weeks. I sought for my mother, inquired about my husband, but lost all trace of them both till I suddenly came across my husband in Brightside Park. But Clarence, if you have formed other ties don't let me come between you and the sunshine. You are free to apply for a divorce; you can make the plea of willful desertion. I will not raise the least straw in your way. I will go back to the convent and spend the rest of my life in penitence and prayer. I have sinned; it is right that I should suffer." Clarence looked eagerly into the face of Annette; it was calm and peaceful, but in it he read no hope of a future reunion.

"What say you, Annette, would you blame me if I accepted this release?"

"I certainly would. She is your lawful wife. In the church of her father you pledged your faith to her, and I do not think any human law can absolve you from being faithful to your marriage vows. I do not say it lightly. I do not think any mother ever laid her first born in the grave with any more sorrow than I do to-day when I make my heart the sepulchre in which I bury my first and only love. This, Clarence, is the saddest trial of my life. I am sadder to-day than when I stood a lonely orphan over my grandmother's grave, and heard the clods fall on her coffin and stood lonely and heart-stricken in my uncle's house, and felt that I was unwelcome there. But, Clarence, the great end of life is not the attainment of happiness but the performance of duty and the development of character. The great question is not what is pleasant but what is right."

"Annette, I feel that you are right; but I am too wretched to realize the force of what you say. I only know that we must part, and that means binding my heart as a bleeding sacrifice on the altar of duty."

"Do you not know who drank the cup of human suffering to its bitter dregs before you? Arm yourself with the same mind, learn to suffer and be strong. Yes, we must part; but if we are faithful till death heaven will bring us sweeter rest." And thus they parted. If Luzerne had felt any faltering in his allegiance to duty he was too honorable and upright when that duty was plainly shown to him to weakly shrink from its performance, and as soon as his wife was able to travel he left A. P., for a home in the sunny South. After Luzerne had gone Annette thought, "I must have some active work which will engross my mind and use every faculty of my soul. I will consult with my dear friend Mrs. Lasette."

All unnerved by her great trial, Annette rang Mrs. Lasette's front door bell somewhat hesitatingly and walked wearily into the sitting-room, where she found Mrs. Lasette resting in the interval between twilight and dark. "Why Annette!" she said with pleased surprise, "I am so glad to see you. How is Clarence? I thought you would have been married before now. I have your wedding present all ready for you."

"Mrs. Lasette," Annette said, while her voice trembled with inexpressible sorrow, "it is all over."

Mrs. Lasette was lighting the lamp and had not seen Annette's face in the dusk of the evening, but she turned suddenly around at the sound of her voice and noticed the wan face so pitiful in its expression of intense suffering.

"What is the matter, my dear; have you and Luzerne had a lover's quarrel?"

"No," said Annette, sadly, and then in the ears of her sympathizing friend she poured her tale of bitter disappointment. Mrs. Lasette folded the stricken girl to her heart in tenderest manner.

"Oh, Mrs. Lasette," she said, "you make me feel how good it is for girls to have a mother."

"Annette, my brave, my noble girl, I am so glad."

"Glad of what, Mrs. Lasette?"

"Glad that you have been so true to conscience and to duty; glad that you have come through your trial like gold tried in the fiercest fire; glad that my interest in you has not been in vain, and that I have been able to see the blessed fruitage of my love and labors. And now, my dear child, what next?"

"I must have a change; I must find relief in action. I feel so weak and bruised in heart."

"A bruised reed will not break," murmured Mrs. Lasette to herself.

"Annette," said Mrs. Lasette, "this has been a fearful trial, but it must not be in vain; let it bring you more than happiness; let it bring you peace and blessedness. There is only one place for us to bring our sins and our sorrows, and that is the mercy seat. Let us both kneel there to-night and ask for grace to help in this your time of need. We are taught to cast our care upon Him for he careth for us. Come, my child, with the spirit of submission and full surrender, and consecrate your life to his service, body, soul and spirit, not as a dead offering, but a living sacrifice."

Together they mingled their prayers and tears, and when Annette rose from her knees there was a look of calmness on her face, and a deep peace had entered her soul. The strange trial was destined to bring joy and gladness and yield the peaceable fruit of righteousness in the future. Mrs. Lasette wrote to some friends in a distant Southern town where she obtained a situation for Annette as a teacher. Here she soon found work to enlist her interest and sympathy and bring out all the activity of her soul. She had found her work and the people among whom she labored had found their faithful friend.

Chapter XX

Luzerne's failure to marry Annette and re-instatement of his wife was the sensation of the season. Some pitied Annette; others blamed Luzerne, but Annette found, as a teacher, opportunity among the freedmen to be a friend and sister to those whose advantages had been less than hers. Life had once opened before her like a fair vision enchanted with delight, but her beautiful dream had faded like sun rays mingling with the shadows of night. It was the great disappointment of her life, but she roused up her soul to bear suffering and to be true to duty, and into her soul came a joy which was her strength. Little children learned to love her, the street gamins knew her as their friend, aged women blessed the dear child as they called her, who planned for their comfort when the blasts of winter were raging around their homes. Before her great trial she had found her enjoyment more in her intellectual than spiritual life, but when every earthly prop was torn away, she learned to lean her fainting head on Christ the corner-stone and the language of her heart was "Nearer to thee, e'en though it be a cross that raiseth me." In surrendering her life she found a new life and more abundant life in every power and faculty of her soul.

Luzerne went South and found Marie's mother who had mourned her child as dead. Tenderly they watched over her, but the seeds of death were sown too deeply in her wasted frame for recovery, and she wasted away and sank into a premature grave, leaving Luzerne the peaceful satisfaction of having smoothed her passage to the grave, and lengthened with his care, her declining days. Turning from her grave he plunged into active life. It was during the days of reconstruction when tricksters and demagogues were taking advantage of the ignorance and inexperience of the newly enfranchised citizens. Honorable and upright, Luzerne preserved his integrity among the corruptions of political life. Men respected him too much to attempt to swerve him from duty for personal advantage. No bribes ever polluted his hands, nor fraud, nor political chicanery ever stained his record.

He was the friend and benefactor of his race, giving them what gold is ever too poor to buy—the benefit of a good example and a noble life, and earned for himself the sobriquet by which he was called, "honest Luzerne." And yet at times he would turn wistfully to Annette and the memory of those glad, bright days when he expected to clasp hands with her for life. At length his yearning had become insatiable and he returned to A. P.

Laura Lasette had married Charley Cooper who by patience and industry had obtained a good position in the store of a merchant who was manly enough to let it be known that he had Negro blood in his veins, but that he intended to give him a desk and place in his establishment and he told his employees that he intended to employ him, and if they were not willing to work with him they could leave. Charley was promoted just the same as others according to his merits. Time had dealt kindly with Mrs.

Lasette, as he scattered his silvery crystals amid her hair, and of her it might be said,

> Each silver hair, each wrinkle there
> Records some good deed done,
> Some flower she scattered by the way
> Some spark from love's bright sun.

Mrs. Larkins had grown kinder and more considerate as the years passed by. Mr. Thomas had been happily married for several years. Annette was still in her Southern home doing what she could to teach, help and befriend those on whose chains the rust of ages had gathered. Mr. Luzerne found out Annette's location and started Southward with a fresh hope springing up in his heart.

It was a balmy day in the early spring when he reached the city where Annette was teaching. Her home was a beautiful place of fragrance and flowers. Groups of young people were gathered around their teacher listening eagerly to a beautiful story she was telling them. Elderly women were scattered in little companies listening to or relating some story of Annette's kindness to them and their children.

"I told her," said one, "that I had a vision that some one who was fair, was coming to help us. She smiled and said she was not fair. I told her she was fair to me."

"I wish she had been here fifteen years ago," said another one. "Before she came my boy was just as wild as a colt, but now he is jist as stiddy as a judge."

"I just think," said another one, "that she has been the making of my Lucy. She's just wrapped up in Miss Annette, thinks the sun rises and sets in her." Old mothers whose wants had been relieved, came with the children and younger men too, to celebrate Annette's 31st birthday. Happy and smiling, like one who had passed through suffering into peace she stood, the beloved friend of old and young, when suddenly she heard a footstep on the veranda which sent the blood bounding in swift currents back to her heart and left her cheek very pale. It was years since she had heard the welcome rebound of that step, but it seemed as familiar to her as the voice of a loved and long lost friend, or a precious household word, and before her stood, with slightly bowed form and hair tinged with gray, Luzerne. Purified through suffering, which to him had been an evangel of good, he had come to claim the love of his spirit. He had come not to separate her from her cherished life work, but to help her in uplifting and helping those among whom her lot was cast as a holy benediction, and so after years of trial and pain, their souls had met at last, strengthened by duty, purified by that faith which works by love, and fitted for life's highest and holiest truths.

And now, in conclusion, permit me to say under the guise of fiction, I have essayed to weave a story which I hope will subserve a deeper purpose than the mere amusement of the hour, that it will quicken and invigorate human hearts and not fail to impart a lesson of usefulness and value.

Notes

1. In the original, this sentence reads: "After she became a wife and mother, instead of becoming entirely absorbed in a round of household cares and duties, and she often said, that the moment the crown of motherhood fell upon her how that she had poured a new interest in the welfare of her race."

2. The original reads "But Mr. Thompson."

3. The original reads "but during her short sojourn in the South."

4. In the original this sentence reads: "Young men anxious for places in the gift of government found that by winking at Frank Miller's vices and conforming to the demoralizing customs of his place, were the passports to political favors, and lacking moral stamina, hushed their consciences and became partakers of his sins."

5. The original reads "Mrs. Larking."

6. The original reads "said Mrs. Larkins, seating herself beside Mrs. Larking."

7. The original reads "continued Mr. Slocum."

8. The original reads "'Isn't your name Benny?'"

9. The original reads "said Charley Hastings."

10. The original reads "scarcely on intellect."

11. The original reads "expensive views."

12. The original reads "Mrs. Harcourt."

13. The original reads "Mrs. Hanson."

14. The original reads "Mr. Thomas."

15. The original reads "Tom Hanson."